P9-CBU-197

THE GODLY ORDER

ALCUIN CLUB COLLECTIONS No. 65

The Alcuin Club exists to promote the study of Christian liturgy in general, and in particular the liturgies of the Anglican Communion. Since its foundation in 1897 it has published over 130 books and pamphlets. Members of the Club receive publications of the current year *gratis*.

Information concerning the annual subscription, applications for membership and lists of publications is obtainable from the Treasurer, 5 St Andrew Street, London EC4A 3AB (telephone 01-583 7394).

President
The Right Reverend E. W. Kemp, D.D., Bishop of Chichester

Committee
The Venerable G. B. Timms, M.A. *Chairman*
The Reverend A. M. Haig, B.D., A.K.C. *Secretary*
The Reverend P. F. Bradshaw, M.A., Ph.D. *Editorial Secretary*
James Holden, Esq., *Treasurer*
The Reverend Canon G. J. Cuming, D.D.
The Reverend Canon D. C. Gray, M.Phil., A.K.C.
The Venerable R. D. Silk, B.A.
The Reverend K. W. Stevenson, M.A., Ph.D.

THE GODLY ORDER

Texts and Studies relating to the
Book of Common Prayer

GEOFFREY CUMING

ALCUIN CLUB/SPCK

First published 1983
for the Alcuin Club
by SPCK
Holy Trinity Church
Marylebone Road
London NW1 4DU

Copyright © Geoffrey Cuming 1983

British Library Cataloguing in Publication Data

Cuming, G. J.
  The godly order. – (Alcuin Club collections; no. 65)
  1. Church of England.   Book of Common Prayer –
History
  I. Title   II. Series
  264'.03   BX5145

  ISBN 0-281-04059-1

Typeset by Oxford Verbatim Limited
Printed in Great Britain by
Spottiswoode Ballantyne Ltd
Colchester and London

Contents

Introduction

In the writing of *A History of Anglican Liturgy* I became aware of various topics which needed investigation in greater depth than time allowed, and treatment at greater length than was available in a textbook. This book is the result of my subsequent investigations. It is chiefly composed of texts which illuminate the origins and development of the Book of Common Prayer, with introductions and comments. The great German liturgist Dom Hieronymus Engberding believed that the clearest and fullest way to demonstrate the relationship between liturgical texts is to set them out in parallel columns, and I have made frequent use of this procedure throughout the book.

Chapter 1 deals with Cranmer's first attempts at reform of the Breviary, and includes English translations of the more important parts of the manuscript. The original text, in Latin, has long been available, but has never, to my knowledge, been published in English. A note is appended on the Office in Lutheranism, a subject to which little attention has been paid.

Chapter 2 prints, again mostly for the first time since the sixteenth century, the canticles and collects from the reforming Primers of the years 1530–45, whose interest as precursors of the Prayer Book forms needs no underlining. There are about fifty editions of these Primers (the exact number depends on the definition of 'edition'), and I have been able to examine in person an example of every one, with the single exception of Redman's Primer of 1535: the only existing copy is in Paris, and for this I was content with a microfilm.

Chapter 3 takes a detailed look at Cranmer's methods of working. F. E. Brightman had already done much good work in this field, and this chapter supplements rather than supersedes his findings.

Chapter 4 assesses the importance of Hermann von Wied's *Simple and Religious Consultation* as a source of the Prayer Book. The sequence of events in Cologne which produced it and were produced by it is traced, with the help of contemporary publications, in fuller detail than has previously been available.

Chapter 5 sets out the Canon of 1549 in relation to its Latin, German and English sources. Here again I am building on Brightman's foundations, but it has proved possible to make a considerable number of additions to his pioneering work.

Chapter 6 shows the reshaping of the Canon from its original form of 1549 via 1552 and 1637 to the final product of 1662.

Chapter 7 was the Durham Cathedral Lecture for 1975, while Chapter 8 originally appeared in the *Church Quarterly Review* (vol. 48 (1962), pp. 29–39).

Chapter 9 is a recasting and conflation of two separate pieces which originally appeared in the *Journal of Ecclesiastical History* (vol. 8 (1957), pp. 182–92) and *Studies in Church History* (vol. 3 (1966), pp. 247–53) respectively.*

Chapter 10 is the spin-off of a long-abandoned study of the genesis of the 1928 Prayer Book. The first part was read to the Ecclesiastical History Society as a 'communication' in 1970; the remainder shows how the Prayer of Consecration in that book reached its final form after five stages of revision.

Oxford, Christmas 1982   *Geoffrey Cuming*

* The note appended to chapter 7 is drawn from a review in the *Journal of Theological Studies* (n.s. vol 69 (1968), pp. 681–3).

1

The Reform of the
Daily Office

The Orders for Mattins and Evensong in the Book of Common Prayer of 1549 were not Cranmer's first attempt at revision of the Breviary. MS Royal 7B.IV in the British Museum contains two such attempts, described on f. 36 as *Festivale et horarum canonicarum series* (referred to below as Scheme A and Scheme B respectively). Unfortunately the manuscript bears no indication of date. F. A. Gasquet and E. Bishop, its first editors,[1] pointed to the fact that the second scheme is more conservative in character than the first, and therefore assumed that it was the earlier of the two and assigned to it a date *c.* 1543; they placed the first, which more nearly resembles the Lutheran pattern, at the end of Henry VIII's reign, *c.* 1546–7. This dating was accepted by W. H. Frere[2] and F. E. Brightman.[3] J. Wickham Legg, who edited the manuscript for the Henry Bradshaw Society,[4] was more cautious in his approach, and wrote: 'There will very likely be a preponderance of opinion that the composition of Part the Second preceded Part the First . . . though there is no exact proof which came into existence before the other'.[5]

The manuscript itself may be analysed as follows:

ff.			
	4–6	Hand A	Calendar
	7–47	Hand B	Scheme A (up to Fourth Lesson for 9 March)
	50–132	Hand C	Scheme A, remainder of Fourth Lessons
	133–50	Hand C	Scheme B
	151–6	Cranmer's own hand	Table of Lessons for Scheme B
	157–9	Hand D	*Calendarium Secundum*

Hand A may be the same writer as Hand B; Hand C has been generally accepted as that of Cranmer's secretary, Ralph Morice;

1

there are also annotations in Cranmer's hand throughout the manuscript. It is a fair copy, with the rubrics in red, but the text of Scheme A is incomplete. Cranmer set out to provide Fourth Lessons for all saints' days, and had done so up to 9 March; for the rest of the year he has provided lessons for only twenty-five days out of seventy-five, and blank spaces are left in the manuscript for the remainder. The change of hand in the manuscript from Hand B to Ralph Morice coincides with a particular stage in Cranmer's work, after which it seems that he left Scheme A incomplete. C. H. Smyth[6] drew attention to a letter of Cranmer's, dated 11 April 1538, in which he speaks of his chaplain, Mr Malet, whom he had left 'occupied in the affairs of our church service, and now at the writing up of *so much as he had to do*'.[7] It seems reasonable to deduce that Malet's task was to copy out the completed part of Scheme A, after which Morice took over; but before Cranmer could prepare the remaining fifty lessons, the negotiations with the Lutherans were broken off, and there was little point in continuing the work. (Morice became Cranmer's secretary in 1528, so his participation in the work is of no help for its dating.) Scheme B could well be associated with the Catholic reaction of 1540–3. This dating was accepted by E. C. Ratcliff.[8]

The manuscript itself affords no grounds for placing either scheme before the other, except that Scheme A does come first. The contents, however, yield some slight indications of the priority of Scheme A. First, there is the use of Quiñones' Breviary in its two forms of 1535 and 1536. Scheme A begins with a preface which owes a good deal to that in the first edition of Quiñones. Only at the very beginning does it seem that Cranmer is using a passage from the second edition which is not found in the first; but even in this one sentence the resemblance is confined to the first words, 'There was never anything by the wit of man so well devised'. Quiñones continues, 'which could not later be rendered more perfect by the added insight of many', while Cranmer goes on, 'which in continuance of time has not been corrupted', the exact opposite of Quiñones' thought. Wickham Legg[9] also points to two Fourth Lessons in Scheme A which are clearly based on the first edition of Quiñones rather than the second. But there seems to be no evidence in Scheme A of the second edition being used in preference to the first. In Scheme B, on the other hand, there are many pointers to the use of the second edition;[10] at only one place does it agree with the first edition against the second, and this is merely in the lengthening of a lesson, a procedure which Cranmer could perfectly well have thought of for himself, and indeed frequently applied to the Epistles and Gospels of the Prayer Book.

Two other pieces of evidence may be adduced. Wickham Legg writes:[11]

> The stanzas in veneration of the Cross in *Vexilla Regis* are retained in the First Part but have disappeared from the Second . . . In 1546 Cranmer tried to persuade Henry VIII by his own royal authority to put down all marks of veneration of the Cross in the Service books . . .

The other piece of evidence is provided by the three calendars in the manuscript. That prefaced to Scheme A includes every chapter of the Bible, even of the Apocrypha. But the calendar immediately following Scheme B omits a large number of chapters, and a similar series of omissions is made in the third calendar ('*Calendarium Secundum*', which also follows Scheme B) and again in 1549. They are tabulated below:

	Scheme B1	Scheme B2	1549
Genesis	10, 36	10	10
Exodus	25–31, 36–9	25–31, 36–9	25–31, 36–9
Leviticus	1–17, 21–7	1–17, 21–7	1–17, 21–7
Numbers	1–9	1–9	1–9
Joshua	13–19, 21	13–19	13
1 Kings	6, 7	6, 7	–
Esther	12	–	10–16
Jeremiah	13, 14, 16, 17, 19, 24, 32, 34, 35	13, 14, 16, 17, 19, 24, 32, 34, 35	–
Ezekiel	The whole book	1, 4, 7, 10, 11, 23, 24, 27, 38–48	1, 4, 5, 8–13, 15–17, 19–32, 35–48
1 and 2 Chronicles	The whole of both books	ditto	ditto
1 and 2 Maccabees	The whole of both books	ditto	ditto

Scheme A is thus very different from the other three in this respect, while the other three are closely related to each other, which suggests that Scheme B is later than Scheme A.

3

Thus the balance of evidence inclines towards giving priority to Scheme A. The use of Quiñones means that Scheme A cannot be earlier than 1535, nor Scheme B than 1536. The letter quoted by Smyth implies 1538 as the date of Scheme A; and there is a remark in the preface of the manuscript, '*dum . . . religiosorum tam multifarie cohortes suum queque seorsim habuerint usum*'[12] ('while the many different bands of monks each had their own separate use'), which points to a date very soon after the suppression of the monasteries *c.* 1538. Both schemes are in Latin, which seems unlikely to have been the case after the appearance of the English Litany in 1544 and *The King's Primer* in 1545. A note written in the margin of Scheme A[13] appears to refer to a book published in 1543, but that does not tell against the existence of the manuscript before that date. Further differences between Scheme A and 1549 are noted below (p. 6).

Scheme A

The manuscript begins with a calendar which includes the table of lessons (three for Mattins, two for Vespers). A good number of less well-known saints have been omitted, but a number of biblical names have been added on days when their names occurred in the appointed lessons. The lectionary has been detached from the church year, and begins on 1 January with Genesis, Isaiah, Matthew and Romans. There is also a column indicating which *senarius* (set of six) of psalms is to be said each day.

There follows a preface (untitled) which, translated into English and abridged, appears as 'The Preface' in 1549. Wickham Legg[14] provides a synoptic table of the prefaces of both editions of Quiñones, the manuscript and 1549 in parallel columns, which shows that Cranmer had already in Scheme A considerably abbreviated Quiñones' rather wordy composition. Below (pp. 8–13) is printed an English translation of the manuscript preface with that of 1549 on the opposite pages; the words peculiar to either version are italicized. In translating Cranmer's Latin, his own English words have been used wherever possible. The alterations made in 1549 show Cranmer gently pruning his more outspoken phrases. He defines his chief object in preparing the revision as follows:

> *ut videlicet sacrae scripturae filum et series ubique quoad fieri potest integre et indivulse continuetur, et ut exoticorum scriptorum quam minime intertexatur.*[15]

(that, so much as may be, the thread and order of holy Scripture shall be continued entire and unbroken, and that as little as possible of non-scriptural writers shall be interspersed.)

This object involves the 'cutting-off' of all antiphons, responsories and *capitula*.

Next come the rules for reading the psalms and lessons (translated below, pp. 14–16). Cranmer arranges for the Psalter to be gone through once a month, at the rate of six psalms a day, which raises two problems: first, of coping with the irregular lengths of the months; and, second, of providing thirty more psalms to make up the required total of 180. The first problem he solves in the same way as in 1549, by starting again with Psalm 1 on 31 January and finishing the Psalter on 1 March, and by repeating the psalms for the 30th day on the 31st in May, July, August, October and December. The second problem received two solutions. Cranmer's original idea was to count Psalm 119 as twenty-two psalms, which provided twenty-one of the thirty extra needed. He then added 'seven holy canticles' (as in Quiñones), divided Psalm 9 into two (Pss. 9 and 10 of the Prayer Book), and finally bisected one of the canticles, thus making up thirty. On second thoughts he discarded the canticles and divided eight more psalms into two (nos. 18, 68, 69, 78, 89, 105, 106 and 107).

The Bible readings are arranged thus:

Mattins   1. Old Testament, except the prophets
            2. Prophets and the Apocalypse ('since it is itself a prophecy').
            3. Gospels and Acts (thrice yearly).
            4. Histories of the saints and seasonal homilies, as appropriate.
Vespers   1. Old Testament, except the prophets (following on from Mattins).
            2. Epistles (thrice yearly).

Here again 130 of the longer chapters have been divided in half, to make up the necessary number of days. No chapters are omitted.

There follows the Order for Mattins:

Lord's Prayer
Domine labia etc.
Hymn

Three psalms
Lord's Prayer, in English
First, Second and Third Lessons, in English
Te Deum
Fourth Lesson, if there be one that day
Benedictus
Quicunque vult (only on Sundays)
Preces
Salutation
Collect
Benedicamus

Each reading is to begin with *Jube Domine* and end with *Tu autem Domine*; and to be read from the *suggestus*, not within the chancel.

Cranmer has here already begun the process of conflating different services within the Office which he carried to its completion in 1549. The items as far as Te Deum come from Mattins in the Sarum rite, *Benedictus* from Lauds, and the rest from Prime. The Little Hours and Compline are dropped altogether. In thus reducing the number of services to two each day, Cranmer claims to be merely following current practice. After the opening Lord's Prayer, which Sarum followed with *Ave Maria* and the Creed, and Quiñones with *Confiteor*, Cranmer proceeds straight to the *preces*. He discards Venite, though he restored it in 1549, but conversely keeps the Office hymn, which he omitted in 1549. He follows Quiñones in prescribing three psalms at each service, but in 1549 he varied the number. Like Quiñones, he keeps the Lord's Prayer after the psalms, but it is to be said in English. Again like Quiñones, he keeps the traditional unit of three lessons, followed by Te Deum; in 1549 he reduced the number to two, and placed Te Deum between them. The Fourth Lesson on saints' days seems to be his own invention, unless it be regarded as the equivalent of the *capitulum* of Lauds. This latter service is cut down even further than in Quiñones, the only element to survive being Benedictus. Prime is reduced to *Quicunque vult, preces*, collect and *Benedicamus*; and even *Quicunque vult* may be omitted to leave more room for the sermon. In 1549 Cranmer restores the Apostle's Creed and the Lord's Prayer before the *preces*, and adds the Collect of the day and a memorial collect from Lauds. Another innovation is the monthly recitation of the Psalter, instead of the previous weekly recitation retained by Quiñones.

Vespers is kept closer to its Sarum form, and the chief difference is the addition of two lessons. Comparison with 1549 is difficult, because the latter is a combination of Vespers and Compline assimilated to Mattins. Besides these adaptations, Cranmer completely omitted the offices of saints' days, prayer for the dead and directions for making the sign of the cross.

The Fourth Lessons were compiled by Cranmer from biblical, patristic and contemporary sources. Full details may be found in Wickham Legg's edition, pp. 212–19.

Scheme B

The *Horarum canonicarum series* is much closer to the traditional daily Office as adapted by Quiñones,[16] and requires little comment. From the point of view of the Prayer Book, the only interesting changes made by Cranmer are the introduction of a lesson at Vespers and the restoration of the *preces*. The latter, however, are not the traditional set (which were still kept in Scheme A), but a set from the Bidding of the Bedes which he continued to use in 1549. Also the two Old Testament lessons at Mattins are both taken from the same book, which paves the way for the reduction to one Old Testament lesson effected in 1549; and the same chapters are omitted as in 1549.

There never was anything by men so carefully devised or so surely established, which in *age and* continuance of time hath not been corrupted. This we see to have come about even in those prayers which we call 'hours' or 'canonical'. The ground whereof, *instituted* by the ancient Fathers of the Church, if a man would *diligently* search out *and examine*, he shall find that the same was not ordained *ineptly or inconveniently.*[17] For they so ordered the matter that all the *holy* Bible should be read over once in the year, and that the circle of canonical scripture should revolve with the circle of the year, intending thereby that the clergy and ministers of congregations should by often reading and meditation of the *sacred writings* be stirred up to *take the steep way of* godliness themselves, and *gain the ability* to exhort others by wholesome doctrine and to confute them that were adversaries. And the people by daily hearing of the *sacred* readings of *God's word* in the *sacred assembly*[18] should continually profit more and more in the knowledge of *divine matters*, and be the more inflamed with the love of *God*.

But *alas, the succeeding age has so befouled and convulsed and as it were torn limb from limb* this *so holy, so beautiful, so well fitting* order of *our ancestors. For the order of the books we nowhere preserve continuous and entire; but we pluck fragments hence and thence, and patch them together, paying no attention to what preceded or followed; or only tasting the beginnings of the books, having gone through scarcely* three chapters, the rest *we pass over.*

In this sort, we begin the Book of Isaiah in Advent and the Book of Genesis in Septuagesima; but we only begin them and do not persevere to the end.

After a like sort *we contaminate the Gospels and all* the Scriptures *of the New Testament; the structure of all the books has been loosened; we mix, transpose, confound everything. Indeed, certain frivolities resembling old wives' tales have been introduced, and held worthy that for them the reading of the divine oracles should be moved from its place.*

For the histories of the saints have been collected with such coarse judgement and described in such uncouth style, that they easily cause disgust to the judicious reader. And furthermore, *when* those ancient Fathers had divided *the Book of* Psalms into seven portions, which they call nocturns; now a few of them *only* are repeated daily, *and they rather with the sound of the lips than with the least thought of the mind*, and the rest are omitted.

There was never anything by *the wit of* man so *well* devised, or so surely established, which (in continuance of time) hath not been corrupted: *as (among other things) it may plainly appear by the common prayers in the Church, commonly called divine service*: the *first original and* ground whereof, if a man would search out by the ancient fathers, he shall find that the same was not ordained, *but of a good purpose, and for a great advancement of godliness*: for they so ordered the matter, that all the *whole* Bible (*or the greatest part thereof*) should be read over once in the year, intending thereby, that the clergy, and *specially such as were* ministers of the congregation, should (by often reading and meditation of *God's word*) be stirred up to godliness themselves, and *be more able* also to exhort others by wholesome doctrine, and to confute them that were adversaries *to the truth*. And *further*, that the people (by daily hearing of *holy Scripture* read in the church) should continually profit more and more in the knowledge of *God*, and be the more inflamed with the love of *his true religion*. But *these many years passed this godly and decent* order *of the ancient fathers hath been so altered, broken and neglected, by planting in uncertain stories, legends, responds, verses, vain repetitions, commemorations and synodals, that commonly when any book of the Bible was begun*: before three *or four* chapters *were read out*, all the rest *were unread*.

And in this sort the Book of Isaiah was begun in Advent and the Book of Genesis in Septuagesima: but they were only begun and *never read through*.

After a like sort *were other books of holy Scripture used. And moreover, whereas St Paul would have such language spoken to the people in the church, as they might understand and have profit by hearing the same, the service in this Church of England (these many years) hath been read in Latin to the people, which they understood not; so that they have heard with their ears only; and their ears, spirit and mind have not been edified thereby*. And furthermore, *notwithstanding that* the ancient fathers had divided the psalms into seven portions, whereof every one was called a nocturn, now *of late time* a few of them have been daily *said* (*and oft* repeated) and the rest *utterly* omitted.

To say nothing, meanwhile, of the number and hardness of the rules, of the manifold changings of the services, *and the other labyrinths of matters, by which the method of* turning the book became so hard and intricate that many times there was more business to find out what should be read, than to read it when it was found. *Things had reached the state that a particular art arose from it, and he needed to be a skilful artificer who truly understood the Ordinal (for so they call the rule-book of that art).*

We therefore, considering these *great* inconveniences, *and desiring* to redress the same, set forth an Order, whereby *we think this may be done with* readiness, having drawn out a calendar for that purpose which is plain and easy to be understood, *having this one object chiefly in view,* that (so much as may be) the *thread and* order of holy Scripture shall be continued entire and unbroken, *and that as little as possible of alien writers shall be interspersed.*

For this cause we have *mostly* cut off Anthems, Responds, Invitatories, *Chapters,* and suchlike things as did break the course of *sacred* reading, *only retaining a few hymns which seemed to possess greater age and beauty*[19] *than the rest, and the undoubted histories of certain chosen and unquestionable saints, which we have caused to be taken and picked*[20] *from suitable Greek and Latin writers. Furthermore, we have rejected those saints whose feasts we see to be kept by the people vainly and superstitiously, or whose life and manners were suspect to us, or whose histories were not to be found in approved authors. Lastly, when two or more fell on the same day we have thought fit to omit those who on every count seemed less suitable or necessary.*

Yet, since *we could not altogether avoid* rules, *we have left them both very* few in number, *and much more* plain and easy to be understanded. So that here you have an order for prayer, *not newly invented by us, but rather that* old *order handed down by the Fathers (if you read* their mind and purpose *aright), restored by us as far as possible to the pristine and primitive usage and splendour, or at any rate another not far different from that old one,* and *altogether* a great deal more profitable and commodious than that which *up to now you have in your hands.* It is more profitable, because here are *purged away* and left out many things *which had been added,* whereof some be *useless,* some uncertain and vain, *and it contains almost* nothing but the pure scriptures *inspired by* God,[21] and those in an order *more clear and direct than hitherto, which helps the*

Moreover the number and hardness of the rules *called the pie*, and the manifold changings of the service, *was the cause* that to turn the book *only* was so hard and intricate *a matter*, that many times there was more business to find out what should be read than to read it when it was found *out*.

These inconveniences therefore considered: here is set forth *such* an order, whereby the same shall be redressed. And for a readiness *in this matter*, here is drawn out a Kalendar for that purpose which is plain and easy to be understanded, *wherein* (so much as may be) the *reading* of holy Scripture *is so set forth that all things shall be done in order*, without breaking *one piece thereof from another*. For this cause be cut off anthems, responds, invitatories and suchlike things as did break the *continual* course of the reading of the Scripture. Yet because *there is no remedy, but that of necessity there must be some* rules: *therefore certain rules are here set forth, which, as they be* few in number, *so they be* plain and easy to be understanded.

So that here you have an order for prayer (*as touching the reading of holy Scripture*) *much agreeable to* the mind and purpose of the old Fathers, and a great deal more profitable and commodious than that which *of late was used*. It is more profitable, because here are left out many things, whereof some be *untrue*, some uncertain, some vain *and superstitious: and is ordained* nothing *to be read*, but the *very* pure *word of* God, *the holy* Scriptures, *or that which is evidently grounded upon the same*; and that in *such* a *language and* order *as is most easy and plain* for the understanding *both* of the readers *and hearers*. It is also more commodious, both for the shortness *thereof*, and for the plainness of the order, and for that the rules be few and easy.

reader's understanding and strengthens his memory. It is also more commodious, both for the *succinct* shortness of *reading*, and for the *simple* plainness of the order, and for that the rules be few and easy. *In additon, we have thus removed that re-cooked cabbage of the same sentences and chants repeated so often like a cuckoo, to the great convenience and relief of the readers.* Furthermore, by this *method* ordered *by us, there will be* no need of other *portuises or breviaries* but the Bible *itself, and so there will be less* charge for *buying* books.

And where heretofore there hath been *so* great diversity in saying and singing *the services that it might seem a confusion of tongues almost worse than Babel*, some following Salisbury use, some Hereford use, some of Bangor, some of York, *and the multifarious cohorts of religious each having had their own separate use*, now all the *churches through this* whole realm shall *easily merge into* one *and the same* use. And if any would judge this *our* way more painful, because that *now nearly* all things must be read upon the book, whereas before, by reason of so often repetition, they *had learnt to* say many things by heart; if those men will weigh their labour with the *greater* profit in knowledge which daily they shall obtain, *and the fruit of contemplation, which is wont to come more greatly to readers than to those who recite words from memory, it will certainly be no burden to tolerate this labour and bear it with equanimity. Farewell and prosper.*

Furthermore, by this order *the curates shall* need none other *books for their public service*, but *this book and* the Bible: *by the means whereof, the people shall not be at so great* charge for books, *as in time past they have been.*

And where heretofore there hath been great diversity in saying and singing *in churches within this realm*: some following Salisbury use, some Hereford use, some the use of Bangor, some of York *and some of Lincoln*: now *from henceforth*, all the whole realm shall *have but* one use. And if any would judge this way more painful, because that all things must be read upon the book, whereas before, by the reason of so often repetition, they *could* say many things by heart: if those men will weigh their labour with the profit in knowledge which daily they shall obtain *by reading upon the book, they will not refuse the pain, in consideration of the great profit that shall ensue thereof . . .*

Scheme A

CANON

We have arranged holy Scripture to be read in divine service in this order.

The Psalter will be repeated twelve times each year, the Gospels, Epistles and the Acts of the Apostles thrice.

The whole of the rest of the holy Bible will be read through once in a year.

OF THE READING OF THE PSALMS

The Psalter shall be gone through once every month, but since there is great inequality in the months, we first propose to reduce them to some equality thus.

Every month will receive as concerning this purpose the exact number of thirty days.

So because January and March exceed thirty by one day, February, which is placed between them and has only twenty-eight days, shall borrow one day from each. So for February the Psalter must be begun the last day of January, and ended the first day of March.

And whereas May, July, August, October and December each have one day in excess, we will that the same psalms be repeated the last days of the said months which were read on the penultimate days, so that the Psalter may be begun again the first day of the month ensuing.

And in that way it will happen that for this purpose all the months are equally confined within the number of thirty days, the last and penultimate days of those five months being always counted as one and the same day.

Now hear how we have adjusted the Psalter to this number of days. We have judged it best that each day should always have six psalms allotted to it, namely three for Mattins and three for Vespers.

But since the Book of Psalms only contains in itself 150 psalms, which would be taken up by the daily reading of five psalms, it was necessary to provide another thirty from elsewhere to fill up the set of six for each day, and we have done it in this was. Psalm 118, already divided into twenty-two parts, is appointed to be said as twenty-two distinct psalms, and thus twenty-one of the desired number of thirty psalms are supplied.

To these will be added seven
holy canticles long sung by custom
among the psalms. And so
twenty-eight are filled up.
In addition the ninth psalm will be divided in two,
according to the Hebrew arrangement,
and there will be
twenty-nine   twenty-two

And so far nothing has been divided by us, for division of which
we have not found a precedent either in the Hebrew text or in
our Bible.

Now, to fill up the one psalm   Now, to fill up the eight psalms
which is still lacking, we have   which are still lacking, we have
cut in two the canticle *Audite*   cut in two the eight longest
coeli quae loquar.   psalms, namely 17, 67, 68, 77,
                                         88, 104, 105 and 106.

And thus the number of thirty psalms, which we wanted, is fully
made up. And we have, in all, enough psalms, when distributed
six a day, to supply that month of thirty days of which we spoke.
So much for the regular reading of the psalms.

OF THE READING OF THE REST OF THE SCRIPTURES

Now you shall hear how we have divided the rest of the Scriptures into lessons. Every day there will be three or four lessons in
the morning, and two in the evening. We have given Evening
Prayer its own lessons so that the people may always learn
something, and may return home from the churches better
instructed in the word of God.

OF THE FIRST LESSONS

In the First Lessons of both Mattins and Vespers, the whole
Old Testament, except the prophets, is read once a year, but
here thirty-nine longer chapters are divided, to make up the
number of days, and two lessons are made out of one.

OF THE SECOND LESSONS

All the prophets of the Old Testament, with the Apocalypse
(which, since it is itself a prophecy, we thought should be joined
to the rest of its kind), will be read in the Second Lessons at
Mattins. But here we have been compelled to divide eighty-five

more wordy chapters so that the number of lessons might square exactly with the number of days. The whole of the Old Covenant is thus included. Further, we have assigned the Pauline and other canonical Epistles to the Second Lessons at Vespers, and we shall run through all of them thrice in the space of one year. Here only one chapter is divided, and that only at the second and third repetition.

OF THE THIRD LESSONS

Lastly, we have shared out the Gospels and the Acts of the Apostles among the Third Lessons of Mattins, and they also will come round thrice in a year in their entirety. Here too we have cut in half five longer chapters, that the number of lessons and days should coincide.

And the whole Bible has been marked out into daily portions in such wise that their end is reached always together with the end of the year. And when the beginning of the year returns, the beginning of the books must always be found again.

It must not be passed over in silence that in leap years that additional day which is inserted in February will have in every way the same service as the day before.

THE ORDER OF THE MORNING OFFICE

Now for the sake of clarity we shall describe from head to foot the order of the Morning Office which we wish to be observed.

Let the Lord's Prayer be said first of all, and in the vernacular tongue, more distinctly than was previously the custom. When this has been ended in the accustomed manner, let *Domine labia* be begun with *Deus in adiutorium*, *Gloria Patri* and *Alleluia*, or from Septuagesima to Easter *Laus tibi Domine* according to the ancient custom of the Church.

Then, leaving out Venite (which it seems enough to recite once a month in its place among the psalms), a *Hymn* will be sung, after which let *three psalms* follow, each ended with its own *Gloria Patri*. After this, let the Lord's Prayer be said again in the common tongue out loud. Then let *three lessons* be read.

When these things have been duly done, let Te Deum be sung, and after that let the *Fourth Lesson* be read, if there is one to be read that day. But it will only be on Sundays, or when the birthday of some saint or some otherwise notable day falls, for which we have thought fit to appoint a fourth lesson; for we have kept this place solely for histories of the saints and homilies and exhortations suitable to the time. Further, let each lesson that is to be sung, whether at Mattins or at Vespers, be begun by the priest with *Jube Domine* and a *Blessing*, and sealed with its usual ending *Tu autem Domine*. And let the whole choir answer, *And according to thy great mercy forgive our sins*. And we consider that the legends or lessons should be read, not within the chancels as today, but outside from the pulpit, as was the custom among the ancients, and in the vernacular speech, that the people, hearing and also understanding, may be edified and, according to Paul's institution, able to answer *Amen*.

After all this shall be sung *Benedictus*, then *Dominus vobiscum* with a *Collect* and *Benedicamus Domino*. And let the response be always *Laudemus et superexaltemus nomen eius in saecula. Amen*.

When Mattins has been thus performed, on Sundays only let the creed *Quicunque vult* be said immediately, and when it has been ended with its own *Gloria Patri*, forthwith the priest shall say these prayers:

V. Lord, show thy mercy upon us.	*R.* And grant us thy salvation.
V. Vouchsafe, O Lord, that day.	*R.* To keep us without sin.
V. O Lord, have mercy upon us.	*R.* Have mercy upon us.
V. O Lord, let thy mercy lighten upon us.	*R.* As our trust is in thee.
V. Turn us again, Lord God of hosts.	*R.* Show thy countenance and we shall be whole.
V. Lord, hear our prayer.	*R.* And let our cry come unto thee.
V. The Lord be with you.	*R.* And with thy spirit.

Let us pray.

Lord, holy Father, almighty, everlasting God, who hast safely brought us to the beginning of this day, save us today by thy power, and grant that this day we fall into no sin nor run into any danger; but that all our doing may be ordered by thy governance, to do always what is righteous in thy sight. Through ...

V. The Lord be with you.	*R.* And with thy spirit.
V. Let us bless the Lord.	*R.* Let us praise and exalt his name above all for ever. Amen.

The order of the evening office

Lord's Prayer. Deus in adiutorium. Gloria Patri or *Laus tibi.* Then *Hymn. Three psalms. Lord's Prayer. Two lessons* with their *Blessings. Magnificat.* Lastly *Collect,* exactly as in the Morning Office.

Further, we think Compline should be omitted altogether, and likewise the customary hours of Prime, Terce, Sext and None; partly because in all of them there is an unprofitable and otiose continual repetition of the same things, partly because it seems like a mockery to keep that division of the hours which the ancient Fathers once observed, when that custom of praying seven times a day has long gone out of use in the Church, and we are wont now to assemble for prayers only twice a day. In the place of Compline we have supplied those two evening lessons, which, being always different, will bring more profit and less boredom to readers and hearers.

We wish no one to be under obligation to say anything for morning or evening offices but what is set forth here.

Canon: Of shortening church prayers for the preaching of the word

Now since in this edition of church prayers we are aiming primarily at this goal, that all things should be done in the Church (according to Paul's counsel) for the edifying of the Church; and since we are persuaded that what we so much desire will come about to the greatest extent if sagacious and learned pastors seriously expend care and diligence in every way that the word of God should be expounded as plainly as possible to an unlearned people, and as studiously as possible to a reluctant people; to ensure that the prolixity of our public prayers here instituted by us should not hinder or in any way delay that work of the good shepherds in teaching their flock, we wish it noted and confirmed by this canon, that whenever any speech of exhortation is to be made to the people or preaching done, then the incumbent may leave out Te Deum, the Fourth Lesson and the creed *Quicunque vult* in those public prayers when the people are present, so that the people, kept too long and wearied by too lengthy reading, should not attend keenly enough, or should not have enough time to hear the preaching of the gospel and the clear showing-forth of the Spirit of Christ.

(There then follow:
Six blessings, one for each lesson, in hexameter verse, possibly composed by Cranmer himself.

Hymns, for each day of the week, Mattins and Vespers, ferial and seasonal.

Collects, one for each season from Advent to Trinity, then one for each Sunday.

Fourth Lessons for days marked in the Calendar before the Preface, some only indicated by titles with no lesson following.)

Scheme B

SEQUENCE OF CANONICAL HOURS

The first Sunday of the Advent of the Lord

AT MATTINS

Before all Hours, whether by day or by night, throughout the whole course of the year, the Lord's Prayer is to be said. Which said, the priest shall immediately begin O Lord, thou shalt open, *etc.*; O God, make speed, *etc.*; Glory be to the Father, *etc.*; *with* Alleluia.

This custom is to be observed all the year, except that from Septuagesima to Easter in place of Alleluia *shall be said* Praise to thee, O Lord, King of eternal glory.

The invitatory O come, let us adore Christ the Lord promised through the prophets. *The psalm* O come let us sing, *etc.*, *with* Glory be to the Father, *etc.*

The hymn The heavenly Word, *etc.*

The psalms appointed, in order. All psalms and canticles throughout the year are to end with Glory be to the Father, *etc.*

The antiphon The night is far spent and the day is at hand. Let us therefore cast off the works of darkness and put on the armour of light.

Three Lessons, to be found in the calendar appointed. The Fourth Lesson from Daniel, ch. 9, 'Seventy weeks . . . desolation shall persevere'.

Blessing for the First Lesson: May the eternal Father bless us with perpetual blessing. *For the Second*: May God the Son of God vouchsafe to bless and help us. *For the Third*: May the grace of the holy Spirit enlighten our senses and heart. *For the Fourth*: May the holy Trinity keep us in perfect charity. *Further, each Lesson, whether at morning hours or evening, shall begin with* Lord, bid a blessing (*the priest adding the blessing*), *and end with* But thou, O Lord, have mercy upon us. *Response*: For thy great mercy's sake.

Then, when the Lessons are finished, the psalm Have mercy on me, O God, *etc.*, *follows. This psalm is to be said here daily until the*

Nativity, and from Septuagesima to Easter; but at other times We praise thee, O God *etc., is to be said.*

When the Lord's Prayer *is finished, the priest shall begin* O God, make speed, *etc., as above at Mattins.*

The psalms appointed, in order, and the canticle Benedictus. *Before* Benedictus *shall be said the* capitulum *from the Wisdom books.* *Response*: Thanks be to God.

The antiphon Rejoice in the Lord always. Let your moderation be known unto all men. The Lord is at hand.

Before every collect The Lord be with you, *etc.*

Let us pray.

Stir up, O Lord, we beseech thee, thy power, and come; that by thy protection we may be rescued and by thy deliverance may be saved from the dangers that hang over us from our sins; who livest, *etc.*

The Lord be with you, *etc.* Let us bless the Lord, *etc.*

Lastly, the prayers shall follow in this way:

Lord, have mercy. Christ, have mercy. Lord, have mercy.

Our Father, *etc.*

Priest And lead us not, *etc.*

Response But deliver us, *etc.*

V. Lord, show us thy mercy.

R. And grant us thy salvation.

V. Lord, save the King.

R. And hear us in the day when we call upon thee.

V. Let thy priests be clothed with righteousness.

R. And let thy saints rejoice.

V. Lord, save thy people.

R. And bless thine inheritance.

V. Give peace, Lord, in our days.

R. Because there is no other to fight for us, but only thou, O God.

Priest. The Lord be with you, *etc.*

Let us pray.

Lord, holy Father, almighty, eternal God, who hast brought us to the beginning of this day, preserve us today by thy power, and grant that in this day we may fall into no sin, nor run into any danger, but that all our doing may always be directed by thy guidance to do thy righteousness; through Christ, *etc.*

After the saying of the Lord's Prayer *the priest shall begin* O God, make speed, *etc., as above at Mattins.*

The hymn Now that the daylight, *etc.*

The psalms appointed, in order; followed on Sundays and Festivals by the Athanasian Creed, Whosoever will be saved, *etc. On other days*, I believe in God, *etc.*

The antiphon All creatures rightly praise and glorify thee, O blessed Trinity.

When the prayers are finished, in place of the martyrology is read the story of the festival, if there is one.

Priest Precious in the sight of the Lord

R. is the death of his saints.

Let us pray.

May holy Mary, mother of our Lord Jesus Christ, and all the righteous saints and elect of God pray for us sinners to the Lord our God, that we may be helped and saved by him, who in perfect Trinity lives and reigns, God through all, *etc.*

The Lord be with you, *etc.*   Let us bless the Lord, *etc.*

AT TERCE

O God, make speed, *etc., as above at Mattins.*

The hymn Come, holy Ghost, *etc.*

The psalms appointed, in order.

The antiphon Praise and eternal glory to God the Father, the Son, and the holy Paraclete, world without end.

Priest The Lord be with you, *etc. The collect of the day follows.*

AT SEXT

The hymn O God of truth, *etc.*

The antiphon Lord, show us thy mercy, and grant us thy salvation.

The rest as above at Terce.

AT NONE

The hymn O strength and stay, *etc.*

The psalms appointed, in order.

The antiphon Bear ye one another's burdens, and so fulfil the law of Christ.

Lord, have mercy. Christ, have mercy *etc. as above after Lauds, except the collect, which is:*

21

Give ear, Lord, to our supplications, and dispose the way of thy servants in the prosperity of thy salvation, that among all the changes of this life we may always be protected by thy help; through our Lord, *etc.*

AT VESPERS

When the Lord's Prayer *has been said, the priest shall begin* O God, make speed, *etc., as above at Mattins.*

The hymn Creator of the starry height, *etc.*

The psalms appointed, in order. Immediately after the psalms the canticle Magnificat *is said with* Glory to the Father, *etc.*

The antiphon Let us live soberly and righteously and piously in this age, awaiting the blessed hope and the advent of the glory of God.

Then before the lesson follows the blessing May the divine help always remain with us; *and this blessing shall be said at Vespers perpetually.*

The lesson from the calendar. The blessing for the lessons of this day do not change the whole year. But you will find the lessons themselves, which change daily, in the calendar, except those which are assigned to be said on certain days separately. The Lord be with you, *etc., follows, with the collect of the day.*

AT COMPLINE

When the Lord's Prayer *has been said, the priest shall say*

Turn thou us, O God of our salvation.

R. And turn away thy wrath from us.

Priest. O God, make speed, *etc., as above at Mattins.*

The hymn O Saviour of the world, *etc.*

The psalms appointed, in order. Immediately after the psalms follows the canticle Nunc dimittis.

The antiphon Save us, Lord, waking; guard us sleeping, that we may wake in Christ and rest in peace.

Then follow the prayers, all kneeling. Lord, have mercy, *etc., as above at Lauds.*

Collect

Lighten our darkness, we beseech thee, Lord God, and mercifully drive away from us the snares of the whole night; through our Lord Jesus Christ your Son, who lives and reigns in the unity of the holy Spirit, God world without end.

Amen.

Priest The Lord be with you.

R. And with thy spirit.

V. Let us bless the Lord.

R. Thanks be to God.

This collect is used on this day in the church hours, and is to be observed through the whole circle of the year, unless warning is given otherwise for a season by a special rule.

Te Deum. Benedictus.

It must be remembered that the canticles Benedictus, Magnificat *and* Nunc dimittis *follow the psalms which precede them in such a way that nothing is inserted, but they are bound to the preceding psalms in continuous course without any gap.*

(Hymns, antiphons, lessons and collects are then set out for the rest of the year.)

Note: THE DAILY OFFICE IN LUTHERANISM

Unlike Cranmer, the Lutheran leaders did not envisage the Daily Office as holding a prominent place in the diet of worship provided for the average adult. This was not surprising in view of the fifteenth-century treatment of the Office, in which the regular recitation of the Psalter and systematic reading through the Bible had given way to frequent repetition of the relatively few psalms and lessons appointed for saints' days and their octaves. Most of the Lutheran Orders provided forms of daily prayer, but these were intended for use in schools and, in some cases (e.g. Denmark), monasteries. Luther set the style with his school services of 1526, set out thus:

Morning	*Evening*
Psalm	Three psalms, with antiphons
	Hymn
New Testament chapter	Old Testament chapter
(first in Latin, then in German)	(ditto)
Antiphon	
Exposition	
Hymn (in German)	Magnificat, with antiphon
Lord's Prayer (said privately)	ditto
Collect	ditto
Benedicamus Domino	ditto

It is noticeable that the only surviving canticle is Magnificat, which accords with the emphasis on Marian feasts in the Lutheran calendars (see below, p. 25).

The later Orders keep this basic scheme, but introduce every kind of variation. All increase the amount of psalmody in the morning, either to three psalms, or to a choice of one, two, or three (presumably according to length). At this stage, no table of daily portions is provided. In the evening, three remains the normal figure, though in some Orders a reduction to one or two is permitted.

There is a tendency to depart from Luther by reading the Old Testament in the morning and the New in the evening. Antiphons are preserved everywhere, and in some places responsories are kept also. Exposition soon drops out, but the German hymn establishes itself almost universally. The collect and *Benedicamus Domino* form the normal ending, with or without Kyrie, Lord's Prayer, and *preces*. In North Germany, Te Deum, Benedictus and *Quicunque vult* are often retained. But in general Luther's original scheme is plainly recognizable behind the minor variations.

Here and there features appear which have been thought to have influenced Cranmer in his various revisions of the Daily Office. Brandenburg–Nürnberg (1533) has a service called 'Common Prayer' (*Gemeingebet*), which is based on the sequence Psalms–Epistle–Hymn–Gospel–Te Deum, and ends with *three* collects. Calenberg–Göttingen (1542) produced an order of service which comes very near to the Mattins of the Prayer Book:

O God, make speed to save us . . .
Venite
Three psalms, with antiphons
Lesson (Old or New Testament)
Responsory
Te Deum
Lesson (New Testament)
Benedictus, with antiphon
Collect
Benedicamus Domino

But Vespers in this Order remains close to Luther's outline.

Denmark (1537) has the same set of versicles after the Lord's Prayer that Cranmer adopted in his Scheme B and in the Prayer

24

Book; its monastic Vespers includes Nunc dimittis as well as Magnificat, and also has the same curious sequence Kyrie–Creed–Lord's Prayer as appears in 1549 Mattins. Its author, Johann Bugenhagen, sent a presentation copy to Henry VIII, so Cranmer may well have been familiar with it. But while all these points may have impressed themselves on that retentive memory, it must be admitted that most, if not all, were likely to occur to anyone who set out to make a constructive reform of the Daily Office.

THE LUTHERAN CALENDAR

In their treatment of the Calendar, the later Orders show their usual tendency to a mildly conservative reaction. Luther himself never tackled the Calendar in detail, but the Orders which appeared in the years 1539–42 have a fuller list of observances than those of 1528 (Ernestine Saxony) or 1533 (Brandenburg–Nürnburg). By 1540 a list of widely accepted feasts has emerged, made up as follows:

The Circumcision, The Epiphany, The Purification, The Annunciation, Easter Day, Ascension Day, Whitsunday, John the Baptist, The Visitation, Christmas Day, Stephen.

Notice the concentration on Christmastide and also retention of the Marian feasts. Less widespread, but still popular are:

All the Apostles, Trinity Sunday, Michaelmas.

Quite rare are:

Maundy Thursday, Good Friday, Easter Monday and Tuesday, Whit Monday and Tuesday, Mary Magdalene, The Innocents.

There are some peculiarities: in Albertine Saxony the observance of the apostles' days is optional; while Brandenburg–Nürnberg keeps the Visitation on the traditional date of the Assumption, thus preserving a popular holy day (and holiday) without accepting its *raison d'être*. (This example is being followed by several Anglican provinces.) Electoral Brandenburg, in keeping with its generally conservative character, has much the fullest list, including:

Corpus Christi, Laurence, The Assumption, The Nativity of Mary, All Saints, Martin and Catherine.

Finally, there is no trace in the Lutheran Orders of any classification into different grades, such as is found in the medieval calendars, and even in the Prayer Book's division into red-letter and black-letter days.

2
The Primers:
Canticles and Collects

An important source of the Book of Common Prayer is the series of reforming Primers which appeared during the years 1530–45. In these books the traditional Hours of our Lady are supplemented by matter derived from Lutheran sources. The proportion of reformed to traditional material varies from Primer to Primer, and in the later examples the Hours themselves are subject to revision. It was a convenient method of introducing Lutheran ideas into England under the guise of traditional piety; but from the point of view of the Prayer Book the great importance of the Primers is that they contain numerous attempts at rendering the Hours into English. Manuscript Primers had included English versions many years before, but these were only available to the wealthy. The invention of printing made vernacular services a much more practical proposition.

About fifty different issues of these Primers have been recorded, twelve of them surviving in only one copy. Several of the issues are almost identical, but unpredictable variations abound, changes of content, or a sudden switchover from one source to another. The later Primers are heavily dependent on two or three of the pioneer issues, and exhibit the most complicated mixture of portions from different predecessors.

The first scholar to realize the importance of these Primers was Edward Burton, who reprinted three of them in 1834 as *Three Primers put forth in the Reign of Henry VIII*: his choice was Marshall's of 1535[1], Hilsey's of 1539 and *The King's Primer* of 1545. Unfortunately, his reprinting of Hilsey and *The King's Primer* is incomplete, as he does not print out in full any form found in Marshall, but gives only the *incipit* and *explicit*. The unwary reader is thus led to suppose that the text of, say, *Te*

Deum is identical in all three books, which is very far from being the case.

A great step forward was taken by the publication in 1901 of Edward Hoskins's *Horae Beatae Mariae Virginis*, a catalogue of Primers, manuscript and printed, in Latin and in English, with details of their contents, which remains an indispensable tool of scholarship. Little further work, however, was done in this field until C. C. Butterworth's *The English Primers (1529–1545)* appeared in 1953. Butterworth inspected every existing Primer, and was able to compare them in detail by the use of microfilm. His chronological analysis is unlikely to be challenged, and his painstaking identification of the various sources of each issue has elucidated the relationship between them once and for all. In only one respect is his work incomplete. His primary interest lay in translations of the Bible, and he first studied the Primers to establish the extent to which the various versions were disseminated. Thus he deals exhaustively with the psalms and lessons which constitute the bulk of the Hours, but he seems not to have felt an equal concern for the canticles and collects, which to the Anglican student are the Primers' most interesting features. The canticles in question are *Venite*,[2] *Te Deum, Benedicite, Benedictus, Magnificat* and *Nunc dimittis*. Also relevant to the Prayer Book are the opening *preces*, the Lord's Prayer, and some half-dozen collects (for which see below, pp. 49–55).

The earliest surviving Primer is the *Hortulus Animae* of 1530, plausibly attributed by Butterworth to George Joye, one of the first English Reformers, who fled to the Continent and published Lutheran material there. His translation of the canticles is taken over *in toto* by the two Primers of William Marshall (1534 and 1535), an associate of Thomas Crumwell and a favourite of Anne Boleyn; and by that of Thomas Godfray (? 1535). It continues to reappear in the Primers of J. Byddell (1537), R. Grafton and E. Whitchurch (1540) and R. Grafton (1542). Joye's translation seems rough compared with the versions familiar from the Prayer Book, but he has already hit upon a few lines which survive right down to the present day:

Our Father, which art in heaven, hallowed be thy name . . .
And forgive us our trespasses as we forgive them that trespass
    against us . . .
We praise thee, O God: we knowledge thee to be the Lord . . .
The glorious company of the Apostles praiseth thee . . .

27

> Thou art the king of glory, O Christ. Thou art the everlasting Son
> of the Father . . .
> In holiness and righteousness before him: all the days of our life.
> For thou shalt go before the face of the Lord to prepare his ways.

Here at any rate the admiration usually lavished on Cranmer belongs to Joye: Cranmer's only contribution was to refrain from altering Joye's phrases.

Robert Redman (1535) starts by using the *Hortulus* version, but introduces several new readings, especially in the gospel canticles, where he follows Tyndale's translation of 1526 and 1534. He is closely followed by J. Gough (1536). The preface of Redman's next edition (1537) says that its predecessor of 1535 had 'the favour and commendation of the more learned sort', and 'seemed to men of authority not inconvenient to pass among the common people' (a new idea for a Primer, hitherto the preserve of the rich). The 1537 edition has been 'more diligently corrected, more purely imprinted and meetly well purged of many things that seemed no small faults therein'.

A further departure from the *Hortulus* text of the canticles is made in a group of Primers beginning with an anonymous edition printed in Rouen (1536). These Primers keep to the *Hortulus* for *Benedicite*, but otherwise incorporate the changes made by Redman in 1535, and add many more of their own ('after the Latin text'), usually restoring the text of the Breviary where this differs from that of the Bible. The Rouen text appears in a slightly altered reprint of 1538, and is used by N. le Roux (four editions, all 1538) and Redman's editions of 1537 and 1538. These 'Rouen' editions show a slight swing back towards traditional Catholicism, exemplified in the substitution of 'priests' for 'ministers'.

John Hilsey (1539) an ex-monk now bishop of Rochester, reacts against this swing, basing his text on that of Byddell (see above, p. 27). His book has a semi-official status, being 'set forth . . . at the commandment of . . . Thomas Crumwell . . . for an universal usage to his Grace's loving subjects' (the first appearance of the idea of a single use for the whole realm). Cranmer read this Primer soon after publication and wrote to Crumwell on 21 July 1539:

> I have overseen the Primer which you sent unto me, and therein I
> have noted and amended such faults as are most worthy of re-
> formation. Diverse things there are besides therein which, if com-
> mitted unto me to oversee, I would have amended. Howbeit, they

be not of that importance but that for this time they may be well enough permitted and suffered to be read of the people. And the book itself no doubt is very good and commendable.

This letter and Redman's preface, taken together, strongly suggest that Cranmer privately approved of the publication of these Primers, but was unwilling to give them official authorization. Hilsey is followed by N. Bourman, J. Mayler and T. Petyt (all 1540).

After Crumwell's fall, the Primers once more adopt the Rouen text; for example, J. Mayler (second edition, also 1540), T. Petyt (1541, 1542 and 1544), W. Bonham (1542) and R. Toye (1542). Mayler's second edition and Petyt's first share unusual readings with le Roux's third; Petyt's second is based on Redman's of 1537, while his third reverts to le Roux. The differences between these 'Rouen' editions are trifling, and all clearly belong to the same family. It would appear that someone was engaged in constant revision and improvement of the text from 1536 to 1540. Who was this anonymous redactor? It is noticeable that the process ceases after 1540, the year in which Redman died, so that it may well have been inspired by him, even if he was not himself the redactor. The letter quoted above shows that it was not Cranmer.

The last of these reforming Primers was *The King's Primer* (1545). Designed to put an end to the 'diversity' of Primers, it draws on the *Hortulus*, 'Rouen' and Hilsey texts, and introduces new changes of its own, to bring the English as close as possible to the Latin. Some of its versions found their way into the Book of Common Prayer with little or no further alteration. Which versions of the canticles were to be used in the book of 1549 seems to have remained undecided until the very last moment. *Venite* and *Benedicite* are printed from the first in their proper places, using the text of the Great Bible. This translation was issued in 1549 with the psalms pointed for liturgical use with the Prayer Book, and it would clearly be inconvenient to have two different versions of Psalm 95 in use; and likewise with *Benedicite*, which could also be said from the Bible if required. At first this latter procedure seems to have been assumed in the case of the gospel canticles: in an early issue of the Prayer Book (Grafton, 8 March 1549) they are not included at all. But the procedure was soon abandoned: another issue of March 1549 has them at the end of the book, after *Certain Notes*. By then it had been decided to keep the translations of *The King's Primer*, complete with subtitles, and with only two tiny changes. Surprisingly, Whitchurch issues of May and June 1549 introduce otherwise unrecorded variant readings in *Te Deum*: 'Heauen and erthe are *replenished* . . .' and 'the holy gost *also being* the Comforter'. These soon disappear in favour of the familiar text. Thus the translation of the canticles was only established by degrees, well after the rest of the Prayer Book had attained its final form.

The texts which follow are set out so as to show the evolution of the translation from the *Hortulus*, on the left-hand page, to *The King's Primer*, on the right-hand. Both these texts are printed in full. The intervening stages are shown in chronological order; sometimes it has seemed worth while to print an entire canticle, but normally single lines suffice. Each source is indicated by the name of its printer or place of issue, followed by the last two figures of its date, thus: *Redman 35*. Only variants of importance are quoted, and each variant is quoted from the earliest Primer in which it appears. It may be assumed to recur in later Primers of the same group, unless the contrary is indicated by a subsequent change. No attempt has been made to reproduce the titles of the canticles, whether in Latin or in English, in view of the very wide range of non-significant variation that they display. Italic type in the text denotes the first appearance or transposition of the words italicized; omissions are indicated by the sign ∧. The original spelling and punctuation have been retained, except that the stroke (/) has been represented by a comma, and the abbreviation ⁻ for 'm' or 'n' has been written out in full. 'Yᵉ' (article) has been retained to avoid confusion with 'ye' (pronoun); and 'yᵗ' because of the possibility of confusion with 'yᵉ' in the original print. The text of *The King's Primer* is that of the Grafton edition of 29 May 1545 (STC 16034).

Notes

VENITE   *Hortulus*, line 11: 'The Gospell preched' is a gloss of the translator's.

lines 22, 23, 27: the phrases italicized represent words found in the Breviary: '*quoniam non repellet Dominus plebem suam*' and '*ploremus coram Domino*'. All the other *Rouen* changes follow closely the text of the Breviary, and so do those of *The King's*.

Hortulus drops the traditional invitatory, 'Hail, Mary', and substitutes 'Come unto me . . .'. The Redman/Rouen group restores 'Hail, Mary';

30

Hilsey reverts to 'Come unto me . . .', and *The King's* once more restores 'Hail, Mary'.

TE DEUM   *Hortulus*, line 34: note the rendering of '*speravi*' by 'truste', which is also found in the collects of the Book of Common Prayer.

Rouen 36, line 28: 'blys' seems to have no justification as a translation.

BENEDICITE   *Hortulus*, line 2: 'loave', i.e. 'praise'.

line 4: 'mought', subjunctive.

Marshall 34: 'love' = 'loave'.

Rouen 36, line 2 misreads 'ye' and prints '*hye* heuens'; *Redman 37* corrects this, but *Petyt 44* prints '*high* heauens'.

BENEDICTUS   *Hortulus* takes Tyndale's translation of 1526 as its starting-point for all the gospel canticles, but soon diverges.

Line 5, 'a long tyme paste': the letter 'p' is defective in the printed text, and *Godfray* reads it as '+'; he also mistakes the long 's' for 'f', and prints 'a long tyme and ofte'.

In the last verse, *Hilsey's* 'gyue' is probably a misreading of 'guyde' (*Rouen 36* onwards).

Several insignificant variations in *Le Roux 38* (STC 16006) are faithfully reproduced in *Petyt 42* and *44*.

MAGNIFICAT   *Redman 35* follows *Tyndale 26*, except for one verse from the 1534 translation.

NUNC DIMITTIS   *Redman 35* follows *Tyndale 34*.

The Canticles

VENITE

Hortulus

Come and let vs ioyfully geue thankes vnto ye lorde: let vs reioyse in god ower sauiour. Let vs approche into his presens with
praise & thankesgeuinge, and singe we vnto hym in the Psalmes.
For god is a grete lorde and a grete kynge over al goddis in whose
5 handes are the hartes of all the creatures of the erthe and the
hyghe hilles are at his commaundement.
The see is his, for he hath made it and his handes haue fasshoned
the erthe also: come therfore and let vs worshipe and fal downe
10 before the lorde which hath made vs: for he is ower god and we are
the flocke of his pasture and the shepe whom he driuethe.
Now (the Gospell preched) yf ye heare his voyce, se y^t ye harden
not
yower hartes, as they did in the place of temptacion in wildernes
bitterly murmuringe and spekinge ageinst god, where yower fathers
15 tempted me and prouoked me to anger ye althoghe they se my
myracles.
Forty yearis was I at debate chydinge with y^t generation. Wherfore
I sayd euer, theyr hartes are gone fro me, they know not my waies:
to whome I swore in my grete anger that they shulde not enter in
to the lande of my reste.

Redman 35

15 . . . althoghe they *saw* my myracles
17 . . . chydinge with *this* generation

Rouen 36

20 Come & let vs ioyfully gyue thankes vnto the lorde: let vs reioyse
in god our sauyoure, let vs approche into his presens with prayse
and thankesgeuynge, and synge we vnto hym in Psalmes.
For god is a great lorde and a great kyng ouer all goddes *which
shall nat forsake his people*, in whose *power* are all the *costes* of
25 the erthe, and *he beholdeth the toppes of mountaynes*.
The see is hys, for he hathe made it, and hys handes haue fasshoned
the earthe also: come therfore and let vs worshyppe and fall downe
before the lorde, *let vs weape before the lorde*, which hathe made vs, for
he is our *lorde* god, and we are *his people* and the shepe *of his pasture*.

30 Nowe ∧ if ye heare his voyce, se yᵗ ye harden nat your hartes as
     they dyd in the *tyme* of temptacyon in wyldernes, bytterly
     murmurynge ∧ agaynst god, where your fathers temptyd me and
     prouoked me to angre, ye although they sawe my myracles.
     Forty yeres was I *a neyghbour vnto* thys generacyon, wherfore I sayd
35 euer, theyr hertes are gone from me, they know nat my wayes:
     to whom I swore in my great angre, that they shulde nat entre
     into ∧ my reste.

Redman 37
25 . . . the toppes of *the* mountaynes
33 . . . prouoked me to angre, *and yet* ∧ sawe *they* my *workes*

Hilsey 39
28 omits: let let vs weape before the lorde
33 . . . prouoked me to angre, ∧ yet sawe they my workes

The King's

Come and let vs *reioyce* vnto the lorde, let vs *ioyfully syng* to God
our sauioure, let vs *come before his face* with *confession* and thankes-
geyng, and syng we *ioyfully* vnto him in Psalmes.
For God is a great lorde & a great kyng ouer all goddes, whiche *doth*
not forsake his people, in whose power are all the costes of the earth,
and he beholdeth the toppes of the mountaynes.
The sea is his, for he hath made it & his handes haue fashyoned the
earth also: come therfore and let vs worshypp and fall downe before
God, let vs wepe before the lorde who hath made vs, for he is our lord
God, and we are his people and the shepe of his pasture.
Today if ye here his voyce, se that ye harden not your hertes as ∧ in
the bitter murmuryng in the tyme of temptacion in wyldernes where
your fathers tempted me, ∧ *proued* me ∧, *and* sawe ∧ my workes.
Forty years was I *greued with* this generation, *and* I sayde euer, *they*
erre in their hertes, they *haue* not knowe*n* my wayes, to whome I swore
in my ∧ angre that they should not entre into my rest.

TE DEUM

Hortulus

    We praise the (O God): we knowledge the to be the Lorde.
    All therthe mought worshippe the, which are the father euerlastinge.
    To the kri forthe all angels: ye heauens & all the powers therin.
    To the thus krieth Cherubin and Seraphin continually.
5 Holy arte thou. Holy arte thou. Holy arte thou.
    Thou arte the lorde god of hosts.
    Heuen and erthe are fulfilled with the glory of thy maiestie.
    The glorious company of the Apostels prayseth the.
    The goodly felawshipe of ye prophetes worshipe the.
10 The fayer felawshipe of martyrs prayse the.
    The holy congregation of ye faithful thorowte al ye worlde
    magnifie y^e.
    They knowledge the to be the father of an infinyt maiestye.
    They knowledge thy honourable and very only sonne.
15 They knowledge thy holy goste to be a counforter.

Marshall 34

  8 . . . Apostels pray*se* the
11 The holy congregation of ∧ faithful . . .

Redman 35

  2 All therthe *doth* worshipe the . . .
10 The *noble army** of martyrs *do* prayse the

Rouen 36

  5 Holy.∧ Holy.∧ Holy.∧ Lorde god of *Sabaothe*
11 . . . of faithful *thoroughe** al ye worlde
15 *And the* holy Ghoste *also** to be a comforter

Redman 37

  3 . . . & all ∧* powers therein
11 The holy *Churche**∧* thoroughe al ye worlde *doth** magnifie the

Hilsey 39

14 . . . honourable and ∧ only sonne
* *No change from* Hortulus.

TE DEUM

The King's

We prayse the ∧ God, we knowledge the to be the lorde.

Al the yearth doth worship the, ∧ the father euerlastyng.

To the ∧ all aungelles *cry aloude*, the heauens and all powers therin.

To the ∧ Cherubin and Seraphin contynually *do cry*.

Holy. Holy. Holy. lorde God of Sabaoth.

Heauen and earth, are *full of* the *maiestie* of thy *glory*.

The gloryous company of the Apostles, praise the.

The goodly felowship of the Prophets, *praise* the.

The noble armye of Martyres, praise the.

The holy church, throughout al the world doth *knowledge* the,

∧ The father of an infinite maieste.

∧ Thy honourable, *true*, & onely son,

Also the holy goost ∧ *the* comforter.

35

Hortulus

 Thou arte ye kinge of glory o christe.

 Thou arte the euerlastinge sonne of the father.

 Thou (when thou shuldste take vpon the ower nature to
  delyuer man) didest not abhorre ye virgins bodye.

20 Thou hast opened the kingedome of heuen to the beleuers (dethes
  darte ouercome).

 Thou sitteste on the right hand of god into the glory of the father.

 Thou art beleued to com ower iuge.

 Wherfore we praye the helpe thy seruauntes whome thou hast

25 redemed with thy precious bloude.

 Make them to be noumbred withe thy sayntes in ioye euerlastinge.

 O Lorde saue thy people and blesse thy heretage.

 Gouerne & also lyft them vp for euer.

 We prayse the euery daye.

30 And we worshipe thy name euer worlde withouten ende.

 O Lorde let it be thy pleasure to kepe vs this daye withoute synne.

 O Lorde haue mercy vpon vs: haue mercy vpon vs.

 O Lorde let thy mercy lyghten vpon vs euen as we truste in the.

 O Lorde I truste in the, let me neuer be confounded.

Redman 35

 20 *When thou hadest* ouercome *the sharpenes of* dethe, thou opene*dest* the
  kingedome of heuen*s* to *them that beleued in the*

 22 . . . god *in* the glory of the father

 23 *We beleue y^t* thou *shalte* come *to be* our iudge.

Marshall 35

 19 . . . ye virgins *wombe.*

 30 . . . worlde without ∧ ende

Rouen 36

 19 . . . abhorre *a* virgyns wombe*

 28 . . . lyfte them vp *into blys euerlastynge*

 34 O lorde in the *haue* I truste*d*: let . . .*

36

Te deum

Redman 37
18 Whan thou *tokest* vpon the our nature to delyuer man, *thou* . . .*
20 (see Redman 35) . . . the kingedome of heuens to *all true beleuers**
24 We *therfore* praye the . . .*
31 *Vouchsaufe good* lorde to kepe vs . . .*

Hilsey 39
* No change from *Hortulus*

The King's

Thou art the kyng of glory, O Chryst.

Thou art the euerlastyng sonne of the father.

When thou tookest vpon the ∧ to delyuer man, thou dydest not
  abhorre the Virgins wombe.

When thou haddest ouercome the sharpenes of death, thou
dyddest open the kyngdome of heau*en* to all ∧ true beleuers.

Thou syttest on the right hande of God in the glory of the father,

We beleue that thou shalt come to be our iudge.

We therefore praye the, helpe thy seruauntes, whom thou hast
  redemed with thy precious blood.

Make them to be nombred with they saints in *glory* euerlastyng.

O Lorde saue thy people and blesse thyne heritage.

Gouerne *them*, and ∧ lyft them vp *for euer*.

Day by day, we *magnifie* the.

And we worshyp thy name, euer worlde without end.

Vouchsafe, *O* Lorde, to kepe vs this day without synne.

O lorde, haue mercy vpon vs, haue mercy vpon vs.

O lorde, let thy mercy lighten vpon vs, ∧ as *our* trust *is* in the.

O lorde, in the haue I trusted, let me neuer be confounded.

37

Hortulus

Prayse ye the lorde all his workes: prayse and extoll him for euer.

Ye angels of the Lorde praise the lorde: ye heuens loaue the lorde.

Ye waters al y^t are aboue heauen prayse ye lorde: al the powers of ye lorde mought prayse the lorde.

5 The sonne the moone prayse ye ye lorde: starres of the firmament loaue ye the lorde.

The raine & the dewe prayse ye ye lorde: all the wyndes of god prayse ye the lorde.

Fier & heate magnify ye the lorde: winter & somer loaue ye ye lorde.

10 Moistnes and ye hore frostes praise the lorde: the froste and colde loaue ye the lorde.

Yse and snowe mought loaue the lorde: nightes and dayes prayse ye the lorde.

The light and derkenes mought prayse the Lorde: lighteninges and 15 clowdes loaue ye the lorde.

The erthe mought prayse the lorde: loaue and extoll hym for euer.

Marshall 34

2 (and throughout) . . . ye heuens *love* the lorde

10 . . . praise *ye* the lorde . . .

Godfray 35

4 (and throughout) ye lorde *might* prayse the lorde

Redman 35

10 . . . the *yse* and colde . . .

Marshall 35

2 (and throughout) restores: loaue

Rouen 36

4 (and throughout) ye lorde *prayse ye* the lorde

5 The sonne *and* the moone . . .

10 Moys*tures*, and ye hore frostes, praise *ye* the lorde: ∧ froste and colde

Redman 37

2 (and throughout) . . . ye heuens *prayse* the lorde

12 Yse and snow *prayse ye* the lorde . . .

14 ∧ Light and derkenes . . .

15 (and throughout) clowdes *laude* ye the lorde

Hilsey 39
  2 Ye angels of *his* praise the lorde . . .
10 *Dewes* and ye hore frostes . . .

The King's

Prayse ye the Lorde all *the* workes *of the lorde*, praise and *exalt* him for euer.

The Aungelles *of the lorde*, praise *ye* the lorde, ye heauens praise the lorde.

Ye waters, all that are aboue heauen, praise the lorde: all the powers of the lorde, praise ye the lorde.

The sonne and ∧ moone, praise ye the lorde, sterres of the firmament, praise ye the lorde.

The rayne and the dewe, praise ye the lorde, al the wyndes of God, praise ye the lorde.

Fyer and heate, *praise* ye the lorde, wynter & sommer, praise ye the lorde.

Dewes and ∧ hoare frostes, praise ye the lorde, froste and colde, praise ye the lorde.

Ise and snowe, praise ye the lorde, nightes and dayes, praise ye the lorde.

Lyght and darkenes, praise ye the lorde, lightenyng ∧ and cloudes, *praise* ye the lorde.

The yearth, praise the lorde: laude and *exalte* hym for euer.

Hortulus

Hilles and mountayns prayse ye the lorde: all that springethe vp
on the erthe loave ye the lorde.

Ye wellis and springes prayse the lorde: sees and flowdes loave
20 ye the Lorde.

Whale fisshes and all that moveth in the waters prayse ye the lorde:
all byrdes of the ayer prayse the lorde.

Al beastes both wilde and tame prayse the lorde: ye chylderne
of men loave the lorde.

25 Israhel prayse thou the lorde: loave hym and extol hym for euer.

Ye ministers of the lorde prayse ye lorde: ye seruantes of the
lorde loave the lorde.

Ye spirites and soules of rightwis men loave the lorde: ye holy
& meke in harte prayse ye the lorde.

30 Anania, Azaryia, Misael prayse ye the Lorde: loave and extol
hym for euer.

O Lorde thou art blessed and praysed in the firmament of
heauen: thou art prayseworthy, glorious and magnified into
worldes withowte ende.

Redman 35

30 Adds (30a): Blesse wee the father ye son with the holy ghost: prayse
we hym & serue we hym withouten ende.

33 . . . magnified worlde ∧ withowte ende.

Rouen 36

26 Ye *preestes* of the lorde . . .

29 & meke in herte prayse ∧ the lorde

30 . . . loave *hym* and extol hym for euer

Redman 37

22 all byrdes of the ayer prayse *ye* the lorde

25 *Let* Israel prayse ∧ the lorde

30a . . . serue we hym *euermore*

32 *Blessed art thou* (lorde) in the firmament . . .

Hilsey 39

21 *Whalles* and all that moveth . . .

30a . . . & serue we hym *for* euermore

The King's
Mountaynes and *hylles*, praise ye the lorde, all that **spryng**eth vpon the yearth, praise ye the lorde.

Ye welles and sprynges, praise ye the lorde, sees & fluddes, praise ye the lorde.

Great fishes and all that *moue* in the waters, praise ye the lorde, all birdes of the ayer, praise ye the lorde.

All beastes *and cattell*, praise *ye* the lorde, ye children of men, praise ye the lorde.

Let Israell praise the lorde, laude hym, and *exalt* him for euermore.

Ye priestes of the lorde, praise the lorde, ye seruauntes of the lorde, praise the lorde.

Ye spirites and soules of rightwise men, praise *ye* the lorde, ye holy and meke in herte, praise *ye* the lorde.

Anania, Azaria, Misael, praise ye the lorde, laude and *exalt* hym for euer*more*.

Blesse we the father, the sonne, *and* the holy goost: praise we him and *exalt* hym for euermore.

Blessed art thou Lord in the firmament of heauen: thou arte prayse-worthie, gloryous and *exalted*, worlde without ende.

Hortulus

Praysed be the lorde, God of Israel: for he hath graciously visited, and redemed his people.

He hath set vp ower mighty helthe: in ye house of Dauid his seruante.

5 Accordynge to his promises, by ye mouthes of his holy prophetes of a long tyme paste.

Promysinge that we shulde be preserued frome ower enymes: and frome the handes of all them that hate vs.

That he wolde thus vse and declare his riche mercy touwerde ower

10 fathers: rememberinge his holy promyses.

And also to performe his othe which he swore to Abraham ower father: and promised hym selfe to give it us.

So that without feare, we delyuerde frome the handes of ower enymes: myght serue and honour him.

15 In holynes and rightwisness before hym: all dayes of ower lyfe.

Rouen 36

Blessyd be the lorde God of Israell, for he hath ∧ visyted and redemed his people.

And hathe reysed vp *an horne of saluacyon vnto vs*: in the house of ∧ his seruaunte *Dauid*.

20 *Euyn as he promysed* by the mouthe ∧ of his holye Prophetes, *which were syns the worlde beganne*.

That we shulde be *saued* frome our enemyes: and from the handes of all that hate vs.

To fulfyll the mercye promysed to our fathers, *and to* remember ∧ his

25 holy *couenaunt*.

And to perfourme *the* othe whiche he sware *vn*to our father *Abraham, that he wolde* gyue ∧ vs.

That ∧ we delyuered *out of* ye handes of our enemyes, myght serue hym *without feare*.

30 In holynes and rightwysenesse before hym: all *the* dayes of oure lyfe.

Redman 37
25 holy *testament*
26 To perfourme ... (omits: And)

Redman 38
26 ... he sware *to* our father Abraham

Hilsey 39
18 *He* hath raysed up ...
23 of *them* that hate us
27 that he wold gyue *hymselfe to* us

Grafton and Whitchurch 40
 1 *Prayse* be *to* the lorde ...

The King's

Blessed be the lorde God of Israel, for he hath visited & redemed his people.

And hath *lifted* vp *the* horne of saluation ∧ to vs, in the house of his seruant Dauid.

∧ As he *spake* by the mouth of his holy Prophetes, which *hath ben* syns the worlde began,

That we should be saued from our enemies, and from the handes of all that hate vs.

To *perfourme* the mercy promysed to our fathers, & to remembre his holy *couenant*.

To perfourme the othe which he sware to our father Abraham, that he woulde geue vs.

That we *beyng* delyuered out of the handes of our enemies, might serue hym without feare.

In holynes and righteousnes before hym, all the dayes of our lyfe.

BENEDICTUS

Hortulus
>And thou (my chylde) shalt be called the prophete of the most hyghest:
>for thou shalt go before the face of the lorde to prepare his wayes.
>To geue the knowledge of the sauinge helth to his people, thorowe
35 the foregeuenes of their sinnes.
>The whiche cometh thorowe thaboundante mercy and goodnes of ower god:
>by the whiche he hathe thus graciously loked upon vs, springinge frome aboue.
40 To geue lyght to them that have sitte in derknes, and in the shadowe of dethe: to directe ower fete into y^e waye of peace.

Redman 35
34 to geve $\wedge$ knowledge . . .

Marshall 35
40 . . . them that have sitte*n* . . .

Rouen 36
31 and thou $\wedge$ chylde, shalt be called the Prophete of the hyest: for
>thou shalt go before the face of the lorde to prepare his wayes.
>*And* to gyue knowledge of *saluacyon vn*to his people: *for the remyssyon*
45 of $\wedge$ synnes.
>$\wedge$ Thoroughe the *tender* mercye $\wedge$ of our god, *whereby the day sprynge from an hye hathe visyted* vs.
>To gyue lyghte to them that sat in darkenes & in the shadowe of deathe: *and* to *guyde* our fete into the waye of peace.

Redman 37
44 To gyue knowledge (omits: And)
48 . . . them that *syt* . . .

Redman 38
45 of *theyr* synnes
46 Thoroughe the tender mercy of god . . . (omits: our)

Hilsey 39
44 . . . for remyssion (omits: the)
46 . . . of *our* god, *by the which* spryng*ynge* from *the* hye . . .
48 . . . syt in *the* darkenesse . . .

BENEDICTUS

The King's

And thou childe, shalt be called the Prophet of the highest,
for thou shalt go before the face of the lorde, to prepare his wayes.
To geue knowledge of saluation vnto his people, for the remission
of their synnes.
Through the tendre mercy of our God, wherby the day spryng
  from an high hath visited vs.
To geue light to them that syt in darkenes & in ye shadow of death,
& to guyde our fete into the way of peace.

Hortulus

    My soule magnifieth the lorde.

    And my spirite reioysethe in god my sauiour.

    For he hath loked on ye poor degre of his hande maiden.

    Beholde nowe frome thenceforthe shall all generations cal me

5 blessid.

    For he y^t is mighty hath magnified me: wherfor blessed be his name.

    And his mercy is ouer them that feare hym: thorowte all

    generations.

    He hath declared his myghte by his power: he hath dispersed y^e

10 proude men by the vayne study of their owne hartes.

    He hath plucked downe men of power from their seates: and hath

    lyfted vp the poore lowly ons.

    The hongry he hath satisfyed with goodnes: and them that appered

    riche he hath lefte voyde.

15 He hath taken up Israel his seruante: thynkynge vpon hym to be

    saued for his mercyes sake.

    Lyke as he promysed to ower fathers: as to Abraham and to his

    seade for euermore.

Redman 35

    My soule magnifieth the lorde.

20 And my spirite *reioysed* in god my sauiour.

    For he hath loked on ye poore degre of his hande mayden: beholde

    now from *hens* forth shall all generacyons call me blessyd.

    For he that is myghty, hathe *done to* me *great thynges*, *&* blessyd

    is his name.

25 And his mercye is *alwayes on* them that fear hym thorowghe out all

    generacyons.

    He hath *showed strengthe with* his *arme*, he hath *scatered them that*

    are proude *in the ymagynacyon* of theyr ∧ hertes.

    He hath *put* downe *the myghty* from theyr seates, and hathe *exalted*

30 *them of lowe degre.*

He hath *fylled the hongry* with good *thynges*: and *hath sent away the* ryche *empty*.

He hathe *remembred mercy: & hath holpen his seruaunt Israel.*

Euen as he promysed to our fathers ∧ Abraham & to his sede for
35 euer ∧.

Redman 37
20 And my spirite *hath* rejoysed . . .
21 For he hath loked on y^e *lowe* degre . . .

The King's

My soule *doth* magnify the lorde.

And my spirit *hath* reioised in God my sauiour.

For he hath *regarded* the *lowlynes* of his handmayden.

For beholde ∧, from henceforth ∧ all generations *shal* cal me
blessed.

For he that is mighty, hath *magnified* me, and *holy* is his name.

And his mercy is ∧ on them that feare him, throughout al
generations.

He hath shewed strength with his arme, he hath scatered *the*
proude in the imagination of their hartes.

He hath put downe the mighty from their seate, and hath exalted
the humble and meke.

He hath filled the hungry with good thinges, and *the riche he* hath
sent *empty* away ∧.

He *remembrying his* mercy, ∧ hath holpen his seruant Israel, ∧ as
he promised to our fathers, Abraham and ∧ his sede for euer.

Hortulus

Nowe letest thou thy seruaunt departe, o lorde, accordinge
to thy promyse, in peace.

For myn eyes have sene the sauiour: sent from the.

Whom thou hast set forthe in the presens of all people.

5 To be a lyght, lyghteninge ye gentils & to be ye glory of thy
people Israel.

Redman 35

Lorde now lettest thou thy seruaunt departe *in peace* accordyng
to thy promes.

For myne yies haue sene ye sauiour sent from the.

10 Whom thou haste *prepared before the face* of all people.

To be a lyght *to lyghten* the gentyls, and ∧ the glory of thy
people Israell.

Rouen 36

9 For myne eyes haue sene *thy sauynge healthe.*

10 *Which* thou haste prepared . . .

11 ∧ A lyght to *be shewed vnto* the gentyles, and *to* the glorye . . .

Redman 38

7 *Nowe* (Lord) *let* thy seruaunt . . .

Hilsey 39

7 *Lorde* nowe *lettest thou* . . .

12 *of* Israell

The King's

Lorde, now lettest thou thy seruaunt depart in peace,
according to thy *worde*,

For myne eyes haue sene thy *saluation*,

Which thou hast prepared, before the face of all *thy* people,

To be a lyght *for* to *lyghten* the Gentyles, and to *be* the glory of
thy people of Israel.

The collects in the Primers do not play as important a part in the prehistory of the Prayer Book as do the canticles. Only a few of the collects in the Prayer Book appeared in any of the Primers. Since the Primers are based on the Hours of the Blessed Virgin Mary, the collect of the Annunciation is normally present, and so are the collects of Whitsunday and Trinity Sunday. The more traditional Primers include a number of collects for saints' days, but the majority of these days and their collects were not carried on into the Prayer Book.

Texts of the Lord's Prayer have been included here for general interest. Petyt's Primer of 1541 contains this note:

> The kynges hyghnesse greatly tenderynge the welthe of his realme hath suffered heretofore the Pater noster, Aue, Crede and the x commaundementes of god, to be had in ye Englysh tongue. But his grace perceyuynge nowe the great diuersyte of the Translacyons hath wylled them all to be taken vp, and in stede of them hath caused an vniforme translacyon of the sayd Pater noster, Aue, Crede and x commaundementes, to be set forth.

The text of the Lord's Prayer referred to is that printed below from *The King's Primer*, which first appeared in Robert Redman's Primer of 1538.

For the conventions of transcription used below, see p. 30. Here all texts are printed continuously, not on facing pages.

PRECES

Hortulus

    O lorde opene thow my lippes: & then shal my mouthe shew
      forth thy prayse.
    O God bende thi selfe into my helpe: lorde haste y^e to helpe
    me.
5 Glory be to y^e $fath^r$, to the sonne, and to the holi goste.
    As it was in the beginninge: as it is now & ev^r shalbe. amen.

Redman 37

1 Lorde opene . . . my mouthe shal pronounce . . .
6 . . . shalbe. So be it.

Hilsey 39

6 . . . and as it is now . . .

The King's

O Lorde open thou my lippes. And ∧ my mouth shal shew ∧ thy prayse.

O God, *to helpe me make good spede.* Lord *make* haste ∧ to *succur* me.

Glory to the father, and to the sonne, and to the holy goost.

As it was in the begynnyng, *and* ∧ is now, and euer shalbe *worlde withoute ende.* Amen.

THE LORD'S PRAYER

Hortulus

Owre father which arte in heauen, halowed be thy name.
Lete thy kyngdome come ouer vs.
Thy wyll be fulfilled as well in erthe as it is in heauen. Geue vs this daye ower sufficiente fode. And forgeue vs ower
5   trespasses as we forgeue them that trespas ageinste vs. And lede vs not into temptacion, but delyure vs from theuel spirit. Amen.

Rouen 36

2   . . . come *vnto* vs
4   . . . our *daylye breade* . . .
6   . . . from *euyll. So be it.*

Redman 37

1   . . . *sanctified* be thy name
2   omit: vnto vs
4   . . . our *offences* . . .
5   . . . that *offende* . . .

Redman 38

1   . . . *halowed* . . .
2   omit: Lete
3   Thy wyll be *done* . . .
4   . . . our *trespasses* . . .
5   . . . that *trespass* . . . *Let* vs nat *be led* into temptacion.

The King's

Our father whiche art in heauen, halowed be thy name. Thy kingdome come. Thy wyll be done ∧ in yearth, as it is in heauen. Geue vs this day our daily breade. And forgeue vs our trespaces as we forgeue them that trespace against vs.

50

And let vs not be led into temptation, but deliuer vs from euyl. Amen.

THE SECOND COLLECT OF EVENSONG
Redman 35

O God, from whom all holy desyres, al good counselles and all iuste workes do procede, gyue vnto vs the same peace whiche the worlde can nat gyue that our heartes beyng obedient to thy commaundementes (& fear of our
5 enemyes taken away) our tyme may be peasyble thorough thy proteccyon. By Christe our lorde. Amen.

Rouen 36
2 . . . gyue vnto *thy seruauntes* that same peace . . .
6 . . . our lorde. *So be it.*

The King's

O God, from whome all holy desires, al good counsels, and all iust workes do procede, geue vnto thy seruauntes that same peace, which the worlde can not geue, that oure hartes being obedient to thy commaundementes, & *the* feare of our enemies taken away, our time may be peaceable *by* thy protection. *Thorough* Christ our lord, Amen.

THE THIRD COLLECT OF EVENSONG
The King's

O Lorde God, we beseche the to lighten our darkenesse, and deliuer vs from all the daungers of this night, O merciful lorde. Through our lord Jesus Christ: who liueth & reigneth with the in unite of the holy spirit, worlde without ende. Amen.

THE SECOND COLLECT AFTER THE LITANY
Redman 35

God to whom it is appropryed to be merciful euer and to spare, take our prayer, & let thy merciful pity assoyle them that ben bounde with the chayne of synnes. By our lorde Jesu Christ. So be it.

Hilsey 39
3 . . . *pitiful mercy* . . .

Redman 35

    Almyghty eternal God, which alone dost great wonders,
graunt vnto thy seruauntes thy bysshoppes, and to all
congregacyons committed vnto them, the spirite of grace;
and to thende that they maye please the, powre out on them
5 ye perpetual dew of thy grace, by Christ. So be it.

Rouen 36

5 ... dew of thy *benediccyon*, by Christ *our Lorde* ...

Redman 37

2 ... *the* bysshoppes ...

Hilsey 39

4 ... and that in *ye truth* they maye ...

The King's *reproduces the text of the 1544 Litany for both these collects; and so does the 1549 Book.*

WHITSUNDAY

Hortulus

    O God, whiche hast instructed ye hartes of faithful men with
the lyghteninge of thy holy goste: graunte vs to sauoure
arighte in the same spirite, and to reioyse euermore of his
holy consolation. whiche lyuest and raignest in ye same
spirit euer. Amen.

Marshall 34

1 ... of *the* faithful men ...

Redman 35

    O God, which hast instructed ye hartes of ye faithful by y^e
inspiracyon of ye holy ghost, vouchsaufe that we in the same
spirite may sauour the truthe. And euermore to reioyse in
hys holy consolacyon. By Christ our Lorde. So be it.

The King's

    O God, which by the *information* of the holy goost, hast
instructed the hertes of *thy* faithfull, *graunt vs* in the same

spirit *to haue right vnderstanding*, and euermore to reioyce in his holy consolation. *Through* Christ our lorde. *Amen.*

TRINITY SUNDAY

Hortulus

O almyghty everlastinge god, which has geven vs thy seruauntes to knowledge the glory of theuerlastinge Trinite with a faithfull knowledge, and to worshipe ye one god in thy almyghty maiesty: we beseche the that thorowe the stedfastnes of this faith, we mought be defended from all aduersites: which lyuest and reignest one god in ye Trinite of persons worlde withoute ende. Amen.

Redman 35

Almyghty & euerlastyng god which hast grauntyd to vs thy seruauntes thoroughe confessyon of the true faythe for to acknowledge the glorye of the eternall Trynite. And in the power of maiestie for to honour the unite. We beseche the, that thorough our stedfastnes in the same faythe, we may alwayes be defendyd from al aduersytes, wherin thou doist raygne our god, worlde without ende. Amen.

The King's

Almighty and euerlasting God which has graunted to vs thy seruauntes *by* confession of the true faith for to acknowledge the glory of the eternal Trinite, and to honour *the, one God* in *thy almighty* maiesty: we beseche the that thorough stedfastnes in the same faith, we may *be* alway defended from al aduersyte, *whiche lyuest and reignest one* God world without ende. Amen.

3 Rouen *and the Whitchurch issue of* The King's *dated 20 July 1546 read* and to honour the one God, *without the comma after* the.

TRINITY 2

Grafton and Whitchurch 40

O Lord make vs to haue a perpetuall feare and loue to thy holy name for thou neuer leuest those destytute of thy gouernayle, whom thou hast fyxed in the stedfastnes of thi loue.

53

Redman 37

O God the protector of al that truste in ye without whome
nothynge is of value, nothynge is holy, multyplye thy mercy
on vs, that thorowe thy gouernaunce & guydynge we may so
passe in temporall goodes, that we lese not the eternall. By
Chryst oure Lorde.

Grafton and Whitchurch 40

O God defender of all that trust in the without whom
nothynge is *stronge* nothynge ∧ holy multiply *ouer* vs thy
mercy that *thou beynge gouerner and leder*, we may so passe ∧
temporall *felicyte* that we lose nat ∧ eternall, *graunt thys for
Jesu Christe the Lordes sake which with the and with the holy gost
lyueth and regneth God for euer and euer. Amen.*

SAINT JOHN THE EVANGELIST

Redman 35

We beseche the, lorde of thy benygnyte to gloryfie thy
churche, that it beyng illumyned with the teachynges of
blessyd saynt Iohan thy apostle and euangelyst, may attayne
the rewardes euerlastynge. By Christe our lorde. So be it.

THE ANNUNCIATION

Redman 35

Lorde we beseche the to poore out thy grace into our heartes,
so y^t we which haue knowlege of the incarnacyon of our lorde
Jesu Christe, by annuncyacyon of thy Aungell, through his
holy passyon & crosse, may be brought vnto the glory of the
laste resurreccyon. By the same lorde Jesu Christ, which
lyueth and reygneth one God with the father & the holy
ghoste worlde without ende. So be it.

Hilsey 39

O Lorde whiche by the annunciacyon of thy aungel haste
gyuen vs knowledge of the Incarnacyon of thy sonne Chryst
(we beseche the) powre thy grace into our hartes that we
trustynge in hym through his passyon and death maye be
brought to the glorye of the laste resurrecyon. By the same
our lorde Jesu Christ whiche lyueth and reygneth one god

with the father and the holy ghost world without ende. So be it.

SAINT MICHAEL AND ALL ANGELS

Redman 35

O God, whiche by a wonderfull order doyst appoynte the seruice both of men and aungelles, of thy excedynge mercy graunte vs, that they whiche attende alway vpon thy seruice in heuyn may defend our lyfe here in erth. By Christe our lorde. So be it.

The King's *does not include any of the previous five collects.*

BURIAL

Redman 37

O God which by the mouth of Saint Paul the apostle hast taught vs not to be sorry for them that sleep in Christ, we beseech thee, that in the coming of thy Son our lorde Jesus Christe, we with all other faithful people being departed may be graciously brought to the ioys euerlasting, which shalt come to iudge the quick and the dead, and the world by fire.

The King's
2 not to *wail* for them . . .
4 . . . Jesus Christ, *both* we *and* all other

3
Cranmer at Work

The Collects

It was against the background of the clumsy translations printed above that Cranmer began his work on the collects. His versions of the medieval collects are generally reckoned to mark the peak of his achievement as a writer of liturgical prose. At times he himself is capable of clumsy literalism, as in the collect of Trinity 3:

> Lord, we beseech thee mercifully to hear us, and unto whom thou hast given an hearty desire to pray: grant that by thy mighty aid we may be defended: through Jesus Christ our Lord.

But in general, the difference in quality between his translations and those of the Primers is quite amazing; and his new compositions are hardly less successful.

Taking Sundays and holy days together, there are eighty-four collects in the 1549 Prayer Book, besides others included in various services, which are not discussed here. Cranmer's treatment of them takes three forms, though the dividing line between them must not be pressed too hard. There are straightforward translations; adaptations; and new compositions. The great majority of the third class are found among the saints' days, for doctrinal reasons; but it is also noticeable that, whereas Cranmer begins the year at once with new collects for Advent 1 and 2, he is content to translate or adapt *all* the collects for the Sundays after Trinity. Either time or enthusiasm for new composition seems to have run out.

Many of the changes Cranmer makes in his translations reveal his theological standpoint. Isaac Williams considered them in Tract 86, 'Indications of a superintending Providence in the preservation of the Prayer Book and in the changes which it has undergone', published in 1842. He summed up the difference in tone between Cranmer's work and the original Latin as follows:

Through all these alterations there runs one prevailing tendency, to put into our mouths the language of servants rather than that of sons.

Entire Collects, or expressions in them, which imply the privileges of the faithful, or spiritual rejoicing, as of sons, are dropped; and prayers substituted in a lower tone (pp. 9–10).

It is the same string which is touched upon in all these changes; instead of the spiritual rejoicing of the festival, the same chord is struck, simple, solemn, and deep; and if there are varied intonations, these are but the varied forms, the particular duties, of obedience (p. 49).

Williams perhaps overstates his case, but he has certainly offered one valid insight. Other points of the same nature emerge from the detailed investigations of J. A. Devereux.[1] Cranmer, he points out, inserts a specific mention of grace or God's goodness:

and also may have *grace and* power (Epiphany 1);
may be mercifully delivered *by thy goodness* (Septuagesima).

(The words in italics are not in the Latin).
The word *mereor* ('deserve') is omitted from the collects for the Sunday next before Easter and Trinity 14. Cranmer was already moving towards this in his Breviary schemes, where he substitutes the word *valeo*;[2] and modern translators have tended to follow his lead in omitting *mereor* altogether. Cranmer makes the point that justification by faith still implies good desires and good works (Easter Day, Trinity 25), but the Lent 1 collect which implied that good works obtain rewards was replaced even in the Breviary schemes.[3]

The memorial character of the Eucharist is stressed: the *annua expectatione* of the first Christmas Mass becomes 'the yearly *remembrance* of the birth' of Christ; and the word *hodie* ('today') is omitted from Epiphany, The Conversion of St Paul, Easter (First Communion), Ascension Day and St Bartholomew, presumably in order to avoid any suggestion of representation. But, as Devereux admits, too much must not be made of this point, as Cranmer keeps *hodie* on The Innocents, The Purification and Whitsunday. The eyes of the worshippers are firmly turned from this world towards heaven:

that we *finally* lose not the things eternal (Trinity 4);
that we may so run to thy *heavenly* promises (Trinity 13).

Of the medieval saints' day collects, some are discarded because they ask for the saint's protection (Mark, James, Thomas) or intercession (Andrew, Barnabas, Mary Magdalene, Matthew, Luke, All Saints), while others claim merit in carrying out the observance (Ash Wednesday, Simon and Jude).

Straightforward translations constitute two-thirds of the *Temporale* and a quarter of the *Sanctorale*. Only three collects could be described as absolutely exact renderings (Trinity 11, Trinity 17, Annunciation). Idiosyncrasies of translation abound which are not attributable to theological reasons. For example, Cranmer has a well-known habit, shared with Bucer, of doubling words ('erred and strayed'). This doubling occurs three times in Advent 4 and Good Friday ii; twice in Epiphany 1, 4, 5, Lent 5, Trinity 7 and Michaelmas; once in seven others. In addition there is Easter 4, where 'sundry and manifold' is not represented in the Latin at all. It is part of Cranmer's constant tendency to expansion and explanation, which shows itself especially in the insertion of adjectives and adverbs which are not in the Latin, the most frequent being 'all' and 'in all things'.

The words 'mercy', 'merciful' and 'mercifully' appear a good deal more often than the Latin warrants. 'Mercifully' is always used to render the frequent Latin word *propitius*, but it also represents the Latin *coelesti pietate* (Epiphany 1) and *benignus* (Trinity 3). 'Merciful' translates *placatus* in Trinity 21. In Advent 4 *gratiae* becomes 'grace and mercy'; 'mercifully' is added in Lent 4, 'merciful' in Easter 5, and 'mercy' in Trinity 7 (of which more below).

Pietas provides another example of questionable rendering. It really means 'fatherly affection', but is rendered 'true religion' in Epiphany 5 and 'godliness' in Trinity 22 and 23 (see also Epiphany 1, above). In Trinity 7, 12 and 25 it is omitted altogether; evidently Cranmer felt ill at ease with the word. *Spero* is translated 'trust' in Trinity 1 and 4; the Primers were already doing this in the last verse of *Te Deum*. *Ecclesia* is sometimes 'congregation' (Trinity 5 and 16), sometimes 'church' (John Evangelist, Good Friday ii, Trinity 15 and 23, Bartholomew). *Familia* is 'church and household' in Epiphany 5, 'household the church' in Trinity 22 and 'people' in Lent 5. Here and there signs of haste are visible, as in the clumsy repetition of 'follow the example' in Sunday next before Easter.

A number of Cranmer's translations are free enough to be fairly described as adaptations. An excellent example is Advent

4, where the words in italics were all added by Cranmer to the Latin:

> Lord, raise up, we pray thee, thy power, and come *among us* and with great might succour us, that whereas through our sins *and wickedness* we be *sore let and* hindered, thy *bountiful grace and* mercy, through the satisfaction *of* thy *Son our Lord,* may speedily deliver us . . .

Neither *auxilium* nor *indulgentia* is translated at all, and 'satisfaction' is not the equivalent of *propitiationis.* The 1661 revisers applied Cranmer's own methods by adding the words 'in running the race that is set before us' and by creating a fourth double in '*help and* deliver us'; but 'speedily deliver' was a fair translation of *acceleret.*

Lent 2 is equally free, but more successful:

> *Almighty* God, which doest see that we have no power *of ourselves to help ourselves:* keep thou us both outwardly *in our bodies* and inwardly *in our souls,* that we may be defended from all adversities *which may happen* to the body, and from *all* evil thoughts *which may assault and hurt* the soul . . .

Here Cranmer unpacks 'outwardly' and 'inwardly', which is quite justifiable; but reverses the order, thus destroying the chiasmus (inwardly . . . outwardly . . . body . . . soul) and substituting a direct parallelism. He excises the word *mundemur* ('may be cleansed') from the last clause, perhaps to avoid a change of metaphor; but makes up for it by introducing two completely new verbs, 'assault' and 'hurt'.

Similar processes may be seen at work in the collects of the Sunday next before Easter, where 'of thy tender love toward man' is pure Cranmer; Easter Day Mattins ('for our redemption', 'by his glorious resurrection', 'so to die daily to sin'); Easter Day First Communion (almost every word is touched up); and Trinity 12 ('which art always more ready to hear than we to pray, and art wont to give more than either we desire or deserve' is literally 'who dost exceed the merits and prayers of thy suppliants by the abundance of thine affection').

In the case of Trinity 7, the result is less happy. To realize the damage that Cranmer has done to this collect, his rendering, which is preserved unaltered in the 1662 Prayer Book, must be set beside a literal translation of the Latin:

God of hosts, to whom belongs all that is best: graft in our hearts
the love of your name, and cause in us an increase of religion; that
you may nourish what is good; and by the zeal of affection may
preserve what has been nourished . . .

Here a Pauline metaphor is carried right through the collect.
The gardener grafts the bud into the stock, nourishes it and
preserves it when grown: the collect asks God to graft love into
our hearts, nourish it and preserve it when grown. Cranmer
starts pretty freely, adds a new thought in '*true* religion'; treats
bona as external good, whereas it means 'the good in us'; and
finally discards the metaphor altogether, once again mistrans-
lating *pietas*, this time as 'great mercy'. The result is a well-loved
collect which has confused the logical progression of the original,
without offering any corresponding improvement.

Other collects are completely new compositions. These include some of the best of the whole series (also, according to
F. E. Brightman,[4] the worst, that of Mary Magdalene); and it is
a pity that Cranmer did not write more of his own. Advent 1 sets
a very high standard at the start of the year. The collect is based
on the antithesis of the First Coming of Christ and his Second
Coming. This is worked out in four points:

in the time of this mortal life	in the last day
thy Son Jesus Christ came	when he shall come again
to visit us	to judge both the quick and the dead
in great humility	in his glorious majesty

Note the chiasmus: visit . . . humility . . . majesty . . . judge. The
description of the Second Coming is drawn from that in *The
King's Book*: 'Christ shall come . . . in his majesty and glory . . .
and shall judge all, quick and dead'.[5] The carefully balanced
clauses are introduced by a quotation from the Epistle of the
day, which already contains a further pair of antitheses:

that we may cast away	the works of darkness
and put upon us	the armour of light

Cranmer could perfectly well have cast his material in strict
collect form:

Almighty God, whose blessed Son Jesus Christ, in the time of this
mortal life, came to visit us in great humility, and in the last day
shall come in his glorious majesty to judge both the quick and the

dead: give us grace that we may cast away the works of darkness and put upon us the armour of life; through the same . . .

Lucid, but tame; and Cranmer wants to relate the past event and the future event to the present, which he can do by emphasizing ('now') that we are 'in the time of' the First Coming. So he plunges straight into the petition:

Almighty God, give us grace . . .

and encloses the comparison of the two Comings in another striking chiasmus, which makes its effect despite its members being separated by two or three lines of vivid imagery:

now, in the time of this mortal
life . . .   we may rise to the life immortal.

Besides these literary antitheses, the whole collect is poised on the theological relationship between Christ and us.

With Advent 2 and elsewhere, Cranmer uses the traditional collect structure, and with complete ease. He does not relate his collects to the liturgical lessons as closely as Cosin and others have suggested. Out of twenty-four new compositions, he alludes to the Epistle of the day in eight, and the Gospel in four others; in the other twelve he alludes to neither, though he includes allusions to other parts of the Bible.

As so often in the Prayer Book, one of Cranmer's sources was *The King's Book*; one instance has been quoted above in Advent 1. Another is Christmas Day Second Communion, which may be compared with:

The said Son of God . . . did take upon him . . . man's nature, and . . . was born of . . . the said most blessed virgin . . .[6]
    We Christian men may be called the children of God by adoption and grace . . .[7]

So also the Sunday next before Easter, though this is an adaptation rather than a new composition:

He did . . . suffer this cross and this kind of death for our example, that we should follow the steps of him in patience and humility . . .[8]

In the second collect of Good Friday, *The King's Book* may be the source of 'govern and sanctify'[9] as in the Prayer Book, where the Missal has *sanctificatur et regitur*; an improvement in rhythm and sense.

An example of self-quotation from a different source is found in Trinity 6, where Cranmer renders *invisibilia* by 'such things as pass man's understanding', an echo of the Blessing in *The Order of the Communion* (1548) and the Prayer Book of 1549, where, however, the phrase is used of 'the peace of God'.

The third collect of Good Friday shows Cranmer drawing on a number of sources, as he did in the Prayer of Humble Access. He begins with a phrase from the Sarum collect *in capite jejunii* which he also used in his collect for Ash Wednesday, continues by quoting Ezekiel 33.11, works in various phrases from the *Orationes solennes* of Good Friday and the Litany, adds a phrase or two of his own, and rounds the collect off with a quotation from John 10.16.

Cranmer has been the subject of much uncritical adulation for his versions of the collects. Sometimes, indeed, he has received credit in popular estimation which was really due to the revisers of 1661. Some of his collects are flat, and one or two downright bad, as he would have been the first to admit: his criticism of his own attempts at translating hymns from the Latin is well known. But considering the lack of good models and probably also the shortage of time (a good collect cannot be thrown off in one sitting), the standard of excellence he maintains is fully worthy of the praise which generations of Englishmen have gratefully bestowed upon it.

The Psalms

In the 1549 Book the Psalter is divided for daily use into sixty portions, each psalm being said once a month. This produces an average of two and a half psalms in each portion. Cranmer's norm was clearly three psalms at each service, as with Quiñones and Scheme A (p. 5, above). This ideal was realized in the case of the proper psalms for great festivals, where Cranmer had freedom of choice; and even in the daily table, twenty-three of the first thirty-eight portions consist of three psalms. After that, the scheme is upset by the occurrence of very long and very short psalms, and becomes unworkable when two fairly long psalms come next to each other (e.g. Psalms 30, 31; 71, 72; 73, 74), or a long psalm is flanked by two of medium length (88, 89, 90).

It has been alleged that there are no proper psalms in the 1549 Book.[10] Certainly there is no table of such, but one can easily be constructed by reference to the section 'Collects, Epistles and Gospels'. Here there are appointed introit psalms for Holy Communion for every Sunday of the year, and also proper psalms for four great festivals, as follows:

	Mattins	Evensong
Christmas Day	19; 45; 85	89; 110; 132
Easter Day	2; 57; 111	113; 114; 118
Ascension Day	8; 15; 21	24; 68; 148 (1552; 108)
Whitsunday	48; 67; 145 (1552 omits)	104; 145

Brightman[11] provides a table showing how Cranmer chose his introit psalms, first by allocating suitable ones where possible and then filling the gaps with short psalms in numerical order. The former are placed in the right-hand column of his table, the latter in the left. Some of the latter are wrongly placed, and should appear in the right-hand column. For example, Psalm 54 is thoroughly appropriate to the Fifth Sunday in Lent, especially to its new Epistle. For the Sunday next before Easter Brightman had lxii wrongly for lxi, which should in any case be in the 'proper' column and is indeed still appointed for Palm Sunday. For Easter Tuesday, the appropriateness of cxiii is not obvious: possibly it is a misprint for lxiii. On Easter 4 Psalm 82 is specially chosen because verse 1, 'God standeth in the congregation of princes: he is judge among gods', foreshadows 'the prince of this world is judged' in the Gospel of the day. Psalm 93 should also be in the right-hand column: it is still set for Ascensiontide. On the other hand, it is not easy to see the relevance of Psalm 128 to St Thomas.

The Daily Lessons

As has been shown (pp. 5–7 above), Cranmer was gradually working in his Breviary schemes towards the simple two-lesson pattern of 1549. His choice of daily lessons evolved in parallel with the pattern. The calendar of Scheme A includes every chapter of the Old Testament, but that of Scheme B omits no less than eighty-five selected chapters, as well as the whole of 1 and 2 Chronicles. These omissions are exactly repeated in 1549. The reasons for omission are various: Genesis 10 is nothing but genealogy; Exodus 25–31 and 36–9 are concerned with details of the Tabernacle; Ezekiel 35–48 with the measurements of the Temple. Leviticus 1–17, 21–7 and Numbers 1–9 deal with rules for sacrifice and ritual purity. 1 and 2 Chronicles duplicate 1 and 2 Kings, while Esther 10 has only three verses. But it is not easy to see why Ezekiel 1, 4, 5, 8–12, 15–17 and 19–32 were left unread, especially after Cranmer's strictures in the Preface against the medieval habit of reading only a few chapters of each book.

Seasonal Material

A number of days have proper lessons at Mattins and Evensong, or at one service. Only six days have the full complement of four proper lessons: Christmas Day, The Circumcision, The Epiphany, Easter Day, St John Baptist and All Saints. Twelve, including Good Friday, Ascension Day, Whitsunday and Trinity Sunday, have two lessons; and six have only one. Fifteen red-letter days have none. In 1552 the lessons were collected in a table and a few fresh choices were made.

It is possible to arrange the red-letter days in their apparent order of importance by bringing together the various forms of proper material. Christmas Day and Easter Day alone have the distinction of two Communion Services. These two, with Ascension Day, Whitsunday and Trinity Sunday, have proper prefaces. These five, with the Epiphany, are appointed for the recitation of *Quicunque vult*. Christmas Day has proper psalms for Mattins and Evensong, and all four lessons are proper. All the others mentioned lack one or more proper lessons, presumably because of the difficulty of finding suitable Old Testament passages. Epiphany and Trinity do not have proper psalms. All the other red-letter days are differentiated solely by the number of proper lessons, ranging from four down to none, in accordance with Cranmer's high standards of relevance.

Thus Cranmer's ranking of holy days is as complex and subtle as that of the medieval rite. In the passing of time, most of his distinctions have been ironed out.

The Epistles and Gospels

The Communion lessons in 1549 are very largely derived from the Sarum Missal, but as with the collects, some have been adapted and some replaced by new choices. Very often the change is simply the continuance of a passage to the end of a verse or to the end of the chapter. At other times a few previous verses are prefaced to the existing passage. The division into chapters and verses was unknown to the medieval liturgists who chose the readings, and so they could choose where to begin and to end a passage without reference to any existing division. Cranmer evidently felt bound to respect the printed text in this matter.

One of his chief aims is to make the break at the most natural point. For example, in the Sarum books the passage 1 Corinthians 9.27–10.13 is shared between Septuagesima and the Ninth Sunday after Trinity, the Septuagesima portion ending at 10.4 and that of Trinity 9 beginning at 10.6. Cranmer keeps the allocation between the two Sundays, but makes the division at the end of chapter 9, a considerable improvement in each case. Another example is the Epistle for Trinity 19, which now includes the whole of the paragraph from which the Sarum reading was taken.

Some additions are quite substantial. On Easter Tuesday the whole of Paul's address at Antioch in Pisidia is now read instead of only the first half. Sometimes the reason for an addition is obviously theological, as with the Gospel for Advent Sunday, where the added verses describe the cleansing of the Temple, an episode which naturally appealed to the Reformers. The reason for the addition of the Gadarene swine to the Gospel of Epiphany 4 remains obscure. In the case of Easter Eve, which had no provision in Sarum, an Epistle and a Gospel are provided for the first time, the latter clipped off the end of the Passion narrative on Palm Sunday.

Changes are relatively few. Passages from the Old Testament or the Apocrypha are replaced by passages from the New Testament (e.g. Hebrews 10 for Exodus 12 on Good Friday); or, in the case of The Purification, simply left blank. On the other hand, St John Baptist is given a new Old Testament passage in place of the previous choice from the New Testament. Matthew, Luke and James have specially chosen readings instead of using the appropriate common, while James and Jude are allotted portions of the Epistles which bear their name. The single unaccountable change is at Trinity 15, where Galatians 6.11–18 replaces 5.25–6.10 from the same Epistle. Both passages are worth reading, but in a context of little change, the present substitution seems surprising.

Cranmer's chief object in drawing up Mattins and Evensong, the Preface tells us, was to secure a comprehensive and systematic reading of Scripture; and he there describes the methods by which he hopes to achieve this object. Further light on some of his presuppositions about public worship can be gathered from the rubrics of the services, as well as from the services themselves.

Mattins and Evensong are to be said 'daily throughout the year': the whole phrase occurs three times in Mattins (not a long service), besides two occurrences each of 'daily' and 'throughout the year'. The services were thus intended for weekdays, and not only for Sundays and holy days; the Preface of 1552 makes it quite plain that they were to be compulsory for the clergy, and that Cranmer hoped and expected that a congregation would be present.

Consequently, stress is laid on audibility. Unlike the pre-Reformation practice, the service is to be read 'distinctly, with a loud voice', 'the minister . . . turning him so as he may be heard'. For this purpose the lessons may even be sung 'in a plain tune'. Psalms and lessons are to be read 'in order as they be appointed . . . by the Kalendar': it is essential to remedy the chaotic and repetitive provisions of the medieval Breviary. In view of the people's ignorance, they are to repeat every petition of the Lord's Prayer after the priest (1552). Bishop Hooper's visitation of the diocese of Gloucester bears out the need for this provision even in the case of the clergy.

From *The Order of the Communion* in 1548 the importance of proper preparation for communion is emphasized. Three themes run through the Communion Service: preparation, repentance and reconciliation. They appear at once in the first three of the introductory rubrics: intending communicants must notify the curate overnight; he is to refuse communion to any 'open and notorious evil liver' until he has truly repented, as also to those 'betwixt whom he perceiveth malice and hatred to reign'. In harmony with this emphasis, the first exhortation of 1549 says: 'Judge therefore yourselves . . . repent you truly . . . be in perfect charity with all men'; while the second exhortation adjures the worshipper to search and examine his conscience, to be truly repentant and to be in love and charity with all the world.

If time is short, the sermon must take priority over 'the Litany, Gloria in Excelsis, the Creed, the homily and the exhortation to the communion'. The spoken word is more important than the word read out.

Lastly, ceremonial has become excessive, but has its value in serving 'to a decent order and godly discipline' and stirring up 'the dull mind of man to the remembrance of his duty to God'. 'Without some ceremony it is not possible to keep any order or quiet discipline'. Elevation 'or showing the Sacrament to the people' is specifically forbidden already in 1549, but kneeling, crossing and other gestures were then left optional. This permission was, however, withdrawn in 1552 and was evidently only a temporary concession.

4
Cologne and Canterbury

In 1572 an anonymous author quoted by Strype wrote about the Book of Common Prayer:

> Find me any form of prayer and administration of sacraments set forth since the apostles' time more full of corruption than this, except it be the Pope's portuise, and a book that one Hermannus, archbishop of Colen, did make (out of both of which you have patched yours).[1]

The archbishop referred to, Hermann von Wied, was born on 14 January 1477, the fourth son of Friedrich, Graf zu Wied. He matriculated at Cologne University in 1493, but does not seem to have distinguished himself at his studies. The general disparagement of his intellectual powers may be traced back to an exasperated remark of Charles V: 'He knows no Latin; all his life he has said only three Masses. He doesn't know the *Confiteor*.'[2] This remark was made at a time when the two men were set on a collision course. Like Cranmer, Hermann was fond of riding, but the catalogue of his library[3] shows that he was by no means the indolent illiterate suggested by Charles's outburst.

In 1515 he was elected archbishop of Cologne, taking the title of Hermann V. By one of the ironies of history, it fell to him to crown Charles V as emperor at Aachen in 1520.[4] As Hermann himself said in later years, he thought less at first of his spiritual duties than of his princely position, setting himself, with marked success, to improve the administration of justice. It was the experience of conflict with popes Clement VII and Paul III over legal matters that opened his eyes to the need for reformation. In 1532 he was appointed administrator of Paderborn, at that time in a state of uproar. He soon restored order, though discouraging persecution of the Protestant faction; and in the years 1535–6 he helped to put down the Anabaptists of Münster.

During these years Hermann's court had become the meeting-place of many followers of Erasmus. A young canonist, Johann

Gropper,[5] was installed as chancellor of the cathedral, and advocated reform within the existing framework of the Church. Hermann, by now nearly sixty, became impatient at the pope's delay in summoning a General Council, and himself in 1536 convened a Provincial Council which, influenced by Gropper, passed a large number of reforming canons. These were published in 1538 with a massive exposition of Christian doctrine and ceremonial contributed by Gropper and entitled *Encheiridion Christianae Institutionis*. The latter work was sufficiently advanced in outlook to be placed on the Index at the end of the sixteenth century. It soon reached England, for when in 1540 Thomas Crumwell appoited a commission of bishops to discriminate between pious and impious ceremonies, they drew freely on Gropper's *Encheiridion* for the section on baptism.[6]

The Canons of 1536, however, were never put into effect. Eager for more radical action, Hermann began to develop a relationship with the Strasbourg reformers Capito, Hedio and Bucer, and with Protestant magnates such as Philip of Hesse. In July 1541 the failure of the Diet of Regensburg and the terms of the Recess provided a definite ground for further action. Hermann invited the cathedral chapter to revise the Canons of 1536, which now seemed inadequate, but after long delays they produced a revision which failed to satisfy Hermann.[7] As a result, in February 1542 he sent for Bucer. According to Hermann, it was the chapter who first recommended this course, and at this stage they welcomed further efforts at reformation.[8] Hermann was anxious to proceed by agreement; Gropper and Bucer had several friendly conversations in the archbishop's palace at Buschhoven; but Gropper had already found himself diverging from Bucer's standpoint at Regensburg, and, probably at his instigation, the theologians of Cologne refused to collaborate. They pointed out that the Canons of 1536 had never been followed up by a visitation.[9] Hermann replied that to do so now would only impede a further reformation.[10]

As the next step, Bucer was asked to draw up a draft scheme, which was sent out on 1 September 1542, under the title *Reformatio*.[11] No copies survive in this form. In December Bucer arrived in Bonn, and began to preach there, arousing the liveliest opposition.[12] Gropper, whose ultimate loyalties were to the chapter and 'the Establishment' rather than to the spiritual needs of the people, became the leader of the dissentients. 'Those who had been architects of the previous provincial reformation' now joined the opposition, Hermann commented, 'thinking nothing right unless they had done it themselves.'[13] The archbishop, who in Bucer's opinion had been somewhat slow to act, was forced by this opposition to commit himself definitely to the Protestant side. The chapter demanded the removal of the *verdammter Lutheraner*, and a furious pamphlet warfare broke out. Bucer summed up the situation succinctly: *'Reiche Ernte, wenig Arbeiter, viel Feinde'* ('Rich harvest, few labourers, many foes').[14]

On 9 January 1543 the chapter issued a reply to Bucer's draft, entitled *Compendium Reformationis*,[15] which also was superseded by later writings and has not survived. Hermann, still hoping to proceed gently, restrained Bucer from inflammatory preaching. Though he had a gift for finding the reconciling formula in conference, Bucer was tactless and made many enemies by inopportune criticisms. The chapter flatly refused to engage in discussion with him. In March Hermann scored a considerable success when the three estates of the Landtag gave strong support to his projects. As a result some priests began to give communion in both kinds; they and the communicants were persecuted by the City Council, and Lutheran books were confiscated. Philip of Hesse appealed to the chapter to support Hermann, but in vain.

He did, however, prevail on Melanchthon to come to Cologne, where he arrived at the beginning of May. He found Bucer engaged in revision of the *Reformatio*,[16] and was invited to contribute chapters on six major heads of doctrine. Pistorius came from Hesse at the same time to join in the work, and by 23 May Melanchthon was able to report that it was nearly finished. Hedio arrived from Strasbourg only at the end of June, and cannot have contributed much of significance. The archbishop examined the revised work with considerable thoroughness, spending five hours a day for five days.[17] He kept Luther's translation of the Bible by him during the review; he made numerous additions and alterations; and he suggested the adoption of the most peaceful solutions to all vexed questions. His aim was always to establish a Protestant régime in his spiritual realm with the greatest regard for all traditional rights, and without attacking the pope.

On 23 July the completed Order was laid before the Landtag,[18] and was accepted by the secular Estates, at whose suggestion Hermann had it printed[19] under the title *Einfaltigs Bedencken*.

About a hundred copies were sent out to interested and influential personages.[20] The chapter refused an invitation to send delegates to discuss the *Bedencken*; instead, they drew up a reply entitled *Gegenberichtung*, which they sent to the archbishop on 1 October, with a request that the *Bedencken* should not be published. On learning that it was already in print, the chapter early in 1544 published the *Gegenberichtung* and followed it up shortly after with a Latin translation, *Antididagma*, by Billick. Though anonymous, the work is almost certainly from the pen of Gropper. Hermann, in return, decided to release the *Bedencken* for general circulation,[21] and an enlarged and improved edition appeared in November 1544. A Latin translation, embodying further alterations, was undertaken by Albert Hardenberg,[22] and appeared in 1545 as *Simplex ac pia Deliberatio*. Bucer composed a reply to the *Antididagma*, entitled *Bestendige Verantwortung*, and this too was translated into Latin by Hardenberg; but it did not appear in print until 1613, when a Latin translation by Brem as *Martini Buceri constans Defensio*, with a preface by Hermann himself, appeared in Geneva.

Meanwhile, in October 1544, the chapter had appealed to the pope and to the emperor. The latter had already taken military steps to isolate the archbishop in 1543, and now made one last attempt to dissuade him from the course he had chosen, but without success. Hermann's counter-appeal, lodged in July 1545, was unsuccessful, and in the following year he was excommunicated and deposed. He retired to his estates at Wied, and died on 15 August 1552, in full sympathy with the Protestant cause.

His Order became a dead letter as far as Cologne was concerned; but in England archbishop Cranmer had been watching the progress of Hermann's project with considerable sympathy. He certainly acquired copies of the *Antididagma* and the *Deliberatio*, possibly also of the *Bedencken*. He copied portions of the *Antididagma* into his commonplace-books,[23] while his copy of the *Deliberatio*, preserved at Chichester Cathdral, contains annotations which show that he did not merely own the book but studied it. Meanwhile, interest was sufficiently widespread in England to encourage John Day to publish an anonymous translation into English under the title *A Simple and Religious Consultation*; this appeared on 30 October 1547.[24] Other publishers were interested in Hermann's Order: in 1548 Anthony Scoloker issued at Ipswich a pamphlet containing Hermann's baptism services, translated from the Latin by Richard Ryce.[25] This is a different translation, better than that in Day's publication. Ryce, who was abbot of Conway for the year preceding the Dissolution, treats his original freely, omitting the larger part of a lengthy address, altering the order of the prayers, and reinstating the Sarum ceremonies of giving a white robe and a candle, each with its appropriate form of words. Hermann had omitted both of these, but the 1549 Prayer Book agrees with Ryce to the extent of retaining the chrisom. Meanwhile, Day's version had appeared in a second, revised edition.[26]

Cranmer's interest in the Cologne Order was thus in no way unusual at that time. But the question may be asked, what was it in Hermann's proposals that attracted him? It is not as though they were in any way an original piece of work. By Hermann's own desire, they were based on the Order for Brandenburg and Nürnberg, which Cranmer had known since before its first publication in 1533. Bucer had also made free use of his own forms of service, written for Strasbourg, which likewise had been known to Cranmer for many years. Perhaps it was precisely this combination of right-wing and left-wing reformed ideas that commended it to Cranmer. It may be also that he recognized the similarities between his position and Hermann's. It is significant that, of the four Orders which he used most extensively in the Book of Common Prayer, two were compiled by personal friends, Andreas Osiander and Justus Jonas, and two by fellow archbishops, Berlin and Cologne. Hermann, like Cranmer, was endeavouring to bring about reform from above. Like Cranmer, he was faced by determined opposition from his clergy. It may well be that Cranmer studied Gropper's *Antididagma*, not as an exposition of moderate Catholic doctrine (as Brightman implies), but as an indication of the sort of arguments which would probably be used by his own antagonists. Hermann was forced by the need for comprehension to retain ceremonies like exorcism and services like Confirmation and Burial, all of which the root-and-branch reformers swept away. Cranmer also kept them all, and for the same reason.

The factor which finally proved decisive may have been a sudden shift in Henry VIII's foreign policy. As Brightman points out, during 1546 Henry told the astonished Cranmer that he and the king of France had decided 'to change the Mass into a Communion', and set him 'to pen a form thereof'.[27] At that moment, the *Deliberatio* must have recently arrived from

Germany. The whole project was soon rendered abortive by Henry's death; but it must surely have prompted the drafting of *The Order of the Communion*, since this is designed for the exact purpose of changing the Mass into a Communion. From what we know of Cranmer's methods of compiling a liturgy, it would be quite natural for him to take Hermann's service as his starting-point. If this suggestion is well founded, it explains why Hermann's Order had so great an influence on the Prayer Book, and also why Cranmer made predominant use of the Latin version of the work.

The question must now be raised, which of the versions of Hermann did Cranmer use: German, Latin or English? The answer is not of great significance, because no doctrinal difference is involved; but the point cannot be passed over without discussion, in view of the statements of earlier scholars. Bishop John Dowden was quite categorical: 'The English Reformers had before them Archbishop Hermann's Order for "the Supper" in German (1543)'.[28] Brightman thought that 'sometimes the German is followed, sometimes the Latin; while perhaps in most cases . . . the influence of the English translation can be detected'.[29] Accordingly, in choosing examples for his column headed SOURCES, he 'aimed at using whichever of the two texts [i.e. German or Latin] corresponds more nearly to the English of the Prayer Book in each case'.[30] But, even if Brightman's view were correct, his choice of version is sometimes surprising: in some places there is nothing in the Prayer Book text to indicate one version rather than the other as the source; and elsewhere (for example, at the Comfortable Words) he has printed the German text when the Prayer Book is demonstrably closer to the Latin. It is pretty clear that he consulted the Latin version only in the later stages of preparing his great work.

There can be little doubt that Cranmer used the Latin version: there are numerous phrases in the Prayer Book whose originals occur only in the Latin and are lacking from the German. The reverse case does not appear to hold: only two significant phrases can be found in the German and not in the Latin. One is the *Sursum corda*, where the German has '*Erheben euwer hertzen. Wir erheben die zum Herren*', while the *Deliberatio* gives the traditional Latin. But the German itself is here a translation from the Latin of the Missal. Bucer had printed this translation as long ago as 1526 in a Strasbourg service which Cranmer certainly knew; and Cranmer could have made it for himself direct from the Latin, just as well as Bucer. The other phrase is 'our self, our souls and bodies', which corresponds almost exactly to the words '*vns selb, vnnsere leib vnnd seel*' in a doctrinal chapter of the *Bedencken* headed *Von heyligen Opfer*. Here the Latin has only '*& corpora & animas nostras*': nothing about 'our self'. But it then goes on to quote Romans 12.1: '*Obsecro uos . . . vt praebeatis corpora uestra*', adding the explanation '*hoc est, uos ipsos*'. Thus the whole of the Prayer Book sentence, 'We offer and present unto thee our self, our souls and bodies, to be a reasonable, holy and lively sacrifice', is present in the Latin, though not in the same order: '*Offerimus . . . praebeatis . . . uos ipsos . . . & corpora & animas nostras . . . hostiam uiuentem Sanctam . . . rationalem*'. While it is perfectly possible that Cranmer had read the *Bedencken*, and that the German phrase had stuck in his mind, it is certainly not proved that this was the case.

The case of the English versions is harder to decide. Here, identity of language can always be explained as being the natural translation of the Latin. They can therefore be claimed as a source for the Prayer Book only if they agree with it against the Latin. No instance of this has been noticed so far in the Book of 1549. If, as Brightman suggests,[31] *The Order of the Communion* was already in existence in the autumn of 1547, this, at any rate, was too early to be influenced by the first English translation, which did not appear until 30 October. By the time that the 1552 revision was under way, Cranmer seems to have ceased to treat Hermann as his primary source, though there are one or two phrases in the new material which suggest that by then he had read the English translation. It is shown below (p. 89) that he himself cannot have been the translator. It seems that the German version (if Cranmer ever read it) was no more than a distant memory when the 1549 Canon was being written; and the English translation only came on the scene for the *Second* Prayer Book of Edward VI. For Cranmer, Hermann's Order is represented by the *Simplex ac pia Deliberatio* of 1545.

This is a sumptuous folio, beautifully printed by Laurentius Mylius at Bonn. It is divided into two parts, *De Doctrina* and *De Administratione Religionis*. The former (in which Melanchthon was concerned) covers the whole field of doctrine except the sacraments, while the latter contains short doctrinal chapters, followed by forms of service. The full text of these is given, in contrast to many of the Lutheran Orders.

Hermann's service of The Lord's Supper is divided into two

74

parts. The first is a preparation to be held on Saturday evening after Vespers, consisting of a hymn, a lesson (the Institution Narrative from one of the Gospels, or a passage from 1 Corinthians 10 or 11, or John 6), a choice of two exhortations and prayers for worthy reception. It is followed by individual confession, which is still compulsory. The Sunday morning service begins with the second Confession from the Strasbourg *Psalter* (the same that Calvin chose), the Comfortable Words from the same source, and a new Absolution. It then follows traditional lines as far as the Gospel, which is followed by the sermon. The chants are sung in Latin by the choir, by the people in German. Before the Creed comes a prayer for all estates of men, in two versions, a longer and a shorter, ending with a paraphrase of the Lord's Prayer. Both these are taken from the Cassel adaptation of the Strasbourg rite. The communicants then put their offerings in some prominent place and gather near the altar, men and women separately. *Sursum corda* has an invariable preface which recalls primitive examples by mentioning the Creation and the Fall. The Words of Institution are then sung in German, with the people answering Amen. The Lord's Prayer and *Pax Domini* are followed by communion in both kinds, the men receiving before the women. *Agnus Dei* is sung, with two Lutheran hymns in German. The service ends with a prayer of thanksgiving and a choice of blessings, all from Brandenburg–Nürnberg. In spite of the strong Strasbourg influence, the overall impression made by the service is a conservative one, which must be attributed to Hermann's personal influence. Luther criticized its eucharistic doctrine as Zwinglian,[32] and indeed Bucer's position became steadily closer to Zwingli's, though he never abandoned his belief in a Real Presence. It is likely that the restraining hand of the archbishop preserved much of the traditional structure, such as the Absolution, which Bucer had long since discarded at Strasbourg.

Cranmer's use of Hermann

As suggested above, it seems clear that Hermann's Order provided the inspiration for *The Order of the Communion*. Cranmer did not accept H's[33] division of the service into two parts: the practice of holding a service on Saturday night has remained characteristic of Lutheranism, but it has never taken root in England. In *The Order of the Communion* Cranmer, like H, has two exhortations; but where **H** placed them as alternatives at the service of preparation, Cranmer directs one to be read the Sunday before, or at least one day before, and the other at the heart of the mass, after the consecration. Beyond this, Cranmer attempts no division into separate services. He bases the preparatory exhoration on the first of **H**'s two, *Brevis Institutio sive Concio de Coena Domini*, originally written for Strasbourg and adapted for Hesse–Cassel, then transferred bodily to **H**. Cranmer adds phrases from the doctrinal chapter *De Coena Domini* and from a subsequent chapter *De conversione a peccatis et vera poenitentia*.

The table that follows shows the phrases in Cranmer's first exhortation which have affinities with **H**. The relevant passages occur on the following folios of the *Simplex ac pia Deliberatio*:

De Coena Domini		82b–88b
De preparatione de Coena Domini		89a–91b
Brevis Insitutio	89b–90b	
Adhortatio alia	90b–91b	
Quo pacto celebranda sit Coena Domini		91b–97a
De conversione a peccatis		99b–101a

First the Parson . . .	Curent Pastores . . .	89a
one day before he shall	pridie eius diei quo Coena	89a
minister the Communion . . .	Domini celebranda fuerit . . .	89a
that they prepare them-	quo communicaturi . . .	89a
selves . . .	praeparentur . . .	89a
upon –day next I do	constituimus . . . die	89a
intend . . .	crastino . . .	
in the remembrance of his	memoriam Christi . . .	
	celebrandam . . .	85a
most fruitful . . . Passion . . .	de sua passione et fructu	
	eius . . .	85a
remission of our sins . . .	remissionem peccatorum . . .	90a
with most hearty thanks . . .	iucunda gratitudine . . .	90a
for his infinite mercy	pro his tantis beneficiis . . .	90a
and benefits . . .		
to give us his said body	donare eis ipsum corpus	
	suum,	85a
and blood . . .	et sanguinem . . .	85a
so divine and holy a	res et actio fit coelestis ac	85a
thing . . .	divina . . .	

a most godly and heavenly banquet . . .	hoc coeleste et beatificum convivium . . .	84b 84b
with an unfeigned heart . . .	ex animo dolere . . .	100b
amendment of your former life . . .	vitae emendationem . . .	100b
reconcile yourselves . . .	reconciliare ei . . .	101a
And if there be any of you . . .	Si quis vero lapsus fuerit . . .	99b
comfort and absolution . . .	consolatio privatae Absolutionis . . .	100b
a minister of God and of the Church . . .	Ego Christi et Ecclesiae Minister . . .	92b 92b

The extent of **H**'s contribution must not be exaggerated: the words quoted above amount to only 92 out of a total of 570. Cranmer's treatment of **H** at this point is typical: he reproduces the opening words literally, then diverges freely from his original, but frequently introduces words and phrases which show that his mind is steeped in what he has read. He does not feel bound to follow the original slavishly, but does seem to require an external stimulus to release the flow of creative activity. Though the general lines of these two exhortations are the same, Cranmer's recommendation of auricular confession is significantly warmer than **H**'s.

For the second exhortation, which begins *The Order of the Communion* proper, Cranmer turned to **H**'s second, *Adhortatio alia*, which was taken from the Order for Brandenburg and Nürnberg, and therefore must have been known to Cranmer for a long time. As before, he also drew on the doctrinal chapter on the Supper, and in addition possibly on Gropper's *Antididagma* (*Ant.* in the table below).

Dearly beloved in the Lord . . .	Quandoquidem charissimi in Domino . . .	90b 90b
what St Paul writeth . . .	sicut nos hortatur D. Paulus . . .	90b
examine themselves . . .	sese explorent . . .	90b
we become guilty of the body and blood of Christ . . .	reusque constituitur corporis et sanguinis Domini . . .	86a 86a
an earnest and lively faith in Christ . . .	fidemque nostram in Christum confirmemus et excitemus . . .	91a 91a

these holy mysteries . . .	hoc sanctissimo mysterio . . .	86a
for the redemption of	pro nobis nostrique	
the world . . .	redemptione . . .	91a
both God and man . . .	Deum et hominem . . .	91a
our Master and only Saviour	unici Salvatoris et Domini	85a
Jesus Christ . . .	nostri . . .	85a
	unicum Magistrum et	
	Dominum	85b
	nostrum . . .	85b
the innumerable benefits	quantaque beneficia	
	nobis . . .	85b
which by his precious	impetrarit . . .	85b
blood-shedding he hath	sanguinisque pretiosi	(*Ant.*
obtained to us . . .	effusione nobis	59b)
	comparavit . . .	
a pledge of his love . . .	Horum omnium pignus . . .	91a
to our endless comfort	ad singularem	90b
	consolationem	
and consolation . . .	et confirmationem . . .	90b
not come to this holy	non possint ad mensam	88a
table . . .	Domini accedere . . .	88a

Cranmer follows the exhortation with a penitential section modelled on **H**'s, though the latter is placed at the beginning of the service, not immediately before reception, as in the 1548 Order. Cranmer starts with an invitation to confession which owes nothing to **H**, but for the Confession itself he follows **H** much more closely than in the exhortations. The form in **H** is Bucer's final version of the prayer which he originally composed for Strasbourg in 1537 (the Latin version of **H** is much altered from the German). As in the exhortations, Cranmer diverges from his original after the opening, but here he soon returns to **H**, preserving the structure of the prayer, though omitting four sizeable passages.

Almighty God, Father of our Lord Jesus Christ, maker of all things, judge of all men, we knowledge and bewail	Omnipotens aeterne Deus, Pater Domini nostri Jesu Christi, Creator rerum omnium, judex cunctorum hominum, agnoscimus et deploramus nos in peccatis conceptos et natos, ideoque ad quaevis mala pronos, et abhorrentes a veris bonis, sancta tua praecepta sine fine et modo

our manifold
sins and wickedness, which
we from time to time most
grievously have committed
by thought, word and deed,
against thy divine majesty,
provoking most justly thy
wrath and indignation
against us: we do earn-
estly repent, and be
heartily sorry, for these
our misdoings:

the remem-
brance of them is griev-
ous unto us, the burthen
of them is intolerable.
Have mercy upon us, have
mercy upon us, most merciful Father, for thy Son
our Lord Jesus Christ's
sake:

forgive us all that is
past, and grant that we
may ever hereafter
serve and please thee
in newness of life,
to the honour and

transgressos esse, contemptu tui
et verbi tui, diffidentia opis
tuae, fiducia nostri et mundi,
pravis studiis et operibus,
quibus maiestatem tuam gravissime offendimus, et proximos nos
tros laesimus. Itaque in mortem
aeternam magis et magis nos
ipsi sepelivimus et perdidimus.
    (peccata omnia et omnes
        iniquitates nostras, 92b)

(gravissime, *above*; contra te admisimus,
below)
(maiestatem tuam, *above*)

    (iram tuam justissimam, 93a)
Id vero nobis ex animo dolet, et
veniam a te oramus omnium quae
contra te admisimus, auxilium
tuum imploramus contra inhabit-
ans in nobis peccatum, et incen-
sorem eius Satanam. Serva nos
ne quid porro contra te admitt-
amus, et reliquam in nobis pravi-
tatem justitia Filii tui con-
tege, et Spiritu tuo in nobis
reprime, tandem poenitus expurga.

Miserere nostri, optime et clementissime Pater, per Filium tuum
Dominum nostrum Jesum Christum.

Da et auge in nobis Spiritum
tuum sanctum, qui doceat nos
vere et penitus peccata nostra
agnoscere, poenitentia eorum
viva conpungi, remissionem
eorum in Christo Domino nostro
vera fide apprehendere et tenere,
ut peccatis indies plenius mori-
entes,
    (veniam a te oramus omnium,
above)
(porro, *above*)
    in nova vita ad gloriam
nominis tui et Ecclesiae tuae
aedificationem tibi serviamus,

glory of thy name,	et complaceamus. Haec enim agnoscimus te a nobis jure tuo requirere, quare eadem praestare cupimus, Dignare tu Pater Coelestis, qui donasti nobis velle dare etiam, ut quae salutis nostrae sunt, ea toto corde praestare studeamus,
through Jesus Christ our Lord.	per Dominum nostrum Jesum Christum.

It may be noted that both Cranmer and the translator of the *Simple and Religious Consultation* render '*optime et clementissime*' by a single adjective ('most merciful' and 'most gentle' respectively); but the latter does not compensate for this abbreviation as Cranmer does, by repeating 'have mercy upon us'.

For the Absolution, Cranmer yet again starts with a phrase from **H**:

Our blessed Lord, who hath left power to his Church to absolve penitent sinners from their sins, and to restore to the grace of the heavenly Father such as truly believe in Christ . . .	Quia Dominus noster benedictus hanc Ecclesiae suae potestatem reliquit, ut eos a peccatis absolvat, et in gratiam Patris coelestis restituat, quicumque peccatorum poenitentes Christo Domino vere credunt . . . f.92a

To this, as Brightman shows, Cranmer appends the whole of the Sarum Absolution from Prime and Compline.

Next follow four texts of Scripture, described as 'comfortable words'. Bishop Dowden pointed out that the German version at this point reads: '*Höret den evangelischen Trost*' ('Hear the comfort of the Gospel'). As the Latin has only '*Audite Evangelium*', he argued that here Cranmer must have been using the German text.[34] But 'This is a true saying . . .' was described as a '*Trostspruch*' ('saying of comfort') in the Strasbourg service of 1537, and the English phrase is already found in *The King's Book* (1543): 'The penitent may desire to hear of the minister the comfortable words of remission of sins.'[35] Dowden's argument therefore has little force.

H has five texts in his penitential section: 'So God loved the world', 'This is a true saying', 'If any man sin', John 3.35 and Acts 10.43. These had been gradually assembled in successive Strasbourg services from 1525 to 1537. **H** places them before the Absolution and regards them as alternatives; Cranmer has them after the Absolution and requires all to be read at every service, replacing **H**'s '*aut*' by 'also'. In Cranmer's Order the rubric 'Then shall the priest stand up, and turning him to the people say thus' occurs twice, once before the Absolution, and again, quite nonsensically, after the Absolution and before the Comfortable Words. This strongly suggests that the latter were originally intended to be in **H**'s place, before the Absolution; and that when they were moved, the rubric was wrongly moved with them, as well as being kept in its proper place. To the three 'words' taken from **H**, Cranmer prefixes 'Come unto me . . .'. As Dowden pointed out,[36] this is quoted by **H** in his doctrinal chapter (f. 87b), but it is more likely that Cranmer took the idea from Zwingli's Latin Mass,[37] where it precedes Communion, as it does in *The Order of the Communion*. It is true that Zwingli's text concludes: '*et ego requiem vobis praestabo*' ('and I will give you rest'), but on his title page he quotes it in the form '*et ego reficiam vos*' ('and I will refresh you').

The penitential section ends with a prayer for worthy reception, in which the only trace of **H** is one of Bucer's favourite phrases: 'We may . . . dwell in him and he in us' (e.g. ff. 83b, 90a). Cranmer's words of administration are those of the Sarum Communion of the Sick, with the phrase 'which was given/shed for thee' inserted; **H** adopted the common Lutheran form, in which the latter words occur, from the Order for Brandenburg and Nürnberg, and it is possible that Cranmer may have derived it directly from the same source. Finally, although **H** offers a choice of four blessings, Cranmer adopts none of them, but provides a form of his own, conflated from two New Testament texts.

Hermann and the Book of Common Prayer

The First Prayer Book of Edward VI followed on *The Order of the Communion* at about a year's distance. It incorporated the *Order* into the Communion Service, which otherwise shows much less signs of **H**'s influence. The first part of the service sticks closely to the medieval pattern, as does **H**, while the new elements, the collects for the king and the offertory sentences, appear to be due to Cranmer. Unlike **H**, Cranmer discards the Gradual. After the *Sursum corda* and *Sanctus*, **H** goes straight on to the Words of Institution, in typical reformed fashion, while Cranmer provides a lengthy prayer equivalent to the Canon of the Mass. After the Lord's Prayer then follows *The Order of the*

Communion, slightly revised, the *Agnus Dei* and the Communion. Both services end with a prayer of thanksgiving and a blessing.

The first traces of **H** appear in the offertory rubrics dealing with alms, separation of men and women, and calculating the right amount of elements to be consecrated.[38] Cranmer's use of **H** in the Canon is discussed in detail below, in Chapter 5. Here it must suffice to say that in the first section, Cranmer is obviously influenced by **H**'s prayer '*pro omnibus hominum Statibus, et necessitatibus Ecclesiae*'. As with the exhortations, it is a diffused memory rather than a copying of the original. The second section, the present Prayer of Consecration, has clearly been constructed by Cranmer from materials other than **H**. This was inevitable, since **H** has no consecratory section other than the Words of Institution. Even so, strong coincidences of language may be found, as is natural given the subject-matter. Behind the third section, the Prayer of Oblation, however, we may discern the *Brevis Institutio* from **H**'s preparation service, which had already provided the basis of the first exhortation of 1548.[39]

Though the rest of *The Order of the Communion* is reproduced with little alteration, the beginning of the Absolution shows a significant departure from **H**. The statement that our Lord left 'power to his Church to absolve penitent sinners' is replaced by the familiar declaration of God's promise of forgiveness. The language is largely drawn from the context, but even so some of it still echoes **H**: '*Patris coelestis . . . poenitentes . . .*' (92a); '*veram fidem . . . remissionem peccatorum*' (92b). The Prayer of Thanksgiving is composed on the principle, by now familiar, of taking **H**'s opening words and then diverging into original composition. But **H** took the prayer verbatim from Brandenburg–Nürnberg, and Cranmer may also have found it there years before. **H**'s sermon before the service of Catechism and Exorcism perhaps supplied the phrase 'the blessed company of all faithful people' ('*beatam sanctorum omnium societatem*', 71b).

For the Blessing, Cranmer now turned to **H**, combining one of his with the text from *The Order of the Communion*. The pronouns employed vary remarkably between the various Orders: the German **H** (quoted verbatim from Brandenburg–Nürnberg) has '*sei mit euch und bleib allezeit mit uns allen*' ('be with you and remain with us'); but the Latin version reads '*sit nobiscum et maneat in aeternum*' ('be with us . . .'). This could be a misprint for '*uobiscum*'. The Latin is fairly translated in the *Consultation* 'be with *us* and remain with *us* for ever'; but 1549 is different again:

'be amongst *you* and remain with *you* always' (my italics throughout). Cranmer may have been led to use the second person by the text from Philippians which he had retained from 1548 ('keep *your* hearts and minds').

Mattins and Evensong in 1549 show virtually no verbal dependence on **H**, the solitary exception being the rubric on the position of the lesson reader.[40] **H** provides skeleton forms for these offices in the chapter *De aliis quibusdam Ecclesiae ritibus* (f. 116). These have not been mentioned by previous writers, probably because they have so much in common with those in a number of Lutheran Orders that it cannot be claimed that they specifically exerted any influence on the Prayer Book services. For Mattins **H** prescribes three psalms, *Te Deum* and *Benedictus* with antiphon and responsory; for Evensong, three psalms, hymn and *Magnificat* with antiphon and responsory; both offices are still to be sung in Latin.

H's baptism service is divided into two, like The Lord's Supper. The first part, entitled Catechism, also takes place on Saturday evening. It begins with a very long address, combining those of Saxony and Brandenburg–Nürnberg, after which the pastor puts the interrogations to the parents and godparents, and exhorts them to bring the child up properly. Next follows the Exorcism, which is extremely brief, with no ceremonies except signing with the cross. Two prayers from Luther's service and the Gospel (from Mark 10), with a short exposition, complete the section. Then the pastor lays his hands on the child's head, and the Lord's Prayer and the Creed are said. After a choice of psalms, a prayer ends the service. The rest takes place the next day at The Lord's Supper, after the Creed; an exhortation, proper Epistle and Gospel and a long prayer (from the Cassel Order) are followed by baptism, a prayer from Luther and a hymn.

For Public Baptism Cranmer made nearly as much use of **H** as in *The Order of the Communion*, and in the same way, rejecting his division of the rite into two parts. Here, however, it is a case of fitting **H**'s prayers into the framework of the medieval service. Cranmer is slightly more conservative than **H**, keeping the chrisom and the anointing, both of which are discarded by **H**. The origins of the reformed elements in the service are not easy to determine, because they may come directly from Luther's *Taufbüchlein*; or from Brandenburg–Nürnberg which borrows from Luther; or via **H**, who takes them over from Brandenburg–

Nürnberg. The first prayer, for example, the so-called 'Flood-prayer', was clearly known to Cranmer from Luther or Brandenburg–Nürnberg, since, although it appears in H with only minor modifications, Cranmer more than once agrees with Luther against H. This suggests that Cranmer had already adopted it before becoming acquainted with H. It is not improbable that he had already drafted reformed services other than the Daily Office during Henry VIII's reign. The parallels with H are fully set out by Brightman in *The English Rite*; no fresh parallels have been noticed since Brightman's day; indeed, it was in this service that archbishop Laurence first detected the influence of H in his Bampton Lectures of 1804. The following page references are to volume ii of Brightman's work, with the folio numbers of the Latin H in brackets:

724 (69a)	Preface
726 (69a, 70a, 73b)	Rubric, Address, 'Flood-prayer'
728 (73b)	Sign of the cross
730 (74a)	Gospel
732 (74a, 70b, 74b)	Exhortation, Prayer
734 (74b, 72b)	Address to godparents, Questions
736 (72b)	Creed
744 (73a)	Final Charge
Vol. i, cxix (77b)	Final Charge

It should be noted that in the Gospel (ii, 730) Cranmer is closer to the Latin than to the German reprinted by Brightman.

As with the Holy Communion, Cranmer does not follow H's order, but uses phrases from different parts of the baptismal section almost at random. Once again he takes from H the opening sentence of an exhortation, but soon abandons it. Elements which may be ascribed to H are the formula of signing, the exposition of the gospel, the prayer which follows the exposition, and the charges to the godparents. Cranmer, however, has laid a stress on the reception of the infant into the Church which is wholly absent from H.

The whole service of Private Baptism in 1549 is derived from the Order for Albertine Saxony of Justus Jonas (1539 and 1540). So is H's, but Cranmer again appears to have gone direct to the original. The evidence is set out at length by Bishop Dowden, who shows conclusively that Cranmer must have been using either the Saxon Order or the German version of H;[41] the Latin H is noticeably less close to the Prayer Book. But since, as was shown above, Cranmer elsewhere invariably used the Latin text, and in view of his personal contacts with Jonas, the obvious inference is that he was here following the Saxon Order, which he also drew on at one point in Public Baptism.[42]

The layout of Confirmation is obviously modelled on H, with an explanatory introduction and a catechism before the service, which itself is of no great length. The introduction leans heavily on H, but the catechism is quite independent, drawing on English sources of the period 1537–47, as Brightman shows.[43] If it had in fact been drafted some years before 1549, it would explain why H's catechism was not used, and also why Cranmer in 1548 published separately his translation of a catechism by Justus Jonas deriving from Brandenburg–Nürnberg, which otherwise could have been incorporated into the 1549 Book. In the service proper, Cranmer follows Sarum closely until the final prayer, which is an abridgment of a prayer in H *before* the laying-on of hands. The first of the final rubrics, about the time of catechizing, may be influenced by H, as Cranmer in his own copy underlined the words:

Nam certa omnino hora diebus Festis tractationi Catechismi assignanda propter rudiores, & propter iuventutem. Constitui uero ea hora Catechismo debet, quae sit populo maxime commoda (f. 68a).

(For a certain hour of the holy days must be appointed for the ruder sort and the youth to have the Catechism declared. And that hour for the Catechism shall be appointed that is most convenient for the people'. *Simple and Religious Consultation*, f. 152a.)

Matrimony, which also follows Sarum very closely, raises the same question as Baptism by appearing to use older Lutheran sources in preference to H, though the differences in the texts are of little intrinsic significance.[44] This again points to a possible early draft. The opening address is based on materials of wide dissemination: Brightman quotes parallels from Chaucer and Gropper's *Encheiridion*.[45] Yet H also seems to be in the background, with his '*Deum ipsum Sacrum Coniugium instituisse, et in paradyso*'; these words immediately precede '*homine adhuc integro et sancto*', which Brightman recognizes as a parallel.[46] Again, on his next page H has '*qui etiam praesentia sua & primitiis miraculorum suorum cohonestauit*'.

The Visitation of the Sick makes use of H's Absolution, in a rather freer translation than that of *The Order of the Communion*. It escaped, however, the modification which the latter underwent in 1549. Burial of the Dead again depends largely on Sarum, but borrows *Media vita* from **H** or from some other Lutheran source. **H** may also have suggested the choice of 1 Corinthians 15 for the lesson, the quotation from Philippians 3 in the committal and phrases in each of the following collects ('whose body we have now committed to the earth', 'we give thanks to thee, almighty God . . . this our brother . . . Grant us, we beseech thee');[47] while 'sure and certain hope of the resurrection to eternal life' is a translation of *'certam spem resurrectionis et vitae aeternae'* in the Catechism of the godparents.[48]

The Book of 1552

The story does not end yet. The Prayer Book of 1552 provides evidence of further use of **H**, notably in the introduction then prefixed to Morning and Evening Prayer. In the opening exhortation, the phrase 'acknowledge and confess our manifold sins and wickedness' is almost identical with the beginning of the Confession in *The Order of the Communion*, which is derived from **H**; the difference is only in reading 'confess' for 'bewail'. 'And although we ought at times humbly to acknowledge our sins before God . . .' is rightly referred by Brightman to a rubric of **H**.[49] 'Wherefore I pray and beseech you, as many as be here present' is a literal rendering of *'Quapropter . . . hortor et obsecro uos, quotquot adestis'* from the sermon at the first part of the Baptism in **H**.[50] 'Which desireth not the death of a sinner' is also quoted by **H** in the chapter *De conversione a peccatis et vera poenitentia*. 'And hath given power . . . to his ministers, to declare and pronounce to his people, being penitent, the absolution and remission of their sins . . .' goes back to *'hanc potestatem reliquit . . . quicunque peccatorum poenitentes . . . Ego Christi & Ecclesiae Minister . . . annuncio remissionem omnium peccatorum'* (cf. p. 80, above). As Brightman points out, the English version renders *'annuncio'* by 'declare and pronounce';[51] it also translates *'poenitentes'* by 'being repentant'. It seems that the *Consultation* was by now becoming familiar. Finally, 'grant us . . . his holy Spirit' may be a reminiscence of *'Da et auge in nobis Spiritum tuum sanctum'* from **H**'s Confession.

In the Communion Service a series of small changes are to be noticed:

earnestly exhort them to remember the poor (659)	exhortandi sunt ad benignitatem in pauperes (99)
Then shall the Churchwardens gather the devotions of the people and put the same into the poor men's box (663)	Quas [oblationes] Praefecti Sacri gazophilacii colligent, et in gazophilacium . . . reponent (95a)
All Christian kings, princes and governors (665)	pro aliis Regibus, Principibus et Magistratibus omnibus (93a)
examine your lives . . . by the rule of God's commandments, and whereinsoever ye shall perceive yourselves to have offended . . . against God (671)	examinare debet de fide sua, atque ordine rogare de decem Praeceptis, atque monere ut homines discant peccatum esse contra Deum, cum quid admiserint contra illa praecepta (101b)
a blasphemer of God, an hinderer or slanderer of his word (679)	Dei . . . blasphemos, irrisores verbi divini (90b)
according to thy Son our Saviour Jesus Christ's holy institution, may be partakers[52] of his most blessed body and blood (693)	secundum institutionem D. nostri Iesu Christi (84b) corpore et sanguine Domini communicent, ita ut ipse instituit (96b)
Take and eat (701)	Accipe et manduca (96b)

(References to Brightman, vol. ii and H Latin)

Taken cumulatively, these instances surely suggest continued attention to the text of H. On the other hand, the parallel noted by Brightman in the new exhortation in the Communion Service must be discarded, since Peter Martyr's original Latin has now been rediscovered;[53] unless, of course, Martyr also had been reading H. Another piece of evidence which might support that possibility is that he includes a phrase '*vos omnes, quotquot adestis, invito vosque obsecro*', which is very like the phrase from H quoted above (p. 86). This raises the further possibility that Martyr was the author also of the exhortation at the beginning of Mattins, whether or not he had read H.

In Public Baptism, the new prayer after the Lord's Prayer is based on Romans 6, verses 4, 6 and 5, in that order; H also quotes them, but in the biblical order, so that there is nothing to show whether H or the Bible is the immediate source.[54] In Private Baptism the new phrase 'in the name of this child' occurs in H as '*infantis nomine*'.[55] The new Confirmation prayer 'Defend, O Lord, this thy child with thy heavenly grace' has a distinct affinity with '*Confirma hunc servum tuum* N. *Spiritu sancto tuo, ut . . . perseveret*'.[56] Similarly, 'The Curate of every Parish, or some other at his appointment shall be diligently . . . instruct and examine' may owe something to H's '*In singulis tamen Ecclesiis*

Parochi cum Symmystis suis . . . diligenter praeparabunt'.[57] In the Burial Service, the new exordium of the committal is taken straight from **H**, and the remodelling of the first prayer may echo **H**'s second.[58]

The parallels in the Occasional Offices are few and less marked than those in the Communion Service and in the introduction to Morning and Evening Prayer; but it seems that the new material of 1552, in proportion to its extent, shows almost as free a use of **H** as does the Book of 1549.

To sum up, Hermann's Order evidently fired Cranmer's imagination. Time and again, he uses **H** as the starting-point of some exhortation or prayer that in the end is largely his own composition. Stray phrases, sometimes from totally different contexts, testify to Cranmer's close knowledge of **H**'s text. Even the structure of the services shows signs of **H**'s influence, which, at its height in 1548, was still noticeably at work in 1549 and 1552.

The English Translations of H

Though no information is given by the translator, the *Simple and Religious Consultation* of 1547 is in fact a translation from the Latin, and takes no account of the German original. The style is workmanlike, but lacking in felicity. While a completely literal translation would have been intolerable, the translator takes more liberties than would be acceptable nowadays. The limitations which prevent the translation from being regarded as a wholly reliable equivalent of the Latin fall under three headings: Non-significant additions and omissions, Idiosyncrasies and Errors.

Non-significant additions and omissions   The use of two almost synonymous words is a stylistic mannerism of Bucer's, and the translator not infrequently feels himself free to omit one of the pair, though he will also on occasion render one word by two. He peppers the text with short explanatory phrases such as 'I mean', 'that is', or 'finally'; and he adds definitions of unfamiliar words like 'Catechism' or '*Eucharistia*'. Many quotations from Scripture are broken off with an etcetera, and some references are suppressed, as are also the concluding formulas of prayers, and Amens. Occasionally an entire subordinate clause has been omitted, perhaps from haste rather than by intention. Above all, he ignores the marginal headings completely.

Idiosyncrasies A whole group of phrases is consistently omitted: '*per meritum Christi*', '*propter Christum*', '*exemplo Christi*', '*in fide Christi*'; '*Spiritu suo*', '*adiutus Spiritu Domini*', '*cum Spiritu sancto*'. The translator seems to have felt that the assistance of the second and third Persons of the Trinity must not be so easily assumed. He is also reluctant to describe any thing or person as belonging to God: '*tuus*' is often rendered by 'the' instead of 'thy', and '*eius*' by 'this' instead of 'his'; possibly, though, these may be misprints. '*Regnum coelorum*' is always translated 'the Kingdom of God'; but the severest treatment is reserved for the words '*consecro*' and '*consecratio*': these are completely omitted in five places, and twice translated as 'give'. In every case the words denote self-dedication; presumably, in the translator's view, only God can consecrate.

Errors Some undoubted mistakes may be due to haste, as when '*reuocare*' is rendered 'renew', as though it were '*renouare*', or '*inuitari*' 'be provoked', as though it were '*incitari*'. Towards the end of his task the translator shows signs of fatigue: as when '*salutarem*' and '*utilem*' are both lamely rendered 'good'; and a number of comparatives are treated as positives. Faulty dictation may have produced 'Lord' for '*lex*', instead of 'law'; and bad writing 'mercie' for '*meriti*', instead of 'merite'. There is no such excuse for translating '*Manichaeam*' by 'monkish'; and it was sheer carelessness to read '*Media vita*' (the title of Notker's famous sequence) as '*media via*', and translate 'in the mid way'. An '*aut*' then has to be suppressed to make sense of the sentence. Here, incidentally, is evidence that Cranmer himself was not the translator: no one with an interest in liturgy could have perpetrated such a blunder.

In 1548, a new edition was issued, 'perused by the translator', according to the title page, 'and amended in many places'. Many of the amendments are tiny and seem to be aimed rather at greater smoothness and clarity than at improvement in accuracy. Quite often, the result is a less accurate rendering. On one page, where the 1547 edition had 'prayer' for '*precatione*', 1548 substitutes 'prayers'; and where 1547 had 'prayers' for '*precibus*', 1548 reads 'prayer'. Another variation introduced in 1548 comes at a point where a form of Mattins is outlined, starting with '*tres Psalmos, Te Deum laudamus, Benedictus*'. 1547 rightly translates: 'three psalms, *Te Deum laudamus, Benedictus*';

but the reviser, wrongly taking *Te Deum* and *Benedictus* to be the psalms in question, alters it to 'these two psalms, *Te Deum laudamus, Benedictus*'. Here again it is clear that he had little knowledge of current liturgical ideas. To the credit of the 1548 revision must be placed the restoration of the great majority of the marginal headings and of an entire paragraph at the end of 'The Preparation to the Supper of the Lord', which directs the hearing of individual confession after the service; 1547 had quietly omitted it.

Select Bibliography

Von Gottes genaden, vnser Hermans Ertzbischoffs zu Cöln, und Chürfursten, &c. einfaltigs bedencken . . . (1543, revised 1544).

Christliche und katholische Gegenberichtung eines ehrwurdigen Domkapitels zu Köln . . . (1544).

Antididagma, seu christianae et catholicae religionis per . . . *Canonicos Metropolitanae ecclesiae Colonien propugnatio* . . . (1544).

Nostra Hermanni ex gratia Dei archiepiscopi Coloniensis, et principis electoris, &c. simplex ac pia deliberatio . . . (1545).

Martini Buceri constans defensio . . . *DELIBERATIONIS de Christiana reformatione* . . . (written 1544, published 1613).

Reverendissimi in Christo Domino Patris ac Domini Hermanni, Sanctae Coloniensis Ecclesiae Archiepiscopi . . . *Appellatio contra certos quosdam homines ex Venerabili Capitulo Coloniensi, Clero item & Universitate* . . . (1545).

A Simple and Religious Consultation of vs Herman by the grace of God Archbishop of Colone, and prince Electour . . . (1547, revised 1548).

The Order for Brandenburg–Nürnberg is in E. Sehling, *Die evangelische Kirchenordnungen*, vol. xi (1955).

The Order for Hesse–Cassel is in M. Bucer, *Deutsche Schriften*, vol. vii (1964), pp. 279–318.

M. Deckers, *Hermann von Wied* (Cologne 1840).

G. Drouven, *Die Reformation in den Cölnischen Kirchenprovinz* (Cologne 1876).

C. Varrentrapp, *Hermann von Wied und sein Reformationsversuch in Köln* (Leipzig 1878).

W. Lipgens, *Kardinal Johannes Gropper* (Münster 1951).

G. J. van de Poll, *Martin Bucer's Liturgical Ideas* (Assen 1954).

M. Köhn, *Martin Bucers Entwurf einer Reformation des Erzstiftes Köln* (Witten 1966).

5
The Canon of 1549

In the 1549 service for Communion of the Sick Cranmer refers to the eucharistic prayer as 'the Canon', and this title confirms what literary analysis strongly suggests, that its model was the Canon of the Mass. For the purposes of this essay, the latter will be treated as beginning with *Te igitur*, as it is in, for example, the 1543 edition of the Sarum Manual. In any case, there is little to say about Cranmer's treatment of the *Sursum corda*, Preface and Sanctus, where he follows the Latin fairly closely. Only in the proper prefaces for Christmas Day and Whitsunday does he have recourse to another favourite source, *The King's Book* (see below, pp. 108–9).[1] Cranmer's Canon falls into three sections, referred to below as I, II and III. I is largely concerned with intercession, II with consecration and III with self-oblation.

There is a close enough similarity of language and structure between the two canons to make it highly probable that Cranmer began work by making a straight translation from Sarum. As may be seen in the synopsis below, instances of direct translation are visible at *Te igitur, Communicantes, Hanc igitur, Quam oblationem, Unde et memores, Supplices te, Memento etiam, Nobis quoque* and *Per quem*. Of the remainder, the sections replacing *Memento Domine* and *Supra quae* use some similar language and thoughts; and Cranmer's Institution Narrative covers exactly the same ground as *Qui pridie*, even though it is probably taken from the English Bible rather than translated from the Missal.

Most of these sections occur in the same order as in Sarum, but Cranmer does not hesitate to make vigorous changes of structure. The most obvious comes in section I of his Canon. Halfway through *Communicantes* he cuts out the list of popes and inserts the whole of *Memento etiam* from a much later point in the Sarum Canon, thus concentrating 'thanks for all men', living or dead, in one place. From this it is an easy transition to the thought of the Last Judgement, perhaps suggested by the last

91

phrase of *Hanc oblationem*, 'bid us be numbered among the flock of thine elect'.

Having removed *Memento etiam* from its original place, Cranmer now finds *Supplices te* leading on to *Nobis quoque*, and proceeds to conflate them. After the first three words of *Supplices te*, he holds back the reference to the heavenly altar and goes straight on to the later part of the section, 'that whosoever shall be partakers . . .'. *Nobis quoque* supplies an allusion to our sins; and then he is ready to introduce the heavenly altar, rounding off the passage with the concluding words of *Nobis quoque*, 'not weighing our merits . . .'.

These omissions and alterations are dictated by theological considerations. Apart from removing obvious excrescences such as the list of popes and the non-scriptural embellishments of *Qui pridie*, the first object of the changes is to excise any reference to the offering of the elements and its reception by God, with which the Canon of the Mass is obsessively concerned. Cranmer's positive aims have been widely misunderstood. For example, F. E. Brightman, who first drew attention to Cranmer's use of the Cologne *Antididagma*, quotes that work as setting out a fourfold sacrifice in the Mass:

> (1) of the material offering of the bread and wine . . . at the Offertory; (2) of thanksgiving . . .; (3) of Christ . . .; and (4) of the whole Church.[2]

Cranmer on the other hand, he suggests, adjusted the Sarum Canon to

> the conception of the eucharistic sacrifice as threefold, namely (a) as a commemoration of our Lord's *historical* self-oblation in his death upon the cross; (b) as a sacrifice of praise and thanksgiving for the benefits of redemption so secured; and (c) as the offering of the Church, of ourselves, our souls and bodies: and concentrating all sacrificial language on these three moments.[3]

This analysis has been accepted by later writers.[4] Brightman's (a), (b) and (c) certainly correspond to nos. 3, 2 and 4 above; no. 1 is omitted. But Cranmer himself in his *Defence* (1550) sets out a *twofold* sacrifice:

> One sacrifice there is, which is called a propitiatory or merciful sacrifice . . . which is the death of the Son of God our Lord Jesus Christ . . .
>
> Another sacrifice there is, which . . . is made of them that be reconciled by Christ, to testify our duties unto God, and to show

ourselves thankful unto him; and therefore they be called sacrifices of laud, praise and thanksgiving . . .[5]

In other words, Brightman's second and third 'moments' are really only one: the 'sacrifice of praise and thanksgiving' *is* 'the offering of . . . ourselves'. This equation is already made in the Cologne *Encheiridion* (1538): The Church's self-offering is 'a eucharistic sacrifice of praise, thanksgiving and the obedience proper to and owed to God'.[6] In the passage just quoted, Cranmer goes on to say: 'This sacrifice generally is our whole obedience to God.'

Cranmer's Canon does have a threefold offering, corresponding to the three sections:

I   our offering of prayer;
II   Christ's offering of himself on the cross; and
III our offering of ourselves.

But our offering of prayer is not a sacrifice in the sense in which the other two offerings are; in fact, I has no specifically eucharistic content at all, and is already suitable for detachment from the rest of the Canon. II and III, however, accurately represent the two kinds of sacrifice described in the *Defence*, and set them firmly in the context of the communion.

In pursuance of his objective of ejecting all offering of the elements, Cranmer almost at once replaces '*haec dona, haec munera, haec sancta sacrificia illibata*' by 'these our prayers'. Since he could not allow any suggestion that the redemption and salvation of men's souls could be achieved by offering a sacrifice of praise, whatever content was attached to that phrase, nor accept that God's protection was more likely to be obtained by the merits and prayers of the saints, he naturally finds the section *Memento Domine* largely useless, and replaces it by detailed intercession. Likewise, although thanks are offered for the virtues of the saints, prayer on their behalf is carefully avoided.

Again, when God is asked to bless and sanctify the bread and wine, they are not referred to as 'this oblation', but as 'these thy gifts and creatures' ('*tua dona ac data*', brought up from *Unde et memores*; not our gifts, but God's). Still less, after the Institution Narrative, can the bread and wine be called 'a pure, holy, immaculate victim . . . a holy sacrifice'; they are still 'these thy . . . gifts', though now qualified as 'holy'. They are not now offered, nor is God asked to accept them; they are for celebrating and making the memorial which Jesus Christ 'willed us to make'.

Above all, Cranmer could not offer 'the holy bread of eternal life and the cup of everlasting salvation'; these are benefits which God offers to us, not we to him. On the other hand, he is able to keep the phrase 'that they may be to us the body and blood of thy most dearly beloved Son Jesus Christ' by placing great stress on the words 'to us', which he expounds in the *Defence* as meaning 'to those who receive worthily'.[7] He is also able to keep two black crosses at 'bless and sanctify', and a rubric directing the priest to take the bread and the cup into his hands at the words of institution. All this is in line with his theology of consecration, which he defines thus:

> Consecration is the separation of any thing from a profane and worldly use unto a spiritual and godly use.[8]

The sacrifice which God *is* asked to accept is that of praise and thanksgiving (the phrase is brought down from the discarded section *Memento Domine*), and its content is 'our self, our souls and bodies'. This sacrifice is described as 'reasonable, holy and lively', a quotation from Romans 12.1 which is perhaps intended to compensate for the previous omission of '*adscriptam, ratam, rationabilem, acceptabilemque*' from *Quam oblationem*. The sacrifice of praise and thanksgiving takes the place of the sacrifices of Abel, Abraham and Melchizedek, which might have provided a scriptural justification of our offering of gifts. It leads naturally to a prayer for worthy reception, for which Cranmer uses the later part of *Supplices te*. He wants to keep the earlier part, 'bid these things to be borne by the hands of your holy angel to your altar on high', but not exactly as it stood. What does it mean by 'these things'? Cranmer adopts the view of Innocent III, that they are the prayers of the faithful,[9] and makes the transition from self-offering and worthy reception in words taken from *Hanc igitur* which he has not used at the equivalent place, 'we beseech thee to accept this our bounden duty and service'. Now he can bring in the angel, who has become 'angels' (as already in Innocent's interpretation), and the altar, which has become a 'holy tabernacle'. The idea of an angel offering the prayers of the saints on the heavenly altar is scriptural (Revelation 8.3), but the word 'altar' has sacrificial associations, and Cranmer substitutes the harmless 'tabernacle' of Hebrews 8.2. As a result of this transposition, 'grace and heavenly benediction' now depend on worthy reception rather than on the ministry of the angel.

The lists of saints in *Nobis quoque* disappears, and with it the prayer that we may join them, leaving isolated the final phrase, 'not weighing our merits, but pardoning our offences', which follows less naturally than in its original context. The first sentence of *Per quem* is omitted, perhaps because of its association with the blessing of inanimate objects, and the Canon ends with the Sarum doxology, only leaving out '*in ipso*'.

If there was ever a point in time at which Cranmer's adaptation of the Sarum Canon could stand by itself as a usable prayer, it is not now possible to reconstruct the form which it then took, except (as above) in the roughest outline. From a very early stage Cranmer must have intended to introduce fresh material in considerable quantity, some of it clearly derived from sources which can be identified. One such source is the Latin version (1545) of the Cologne Order commissioned by Hermann von Wied, *Simplex ac pia Deliberatio* (see Chapter 4, above); rather surprisingly, since Hermann's service contains no canon. Some of the apparent parallels may be dismissed as inevitable in sixteenth-century writing about the Eucharist; and the same is true of the counterblast by Hermann's opponents, the *Antididagma* of 1544.

The principal contribution of the *Deliberatio* to the Canon is the concept of a lengthy intercessory prayer, though there it is free-standing and not in any way linked to the Sanctus or the Institution Narrative. Cranmer, as usual in his dealings with Hermann, takes the first words as his starting-point, and then only uses a stray phrase from Hermann here and there. In II, when he deals with Christ's sacrifice, the *Antididagma* seems closer than the *Deliberatio* to Cranmer's actual wording; but in III both sources produce a number of parallels and there is one phrase, 'our self, our souls and bodies', which may have been translated directly from the original German version of the *Deliberatio* (but see p. 74, above). It seems on the whole, though, that Cranmer was much less influenced by Hermann in writing the Canon than in preparing *The Order of the Communion*. One other possible German source is the Order for Brandenburg–Nürnberg (1533), which has been suggested as the origin of Cranmer's Institution Narrative. While it is certainly very similar, it seems most probable that Cranmer produced his text of the Narrative simply by harmonizing the four New Testament accounts, and Osiander at Nürnberg may well have done exactly the same thing.[10]

There are two passages in the Canon which have been thought to show the influence of the Greek liturgies; and indeed the Act of Uniformity speaks of having 'eye and respect . . . to the usages in the primitive Church'. The more striking of the two passages consists of the words:

> Hear us, O merciful Father, we beseech thee: and with thy holy Spirit and word vouchsafe to bless and sanctify these thy gifts and creatures of bread and wine, that they may be unto us the body and blood of thy most dearly beloved Son Jesus Christ.

At first sight this looks very like an Eastern epiclesis or invocation of the Holy Spirit upon the elements, such as is found in *St Basil*: 'We beseech thee . . . that thy all-holy Spirit may come upon us and upon these gifts set forth, and bless and sanctify them.' Brightman at first suggested *St Basil* as the source of Cranmer's phrase, but later retracted this view on the ground that there is no word or idea in the passage which cannot be convincingly paralleled from Western services or writers.[11] Recent scholars have tended to follow his later view; and it may be added that in *St Basil* the invocation comes *after* the words of institution, not before (as in 1549), which implies a different theology of consecration. Further, in *St Basil* it is the Spirit himself who is to come and sanctify the elements, whereas the 1549 prayer asks the Father to sanctify them with his Spirit and word. This makes no difference theologically, but is a surprising change if Cranmer was following *St Basil* at all closely. It is in fact closer to the wording of *St John Chrysostom*, 'changing it *by* your Holy Spirit'.

A later passage in the Canon runs: 'humbly beseeching thee that whosoever shall be partakers of this holy Communion may worthily receive the most precious body and blood of thy Son Jesus Christ and be . . . made one body with thy Son Jesus Christ, that he may dwell in them and they in him'. Brightman compares a passage in *St Basil* which leads up to the Lord's Prayer: 'that . . . we may be united to the holy body and blood of thy Christ, and, receiving them worthily, may have Christ dwelling in our hearts'. But the context of the 1549 passage is all supplied by the Roman Canon and St John's Gospel; and the material actually shared with *St Basil* is concerned with the general and not uncommon ideas of worthy reception and union with the body of Christ.

Several striking parallels may be found in English documents of the period. Already in the Exhortation which precedes the English Litany of 1544 Cranmer quotes 1 Timothy 2.1 as enjoining prayers, supplications and thanks for all men, and first of all, for kings; and one or two other phrases suggest that this Exhortation was still fresh in his memory. Then there is a whole series of doctrinal works, beginning with the *Ten Articles* of 1536. These, with a good deal of Lutheran material, were incorporated into *The Bishops' Book* (1537); and a revised edition of this, *The King's Book*, appeared in 1543.[12] The latter adopts a more orthodox Catholic line, except of course with regard to the papacy. Cranmer must have been intimately concerned in the production of all these doctrinal statements. Some of the parallels between them and the Canon are so close as to suggest that Cranmer had at any rate *The King's Book* open on the table in front of him.

But again, it may be simply that this was the kind of language which came naturally to him when writing about the Eucharist. It is noticeable that the parallels are most compelling exactly at those points where he has departed furthest from the Latin text. Unlike the parallels in Hermann, which nearly all occur closely together in the original, the parallels in *The King's Book* are scattered all over the work. The closest parallels to individual phrases are shown in the synopsis below, but the whole movement of thought in the opening of II is very close to such passages in *The King's Book* as this, from 'The Sacrament of the Altar':

> . . . according to the intent of Christ's institution: who, . . . that we should have continual remembrance of his most dear charity showed towards us in his death and passion, did institute this sacrament as a permanent memorial of his mercy and the wonderful work of our redemption . . .[13]

On the whole, the most likely explanation seems to be that Cranmer remained familiar with the wording of *The King's Book*, so that it naturally came into his mind when treating the same subjects. But it would be hard to prove that he did not deliberately consult it when writing the Canon. The reader must inspect the synopsis and judge for himself.

Apart from a very few biblical allusions, the only other identifiable English source is Hilsey's Primer of 1539, which Cranmer certainly used for the conclusion of I. It will be noticed that the English and German sources most freely employed all belong to the years 1543–5, which accords very well with the *a priori* probability that Cranmer was drafting the Canon in the years before 1548.

List of sources and sigla

In the synopsis, column 1 is chiefly devoted to extracts from the Sarum Canon, from which all quotations not otherwise ascribed are taken; the remainder come from the Missal, the Breviary and the Manual.

Column 2 is all from the Cologne *Deliberatio* and *Antididagma*, except for one excerpt from the Brandenburg–Nürnberg Order, which I have translated myself.

Column 3 contains the English sources. The *Ten Articles, The Bishop's Book* and *The King's Book* are quoted from C. Lloyd, *Formularies of Faith*, 1825; the 1544 Litany from W. K. Clay, *Private Prayers of the Reign of Queen Elizabeth* (Parker Society), 1851; Hilsey's Primer from E. Burton, *Three Primers of the Reign of Henry VIII*, 1834; and the *Rationale of Ceremonial* from the edition of C. S. Cobb (Alcuin Club), 1910.

Column 4 contains the text of 1549 with spelling and punctuation modernized.

A	*Antididagma*, 1544 edn
BB	*The Bishops' Book*, as above
EB	*Einfältiges Bedenken*, 1543 edn (German original of *Deliberatio*)
H	*Hermann von Wied, Simplex ac Pia Deliberatio*, 1545 edn
KB	*The King's Book*, as above
L	*The Litany*, as above (including the preceding Exhortation)

SYNOPSIS

Sarum

... et primo pro universali statu Ecclesiae. *Orationes solennes*

Te igitur, clementissime Pater ... supplices rogamus ac petimus uti accepta habeas et benedicas haec dona ... quae tibi offerimus pro Ecclesia tua sancta catholica, quam pacificare, custodire, adunare, & regere digneris toto orbe terrarum ...

... rege nostro *N*. ...

(Memento, Domine, famulorum famularumque ...)

... sanctis omnibus qui in terra sunt ab exordio mundi procreati ... *Mattins for All Saints, Fourth Lesson* Communicantes et memoriam venerantes imprimis gloriosae semperque virginis Mariae genetricis Dei et Domini nos-

German

Oratio pro omnibus hominum Statibus, & necessitatibus Ecclesiae.
   Omnipotens sempiterne Deus ... qui per Filium tuum ... & eius Apostolos mandasti ... H, f. 92^v

... in conspectu divinae maiestatis tuae ... pro Ecclesiis tuis ...

in unitate verae fidei ... *H*, f. 94^r

... pro servis tuis ... et Rege nostro ...

pro consiliariis eius et praefectis ... H, f. 94^v

... cum omni pietate et honestate ... *H*, f. 93^r

... serviamus omni sanctitia & iustitia ... H, f. 94^v

... consolare et erige animos ... cruce et afflictione ... egestate ... morbis, aliisque calamitatibus et infortuniis ...

... qui hic ... convenimus ... in tuo nomine vere conveniamus ... *H*, f. 94^r
... memoriam ... celebremus ... *H*, f. 90^v
... quas possumus tibi gratias habemus, quod illis ... tam admirabilem gratiam dedisti ... *A*, f. 61^r

100

Let us pray for the whole state of Christ's Church.

Almighty and everliving God, which by thy holy Apostle hast taught us to make prayers and supplications, and to give thanks for all men:

. . . as Saint Paul exhorteth us . . . Let us make our prayers and supplications, rendering and giving of thanks for all men . . . *L*, p. 566 (= 1 Tim. 2.1)

we humbly beseech thee most mercifully to receive these our prayers which we offer unto thy divine majesty, beseeching thee to inspire continually the universal Church with the spirit of truth, unity and concord;

. . . unity, concord and charity . . . *KB*, p. 267
. . . unity, peace and concord . . . *L*, p. 573

and grant that all they that do confess thy holy name may agree in the truth of thy holy word, and live in unity and godly love. Specially we beseech thee to save and defend thy servant Edward, our King, that under him we may be godly and quietly governed. And grant unto his whole council, and to all that be put in authority under him, that they may truly and indifferently minister justice, to the punishment of wickedness and vice, and to the maintenance of God's true religion and virtue. Give grace, O heavenly Father, to all Bishops, Pastors and Curates, that they may both by their life and doctrine set forth thy true and lively word, and rightly and duly administer thy holy sacraments. And to all thy people give thy heavenly grace, that with meek heart and due reverence they may hear and receive thy holy word, truly serving thee in holiness and righteousness all the days of their life.

. . . and namely, for kings
. . . that we all that are their subjects may live in peace and quietness with all godliness and virtue . . . *L*, pp. 566–7
. . . all such as be in authority under their prince . . . *KB*, p. 316
. . . that justice be ministered unto them indifferently . . . the right religion and true doctrine . . . *KB*, p. 315

. . . due reverence and faith . . . *KB*, p. 267
When ye received the word of God which ye heard from us . . .
1 Thessalonians 2.13
in holiness and righteousness before him all the days of our life.
Luke 1.74

And we most humbly beseech thee, of thy goodness, O Lord, to comfort and succour all them which in this transitory life be in trouble, sorrow, need, sickness or any other adversity. And especially we commend unto thy merciful goodness this congregation which is here assembled in thy name, to celebrate the commemoration of the most glorious death of thy Son. And here we do give unto thee most high praise and hearty thanks for the wonderful grace and virtue declared in all thy saints, from the beginning of the world; and chiefly in the glorious and most blessed virgin Mary, mother of thy Son Jesus Christ, our Lord and God, and in the holy Patriarchs, Prophets, Apostles and

. . . from sin, sickness, dearth and all other adversities of body and soul. *L*, p. 567
. . . we are here at this time gathered together . . . *L*, p. 565
. . . to praise Christ in them for their excellent virtues which he planted in them . . .
Ten Articles, 1536, p. xxix

Holy virgin Mary, mother of God our Saviour Jesus Christ . . .
All holy Patriarchs and Prophets,

101

Sarum	German

Sarum

tri Iesu Christi, sed et beatorum
apostolorum ac martyrum tuorum . . . et
omnium sanctorum tuorum . . .

Memento etiam, Domine, famulorum famularumque tuarum *N*. et *N*., qui nos
precesserunt cum signo fidei et
dormiunt in somno pacis: ipsis, Domine,
et omnibus in Christo quiescentibus
locum refrigerii, lucis, et pacis ut
indulgeas deprecamur.
(Hanc igitur oblationem . . .)
et in electorum tuorum iubeas
grege numerari.
. . . ut in die iudicii ad dexteram
tuam statuti a te audire mereamur
illam vocem dulcissimam: Venite,
benedicti, in regnum patris mei . . .
Missa de quinque vulneribus Christi

German

. . . eundem unicum mediatorem nostrum . . .
H, 94^r

. . . per Christum semel in cruce . . . plenarie
& sufficienter impetrata . . . qui seipsum
Deo Patri coelesti cruentum sacrificium
pro peccatis mundi obtulit . . . semel in
cruce oblatum . . .
A, ff. 56^v, 63^v
. . . semetipsum tibi in cruce pro peccatis
nostris obtulisse, & pro eis satisfecisse . . .
H, f. 93^v

. . . praecepitque ut sanctissimum illud
sacrificium Patri coelesti iterum atque
iterum ac semper quosque veniat, spirit-
ualiter & commemorativè offeramus.
A, f. 56^v

. . . in verbo efficitur Creatoris et
in virtute Spiritus sancti . . .
*Mattins for Sunday in octave of
Corpus Christi, Fourth Lesson*
. . . benedic et sanctifica hanc cre-
aturam carnis . . .
Sarum Manual: Benedictio carnis
Quam oblationem . . . benedictam . . .
facere digneris, ut nobis corpus
et sanguis fiat dilectissimi
Filii tui Domini nostri Iesu
Christi;

Our Lord Jesus, in the night that he was
betrayed, took bread, gave thanks, and brake

Apostles, Martyrs, Confessors and
Virgins . . . pray for us. *L*, p. 571.

. . . we meekly beseech thee that
in the day of judgement we
(. . . the mystical body of Christ
. . . *KB*, *passim*, e.g. p. 257) may be
on the right hand and hear thy
sweet sentence: Come, ye blessed
of my Father, enjoy ye the kingdom
prepared for you from the beginning of the world . . .
Hilsey's Primer, p. 350 (Terce);
Matthew 25.34
. . . the only mediator between God
and mankind, the redeemer, inter-
cessor and advocate . . . *KB*, p. 237
. . . our mediator and advocate. *L*, p. 575
. . . our Saviour Christ hath offered himself upon the cross a sufficient redemption and satisfaction for the sins of the world . . .
KB, p. 365
. . . suffered upon the cross for
our redemption. *BB*, p. 100
. . . although Christ and his death be
the sufficient oblation, sacrifice,
satisfaction and recompence . . .
BB, p. 98
. . . he hath made sacrifice and
oblation on the cross . . . *KB*, p. 230
. . . did institute
this sacrament as a permanent
memorial of his mercy . . . *KB*, p. 264
For the mass . . . is celebrate in the
Church for a perpetual memory of
his death and passion. *KB*, p. 310.
But in this most high sacrament of
the altar, the creatures which be
taken to the use thereof, as bread
and wine, do not remain still in
their own substance, but by the
virtue of Christ's word in the
consecration be changed and turned
to the very substance of the body
and blood of our Saviour Jesus
Christ. *KB*, pp. 262–3
   *The four New Testament accounts
in the translation of the* Great Bible

Martyrs, whose examples, O Lord, and steadfast-
ness in thy faith and keeping thy holy commandments, grant us to follow.
   We commend unto
thy mercy, O Lord, all other thy servants
which are departed hence from us with the
sign of faith, and do now rest in the sleep
of peace: grant unto them, we beseech thee,
thy mercy and everlasting peace,

   and that
at the day of the general resurrection we
and all they which be of the mystical body
of thy Son may altogether be set on his
right hand and hear that his most joyful
voice: Come unto me, O ye that be blessed
of my Father, and possess the kingdom which
is prepared for you from the beginning of
the world;
   grant this, O Father, for Jesus
Christ's sake, our only mediator and advocate.

   O God, heavenly Father, which of thy tender
mercy didst give thine only Son Jesus
Christ to suffer death upon the cross for
our redemption, who made there, by his one
oblation once offered, a full, perfect and
sufficient sacrifice, oblation and satisfaction for the sins of the whole world;

and did institute, and in his holy gospel
command us to celebrate a perpetual memory
of that his precious death, until his coming
again:

   hear us, O merciful Father, we beseech
thee, and with thy holy Spirit and word
vouchsafe to bless and sanctify these thy
gifts and creatures of bread and wine, that
they may be unto us the body and blood of
thy most dearly beloved Son Jesus Christ.

Who in the same night that he was betrayed,
took bread, and when he had blessed and

103

Sarum

Qui pridie quam pateretur, accep-
it panem . . . tibi gratias agens,
benedixit, fregit, deditque discipulis suis, dicens: Accipite et
manducate
ex hoc omnes, hoc est enim corpus
meum. Simili modo postquam coena-
tum est, accipiens . . . calicem . . .
tibi gratias agens, benedixit,
deditque discipulis suis, dicens:
hic est enim calix sanguinis mei,
novi et aeterni testamenti . . . qui
pro vobis et pro multis effundetur
in remissionem peccatorum. Haec
quotiescumque feceritis, in mei
memoriam facietis.
Unde et memores, Domine, nos servi
tui, sed et plebs tua sancta, eius-
dem Christi Filii tui, Domini nostri, tam beatae passionis, necnon
ab inferis resurrectionis, sed et
in caelos gloriosae ascensionis:
offerimus praeclarae maiestati
tuae de tuis donis ac datis,

(Supra quae . . .) respicere digneris
et accepta habere . . .
hoc sacrificium laudis . . .
Memento Domine

. . . ut merear . . . remissionem omnium
peccatorum meorum accipere . . .
Prayer before the Peace
. . . in sui cordis penetralibus
hostiam vivam Deoque placentem, id
est semetipsos . . . offerre non de-
sistant.
Mattins of All Saints' Day, Seventh Lesson
. . . sanctum sacrificium . . .
Supplices te rogamus . . . ut quotquot
ex hac altaris participatione sacro-
sanctum Filii tui corpus et sang-
uinem sumpserimus, omni benedictione
caelesti et gratia repleamur.

Nobis quoque peccatoribus . . .
Hanc igitur oblationem servitu-
tis nostrae . . . quaesumus, Domine,
ut placatus accipias . . .
iube haec perferri per manus

German

it, and gave it to his disciples, and said:
Take and eat, this is my body, which is given
for you: do this in remembrance of me.
Likewise he took also the cup
after supper, and gave thanks, and gave it
to them, and said: Drink ye all from this,
this is my blood of the new testament,
which is shed for you and for many, for
remission of sins; do this as often as ye
drink in remembrance of me.
Church Order for Brandenburg–Nürnberg, 1533

. . . instituto eius celebramus . . . *H*, f. 90ʳ
. . . secundum institutionem Domini nostri
Iesu Christi . . . *H*, f. 84ᵛ
. . . haec dona caelestia . . . memoriam cele-
tremus . . . *H*, f. 90ʳ

. . . gratiarum actio . . . pro eximiis beneficiis . . . *A*, f. 60ᵛ
. . . his tantis beneficiis . . . *H*, f. 90ʳ

. . . commune laudis et gratiarum actionis sacrificium . . . *A*, f. 58ʳ
. . . omneque meritum suum . . . *H*, f. 90ʳ

. . . remissionem peccatorum . . . *H*, f. 90ʳ

Ecclesia tradit et offert seipsam patri
hostiam vivam votis spiritualibus . . . *A*, f. 70ʳ
. . . offerimus . . . praebeatis . . . vos ipsos . . .
corpora et animas nostras . . . rationalem . . .
hostiam viventem, sanctam . . . *H*, f. 60ʳ
. . . uns selb, unsere Leib und Seele . . . *EB*, f. 69ᵛ

. . . communicantes (*Eng. trans*: be partakers)
corpori ipsius et sanguini . . . simusque
plenius corpus ipsius . . .

in ipso maneamus . . . ac ipse in nobis.
H, f. 90ʳ

are printed in parallel columns in The English Rite, *vol. i, p. cviii.*

given thanks, he brake it, and gave it to his disciples, saying: Take, eat, this is my body which is given for you: do this in remembrance of me. Likewise after supper he took the cup, and when he had given thanks, he gave it to them, saying: Drink ye all of this, for this is my blood of the new testament, which is shed for you and for many, for remission of sins: do this as oft as you shall drink it, in remembrance of me.

Wherefore, O Lord and heavenly Father, according to the institution of thy dearly beloved Son, our Saviour Jesus Christ, we thy humble servants do celebrate and make here before thy divine majesty with these thy holy gifts the memorial which thy Son hath willed us to make; having in remembrance his blessed passion, mighty resurrection and glorious ascension,

... according to the intent of Christ's institution ... *KB*, p. 263

rendering unto thee most hearty thanks for the innumerable benefits procured unto us by the same, entirely desiring thy fatherly goodness mercifully to accept this our sacrifice of praise and thanksgiving; most humbly beseeching thee to grant that, by the merits and death of thy Son Jesus Christ, and through faith in his blood, we and all thy whole Church may obtain remission of our sins and all other benefits of his passion.

... by the merits and passion of our Saviour Christ. *KB*, p. 365; Romans 3.25

... and all other benefits which Christ by his passion hath merited and deserved for us ... *KB*, p. 243 Romans 12.1

Then followeth the offertory, whereby we be learned to prepare our self ... to be an acceptable oblation to him, to the intent we may be partakers of the blessed sacrifice which Christ offered for us upon the cross ... *Rationale of Ceremonial*, p. 22

And here we offer and present unto thee, O Lord, our self, our souls and bodies, to be a reasonable, holy and lively sacrifice unto thee,

... all such as in due manner receive this sacrament. (... the most precious body and blood of ... Jesus Christ ... *KB*, p. 293) For they that do so be made one with Christ, and dwell in him and he in them ... *KB*, p. 266 John 6.56

... according to our bounden duty ... *L*, p. 569

humbly beseeching thee that whosoever shall be partakers of this holy communion may worthily receive the most precious body and blood of thy Son Jesus Christ, and be filled with thy grace and heavenly benediction, and made one body with thy Son Jesus Christ, that he may dwell in them and they in him. And although we be unworthy, through our manifold sins, to offer unto thee any sacrifice, yet we beseech thee to accept this our bounden duty and service; and command these our prayers and supplications, by the ministry

Sarum	German

sancti angeli tui in sublime al-
tare tuum in conspectu divinae
maiestatis tuae . . .
. . . non aestimator meriti, sed
veniae, quaesumus, largitor . . .
Per Christum Dominum nostrum . . .
Per ipsum, et cum ipso, et in
ipso, est tibi Deo Patri omnipot-
enti, in unitate Spiritus sancti,
omnis honor et gloria per omnia
saecula saeculorum. Amen

Revelation 8.3; 15.5

of thy holy angels, to be brought up into
thy holy tabernacle before the sight of
thy divine majesty;

        not weighing our merits,
but pardoning our offences, through Christ
our Lord, by whom and with whom, in the
unity of the holy Ghost, all honour and
glory be unto thee, O Father almighty, world
without end. Amen.

There is a close verbal relationship between many passages in *The King's Book* and the Book of Common Prayer. Some have been pointed out in the collects (pp. 60–1); and others are set out above in the Canon (pp. 97–105). Several more are listed by Brightman in *The English Rite*, of which the most noteworthy are:

KB The penitent may desire to hear of the minister the comfortable words of remission of sins.
BCP Hear what comfortable words our Saviour Christ saith. *ER*, p. 698; *KB*, p. 260)

KB And when they be weary of prayer . . . let them occupy their minds with wholesome and godly meditations.
BCP And there with devout prayer, or godly silence and meditation, to occupy themselves. (*ER*, p. 718; *KB*, p. 308)

KB If they die in the state of their infancy, they shall thereby undoubtedly be saved.
BCP Children being baptized (if they depart out of this life in their infancy) are undoubtedly saved. (*ER*, p. 778; *KB*, p. 254)

KB The first institution of matrimony, as it was ordained by God in Paradise . . . it doth signify this other conjunction which is between Christ and his Church . . . Christ . . . being invited to a certain marriage, made in Cana a town of Galilee, did vouchsafe, not only . . . to honour the said marriage with his corporal presence . . . but there he began also . . . first to work miracles.
BCP An honourable estate, instituted of God in Paradise . . . signifying unto us the mystical union that is betwixt Christ and his Church . . . which holy estate, Christ adorned and beautified with his presence, and first miracle that he wrought, in Cana of Galilee . . . (*ER*, p. 800; *KB*, pp. 272–3)

KB for their mutual aid and comfort
BCP for the mutual society, help and comfort (*ER*, p. 802; *KB*, p. 269)

Besides these, a few parallels may be noted which are not mentioned by Brightman, chiefly from the Prayer of Thanksgiving in Holy Communion:

KB　are incorporated into the mystical body of Christ
　　the lively members of Christ's mystical body
　　still members of the same mystical body of Christ
BSP　we be very members incorporate in the mystical body
(*KB*, pp. 257, 293, 376; cf. *ER*, p. 708)

KB　by the merits and passion of Christ
BCP　by the merits of the most precious death and passion of
thy dear Son (*KB*, p. 365; cf. *ER*, p. 708)

KB　such outward and inward works as God hath prepared for
us to walk in.
BCP　All such good works as thou hast prepared for us to walk
in (*KB*, p. 370; cf. *ER*, p. 708)

KB　because all men be born sinners (*followed by John 3.5*)
BCP　forasmuch as all men be conceived and born in sin
(*followed by John 3.5*) (*KB*, p. 253; cf. *ER*, p. 716)

The cumulative effect of all these parallels, especially those
noted in the Canon, is to make it clear that there is some close
connection between the two books, even if we cannot now state
its precise nature.

6

From Canon to Prayer of Consecration, 1549–1662

The synopsis which follows presents the eucharistic prayers of the 1549, 1552, 1637 and 1662 Communion Services in parallel columns, after the style of *The English Rite*. It was no part of Brightman's plan to include the Scottish Liturgy of 1637 in his synopsis, except for such odd phrases as were actually incorporated into 1662. Further, his *modus operandi* did not allow him to place the three separate prayers of 1552 and 1662 opposite their originals, the three sections of the 1549 Canon. Instead, he prints the three prayers in the places where they occur in 1552 and contents himself (for the first and third of them) with a mere page reference in the 1549 column. Yet it is only when the 1549 and 1552 prayers are placed side by side that the full extent of the surgery inflicted in 1552 becomes visible; and when 1549 and 1637 are placed side by side that the subtlety of the Scottish adaptation is revealed. Finally, some brief quotations from the 'Durham Book' have been added to show the compilers adapting the Scottish text in the interests of their own ideas.

The changes made in 1552 have often been discussed[1] and only the outstanding points need be noted here. Some are simple improvements or adjustments: 'accept our alms' reflects the new position of the prayer; 'all Christian kings' follows up the teaching of the 'Apostle' (1 Tim. 2.2); 'especially to this congregation' is now felicitously placed after 'all thy people'; and 'of himself' defines the word 'oblation' beyond all cavil.

The addition of 'militant here in earth' and the removal of any mention of the departed rules out any idea of asking for the prayers of the saints or of purgatory. (It also deprives 'to give thanks for all men' of any content.) Such words as 'celebrate', 'bless' and 'sanctify' are removed. The congregation are now assembled to hear the Word, not 'to celebrate the commemoration' of Christ's death; we are to 'continue a perpetual memory', not to 'celebrate' it. In 1549 we are 'to celebrate according to our Saviour Christ's holy institution'; in 1552 'to receive these thy creatures' in this manner. Twice the word 'gifts' is deleted.

The epiclesis disappears and is replaced by a sort of anamnesis, in an unprecedented position before the Institution Narrative (unless *The Apostolic Constitutions* provides a precedent, but it is not clear that Cranmer knew that work).

The stress is now laid on the communicants rather than the elements; 'that we, receiving these thy creatures . . . may be partakers of his body and blood' instead of 'whosoever shall be partakers of this holy communion may worthily receive the most precious body and blood'. The removal of the words 'that they may be made one body with thy Son Jesus Christ, that he may dwell in them, and they in him', despite Bucer's eloquent entreaties, denies any presence. Similarly, all reference to a heavenly altar is excised. The 1552 rite is indeed an uncompromising statement of Protestant eucharistic doctrine.

Many Laudian churchmen felt that, in the words of Jeremy Taylor, 'in the second liturgy . . . they did cast out something that might, with good profit, have remained'.[2] The preparation of the Scottish Liturgy of 1637 offered an opportunity to restore this element which James Wedderburn, bishop of Dunblane, persuaded the Scottish bishops to grasp.

The Prayer for the Church remains in its 1552 position, and basically with the 1552 wording, though there are two important changes. First, the sentence about 'this congregation' is restored to its original place, though bracketed for omission when no Communion is to follow. Second, thanksgiving for the saints returns, now phrased in a more cautious manner, leaving out any mention of the Blessed Virgin Mary or of 'the sleep of peace', and introducing quotations from Acts 9.15 and Cosin's *Devotions*.[3] The passage is rewritten and improved in various minor ways (see below).

In the sacramental prayer, 1637 restores the 1549 epiclesis, while retaining most of the receptionist language introduced by 1552 at this point. The manual acts are revived, in rather more detail. The third section follows immediately, as in 1549, now named 'This Memorial, or Prayer of Oblation'. It is a verbatim reproduction of the 1549 prayer, with the exception of the passage about the heavenly altar, which is omitted, and two tiny stylistic alterations. The whole prayer (or prayers) in all its sections is thus a skilful blending of 1549 and 1552.

The 'Durham Book' follows the Scottish Liturgy throughout the three sections of the prayer, with the following exceptions: the epiclesis is a mixture of 1549 and 1637, with the addition of 'by the power of (thy holy Word)' and the omission of 'that they may be unto us the body and blood . . .', thus moving back a little towards 1552; the reading 'in remembrance of Him and to shew forth his death and passion'[4] was suggested by Matthew Wren; and in the Prayer of Oblation[5] the Scottish text is touched up with phrases from Cosin's *Devotions*,[6] including Cosin's favourite concept of representation, and a quotation from Romans 8.34.

The revisers of 1662 rejected all these changes, whether in the form of the Scottish Liturgy or the 'Durham Book', only adding to the 1552 text a much watered-down version of the thanksgiving for the departed taken from the bidding prayer in Canon 55 of 1604. Although the new rubrics assume that the elements are consecrated, the words of the prayer (and presumably its theology) remain unchanged from the Book of 1552.

1549	1552

1549

Let us pray for the whole state of Christ's Church.
Almighty and everliving God, which by thy holy Apostle hast taught us to make prayers and supplications, and to give thanks for all men; we humbly beseech thee most mercifully
to receive these our prayers, which we offer unto thy divine majety, beseeching thee to inspire continually the universal Church with the spirit of truth, unity and concord; and grant that all they that do confess thy holy Name may agree in the truth of thy holy word, and live in unity and godly love. Specially we beseech thee to save and defend
thy servant Edward our King, that under him we may be godly and quietly governed: and grant unto his whole Council, and to all that be put in authority under him, that they may truly and indifferently minister justice, to the punishment of wickedness and vice, and to the maintenance of God's true religion and virtue. Give grace, O heavenly Father, to all bishops, pastors and curates, that they may both by their life and doctrine set forth thy true and lively word, and rightly and duly administer thy holy sacraments; and to all thy people give thy heavenly grace,

that with meek heart and due reverence they may hear and receive thy holy word, truly serving thee in holiness and righteousness all the days of their life.

And we most humbly beseech thee, of thy goodness, O Lord, to comfort and succour all them which in this transitory life be in trouble, sorrow, need, sickness or any other adversity. And especially we commend unto thy merciful goodness this congregation which is here assembled in thy Name, to celebrate the commemoration of the most glorious death of thy Son.

1552

Let us pray for the whole state of Christ's Church *militant here in earth*.
Almighty and everliving God, which by thy holy Apostle hast taught us to make prayers and supplications, and to give thanks for all men: we humbly beseech thee most mercifully *to accept our alms* *and* to receive these our prayers, which we offer unto thy divine majesty, beseeching thee to inspire continually the universal Church with the spirit of truth, unity and concord; and grant that all they that do confess thy holy Name may agree in the truth of thy holy word, and live in unity and godly love.
We beseech thee *also* to save and defend *all Christian kings, princes and governors, and* specially thy servant Edward our King, that under him we may be godly and quietly governed: and grant unto his whole Council, and to all that be put in authority under him, that they may truly and indifferently minister justice, to the punishment of wickedness and vice, and to the maintenance of God's true religion and virtue. Give grace, O heavenly Father, to all bishops, pastors and curates, that they may both by their life and doctrine set forth thy true and lively word, and rightly and duly administer thy holy sacraments; and to all thy people give thy heavenly grace, and especially *to* this congregation here *present*, that with meek heart and due reverence they may hear and receive thy holy word, truly serving thee in holiness and righteousness all the days of their life.

And we most humbly beseech thee, of thy goodness, O Lord, to comfort and succour all them which in this transitory life be in trouble, sorrow, need, sickness or any other adversity:

114

1637	1662
Let us pray for the whole state of Christ's Church militant here in earth. Almighty and everliving God, which by thy holy Apostle hast taught us to make prayers and supplications, and to give thanks for all men: we humbly beseech thee most mercifully (to accept our alms, and) to receive these our prayers, which we offer unto thy divine majesty, beseeching thee to inspire continually the universal Church with the spirit of truth, unity and concord; and grant that all they that do confess thy holy Name may agree in the truth of thy holy word, and live in unity and godly love.	Let us pray for the whole state of Christ's Church militant here in earth. Almighty and everliving God, *who* by thy holy Apostle hast taught us to make prayers and supplications, and to give thanks for all men: we humbly beseech thee most mercifully (to accept our alms *and oblations*, and) to receive these our prayers, which we offer unto thy divine majesty, beseeching thee to inspire continually the universal Church with the spirit of truth, unity and concord; and grant that all they that do confess thy holy Name may agree in the truth of thy holy word, and live in unity and godly love.
We beseech thee also to save and defend all Christian kings, princes and governors, and specially thy servant *Charles* our King, that under him we may be godly and quietly governed: and grant unto his whole Council, and to all that be put in authority under him, that they may truly and indifferently minister justice, to the punishment of wickedness and vice, and to the maintenance of God's true religion and virtue. Give grace, O heavenly Father, to all bishops, *presbyters* and curates, that they may both by their life and doctrine set forth thy true and lively word, and rightly and duly administer thy holy sacraments; and to all thy people give thy heavenly grace,	We beseech thee also to save and defend all Christian kings, princes and governors, and specially thy servant Charles our King, that under him we may be godly and quietly governed: and grant unto his whole Council, and to all that *are* put in authority under him, that they may truly and indifferently minister justice, to the punishment of wickedness and vice, and to the maintenance of *thy* true religion and virtue. Give grace, O heavenly Father, to all bishops and curates, that they may both by their life and doctrine set forth thy true and lively word, and rightly and duly administer thy holy sacraments; and to all thy people give thy heavenly grace, and especially to this congregation here
that with meek heart and due reverence they may hear and receive thy holy word, truly serving thee in holiness and righteousness all the days of their life. (And we commend especially unto thy merciful goodness *the* congregation which is here assembled in thy Name, to celebrate the commemoration of the most *precious* death *and sacrifice* of thy Son *and our Saviour Jesus Christ.*) And we most humbly beseech thee, of thy goodness, O Lord, to comfort and succour all them which in this transitory life be in trouble, sorrow, need, sickness or any other adversity.	present, that with meek heart and due reverence they may hear and receive thy holy word, truly serving thee in holiness and righteousness all the days of their life.

And we most humbly beseech thee, of thy goodness, O Lord, to comfort and succour all them *who* in this transitory life *are* in trouble, sorrow, need, sickness or any other adversity. |
| *And we also bless thy holy Name for* all *those* they serv- | And we also bless thy holy Name for all   thy serv- |

115

And here we do give
unto thee most high praise and hearty
thanks for the wonderful grace and
virtue declared in all thy saints
from the beginning of the world.

and chiefly in the glorious and
most blessed Virgin Mary, mother of
thy Son Jesus Christ our Lord and God,
and in the holy patriarchs, prophets,
apostles and martyrs,

whose examples, O Lord, and stedfastness in thy faith and keeping thy
holy commandments, grant us to follow.
We commend unto thy mercy, O Lord, all
other thy servants which are departed hence from us with the sign of
faith, and do now rest in the sleep of
peace: grant unto them, we beseech
thee, thy mercy and everlasting peace,
and that at the day of the general
resurrection we and all they which be
of the mystical body of thy Son, may
altogether be set on his right hand,
and hear that his most joyful voice:
Come unto me, O ye that be blessed of
my Father, and possess the kingdom
which is prepared for you from the
beginning of the world. Grant this,
O Father, for Jesus Christ's sake,
our only mediator and advocate.
O God,   heavenly Father, which
of thy tender mercy didst give thine
only Son Jesus Christ to suffer death
upon the cross for our redemption;
who made there, by his one oblation
         once offered, a full, perfect
and sufficient sacrifice, oblation
and satisfaction for the sins of the
whole world; and did institute, and in
his holy gospel command us to celebrate, a perpetual memory of that his
precious death   , until
his coming again: hear us, O merciful
Father, we   beseech thee,
and   with thy
Holy Spirit and word vouchsafe   to
bless and sanctify these thy gifts
and creatures of bread and wine, that
they may be unto us the body and blood
of thy most dearly beloved Son Jesus
Christ;

Grant this,
O Father, for Jesus Christ's sake,
our only mediator and advocate. *Amen.*
Almighty God, *our* heavenly Father, which
of thy tender mercy didst give thine
only Son Jesus Christ to suffer death
upon the cross for our redemption;
who made there, by his one oblation *of*
himself once offered, a full, perfect
and sufficient sacrifice, oblation
and satisfaction for the sins of the
whole world; and did institute, and in
his holy gospel command us to *contin-*
ue, a perpetual memory of that his
precious death   , until
his coming again: hear us, O merciful
Father, we   beseech thee,
and

                              grant
that we, receiving these thy
         creatures of bread and wine,

according to thy Son our Saviour Jesus

1637

ants, *who having finished their course*
in faith, do now rest *from their la-*
bours. And we *yield* unto thee most
high praise and hearty thanks for the
wonderful grace and virtue declared
in all thy saints, *who have been the*
choice vessels of thy grace and the
lights of the world in their several
generations:

　　　　　　　　　most humbly
beseeching thee that we may have
grace to follow the example *of their*
stedfastness in thy faith and *obed-*
ience to thy holy commandments;

that at the day of the general
resurrection we and all they which *are*
of the mystical body of thy Son, may
　　　be set on his right hand,
and hear that his most joyful voice:
Come,　　　　ye　　　　blessed of
my Father, *inherit* the kingdom
　　　　prepared for you from the
foundation of the world. Grant this,
O Father, for Jesus Christ's sake,
our only mediator and advocate. Amen.
Almighty God, our heavenly Father, which
of thy tender mercy didst give *thy*
only Son Jesus Christ to suffer death
upon the cross for our redemption;
who made there, by his one oblation of
himself once offered, a full, perfect
and sufficient sacrifice, oblation
and satisfaction for the sins of the
whole world; and did institute, and in
his holy gospel command us to continue a perpetual memory of that his
precious death, *and sacrifice,* until
his coming again: hear us, O merciful
Father, we　　　　　　beseech thee,
and *of thy almighty goodness* vouchsafe
so to bless and sanctify with thy
word and Holy Spirit these thy gifts,
and creatures of bread and wine, that
they may be unto us the body and blood
of thy most dearly beloved Son
　　; *so* that we, receiving *them*
according to thy Son our Saviour Jesus

1662

ants, departed *this life in thy* faith
and fear;

beseeching thee *to give us*
grace *so* to follow their *good* examples,

　　　　　　　　　that with them we may
be partakers of thy heavenly kingdom.

　　　　　　Grant this,
O Father, for Jesus Christ's sake,
our only mediator and advocate. Amen.
Almighty God, our heavenly Father, *who*
of thy tender mercy didst give *thine*
only Son Jesus Christ to suffer death
upon the cross for our redemption;
who made there, by his one oblation of
himself once offered, a full, perfect
and sufficient sacrifice, oblation
and satisfaction for the sins of the
whole world; and did institute, and in
his holy gospel command us to continue, a perpetual memory of that his
precious death　　　　　, until
his coming again: hear us, O merciful
Father, we *most humbly* beseech thee,
and

　　　　　　　　　　　grant
that we, receiving these thy
　　creatures of bread and wine,

according to thy Son our Saviour Jesus

*Christ's holy institution, in remem-
brance of his death and passion,* may be
partakers of his most blessed

who in the same
night that he was betrayed,[a] took
bread and when he had blessed and
given thanks, he brake it and gave it
to his disciples, saying, Take, eat,
this is my body, which is given for
you; do this in remembrance of me.
Likewise after supper he[d] took the
cup, and when he had given thanks, he
gave it to them, saying, Drink ye all
of this, for this is my blood of the
new testament, which is shed for you
and for many, for   remission of
sins; do this as oft as you shall
drink it, in remembrance of me.
Wherefore, O Lord and heavenly Father,
according to the institution of thy
dearly beloved Son, our Saviour Jesus
Christ, we thy humble servants do
celebrate and make here before thy
divine majesty, with these thy holy
gifts, the memorial which thy Son
hath willed us to make, having in
remembrance his blessed passion,
mighty resurrection and glorious
ascension, rendering unto thee most
hearty thanks for the innumerable
benefits procured unto us by the same,

        entirely desiring thy fatherly
goodness mercifully to accept this
our sacrifice of praise and thanksgiving; most humbly beseeching thee
to grant that by the merits and death
of thy Son Jesus Christ, and through
faith in his blood, we and all thy
whole Church may obtain remission of
our sins and all other benefits of
his passion. And here we offer and
present unto thee, O Lord, our self,
our souls and bodies, to be a reasonable, holy and lively sacrifice unto
thee; humbly beseeching thee that
whosoever shall be partakers of this
holy communion may worthily receive
the most precious body and blood of
thy Son Jesus Christ, and be fulfilled
with thy grace and heavenly benediction, and made one body with thy
Son Jesus Christ, that he may dwell
in them, and they in him. And although
we be unworthy, through our manifold
sins, to offer unto thee any sacrifice,
yet we beseech thee to accept this
our bounden duty and service; and

body and blood; who in the same
night that he was betrayed, took
bread and when he had
given thanks, he brake it and gave it
to his disciples, saying, Take, eat,
this is my body, which is given for
you; do this in remembrance of me.
Likewise after supper he took the
cup, and when he had given thanks, he
gave it to them saying, Drink ye all
of this, for this is my blood of the
new testament, which is shed for you
and for many, for   remission of
sins; do this as oft as *ye* shall
drink it, in remembrance of me.
        O Lord and heavenly Father,

        we thy humble servants

        entirely desire thy fatherly
goodness mercifully to accept this
our sacrifice of praise and thanksgiving; most humbly beseeching thee
to grant that by the merits and death
of thy Son Jesus Christ, and through
faith in his blood, we and all thy
whole Church may obtain remission of
our sins and all other benefits of
his passion. And here we offer and
present unto thee, O Lord, our sel*ves*,
our souls and bodies, to be a reasonable, holy and lively sacrifice unto
thee; humbly beseeching thee that
all we which be partakers of this
holy communion may

        be fulfilled
with thy grace and heavenly benediction.

        And although
we be unworthy, through our manifold
sins, to offer unto thee any sacrifice,
yet we beseech thee to accept this
our bounden duty and service;

1637

Christ's holy institution,
                                        may be
partakers of *the same* his most *precious* body and blood; who in the
night that he was betrayed[a], took
bread, and when he had
given thanks, he brake it and gave it
to his disciples, saying, Take, eat,
this is my body, which is given for
you; do this in remembrance of me.
Likewise after supper he[d] took the
cup, and when he had given thanks, he
gave it to them, saying, Drink ye all
of this, for this is my blood of the
new testament, which is shed for you
and for many, for *the* remission of
sins; do this as oft as ye shall
drink it, in remembrance of me.
Wherefore, O Lord and heavenly Father,
according to the institution of thy
dearly beloved Son, our Saviour Jesus
Christ, we thy humble servants do
celebrate and make here before thy
divine majesty, with these thy holy
gifts, the memorial which thy Son
hath willed us to make, having in
remembrance his blessed passion,
mighty resurrection and glorious
ascension, rendering unto thee most
hearty thanks for the innumerable
benefits procured unto us by the same.
And we entirely desire thy fatherly
goodness mercifully to accept this
our sacrifice of praise and thanksgiving; most humbly beseeching thee
to grant that by the merits and death
of thy Son Jesus Christ, and through
faith in his blood, we and all thy
whole Church may obtain remission of
our sins and all other benefits of
his passion. And here we offer and
present unto thee, O Lord, our selves,
our souls and bodies, to be a reasonable, holy and lively sacrifice unto
thee; humbly beseeching thee that
whosoever shall be partakers of this
holy communion may worthily receive
the most precious body and blood of
thy Son Jesus Christ, and be fulfilled
with thy grace and heavenly benediction, and made one body with *him*
                                        , that he may dwell
in them, and they in him. And although
we be unworthy, through our manifold
sins, to offer unto thee any sacrifice,
yet we beseech thee to accept this
our bounden duty and service;

1662

Christ's holy institution, in remembrance of his death and passion, may be
partakers of his most *blessed*
body and blood; who in the *same*
night that he was betrayed,[a] took
bread, and when he had
given thanks,[b] he brake it and gave it
to his disciples, saying, Take, eat,
ᶜthis is my body, which is given for
you; do this in remembrance of me.
Likewise after supper he[d] took the
cup, and when he had given thanks, he
gave it to them, saying, Drink ye all
of this, for this[e] is my blood of the
new testament, which is shed for you
and for many, for the remission of
sins; do this as oft as ye shall
drink it, in remembrance of me. *Amen.*
            O Lord and heavenly Father,

                    we thy humble servants

                    entirely desire thy fatherly
goodness mercifully to accept this
our sacrifice of praise and thanksgiving; most humbly beseeching thee
to grant that by the merits and death
of thy Son Jesus Christ, and through
faith in his blood, we and all thy
whole Church may obtain remission of
our sins and all other benefits of
his passion. And here we offer and
present unto thee, O Lord, our selves,
our souls and bodies, to be a reasonable, holy and lively sacrifice unto
thee; humbly beseeching thee that
all we who are partakers of this
holy communion may

                    be fulfilled
with thy grace and heavenly benediction.

                    And although
we be unworthy, through our manifold
sins, to offer unto thee any sacrifice,
yet we beseech thee to accept this
our bounden duty and service;

command these our prayers and supplications, by the ministry of thy holy
angels, to be brought up into thy
holy tabernacle before the sight of
thy divine majesty; not weighing our   not weighing our
merits, but pardoning our offences,   merits, but pardoning our offences,
through Christ our Lord; by   through *Jesus* Christ our Lord; by
whom and with whom, in the unity of   whom and with whom, in the unity of
the Holy Ghost, all honour and glory   the Holy Ghost, all honour and glory
be unto thee, O Father almighty,   be unto thee, O Father almighty,
world without end. Amen.   world without end. Amen.
[a]Here the priest

                          must take the
bread into his hands.

[d]Here the priest shall
    take the cup into his hands.

not weighing our
merits, but pardoning our offences,
through Jesus Christ our Lord; by
whom and with whom, in the unity of
the Holy Ghost, all honour and glory
be unto thee, O Father almighty,
world without end. Amen.
*ᵃAt these words 'took bread' the pres-
byter that officiates is to* take the
paten in his hand.

*ᵈAt these words 'took the cup' he is
to* take the *chalice* in his hand,
and lay his hand upon so much, be it in
chalice or flagons, as he intends to
consecrate.

not weighing our
merits, but pardoning our offences,
through Jesus Christ our Lord; by
whom and with whom, in the unity of
the Holy Ghost, all honour and glory
be unto thee, O Father almighty,
world without end. Amen.
ᵃHere the *priest*
                               is to take the
paten in*to* his hand*s*.
*ᵇ*And here to break the bread.
*ᶜ*And here to lay his hand upon all the
bread.
ᵈHere   he is
to take the *cup* into his hand. *ᵉ*And *here
to* lay his hand upon *every vessel* (be it ,
chalice or flagon) *in which there is
any wine* to be consecrate*d*.

and sufficient sacrifice, oblation
and satisfaction for the sins of the
whole world; and did institute, and in
his holy gospel command us to continue a perpetual memory of that his
precious death and sacrifice, until
his coming again; hear us, O merciful
Father, we *most humbly* beseech thee,
and *by the power of* thy holy word and
Spirit vouchsafe so to bless and
sanctify these thy gifts
and creatures of bread and wine,

that we, receiving them
according to thy Son our Saviour Jesus
Christ's holy institution, *in remembrance of him, and to show forth his
death and passion,* may be partakers of
his most blessed body and blood . . .
the memorial which thy Son hath
willed *and commanded* us to make; having
in remembrance his *most* blessed passion
and sacrifice, his mighty resurrection
and *his* glorious ascension *into heaven*;
. . . most humbly beseeching thee to grant
that by the merits and death of thy Son
Jesus Christ *now represented unto thee,*
and through faith in his blood, *who maketh
intercession for us at thy right hand,* we
and all thy whole Church may obtain . . .

7
The Anglicanism of John Cosin

He would be a rash man who undertook to say something completely new about John Cosin. The Victorians published almost everything he wrote and discussed it at great length. They pictured him as a 'Tractarian before his time', a seventeenth-century precursor of the Ritualists, like them a martyr for the cause of ceremonial, who fell foul of the law, was imprisoned and brought to trial. But *his* story, unlike those of Purchas and Mackonochie, had a happy ending. In short, a most satisfactory hero for oppressed Anglo-Catholics.

A mild corrective to this romatic picture was administered in the biography by P. H. Osmond[1] (published in 1913), which sticks commendably close to the documents and so gets considerably nearer to the real Cosin. More recently, in C. W. Dugmore's gallery of seventeenth-century divines[2] Cosin is placed in the room entitled 'Central Churchmen', though Dugmore believes, like Osmond, that Cosin began his career as a 'High Churchman'. This view has been challenged by the editors of the recent reprint of Cosin's *Devotions*, P. G. Stanwood and Daniel O'Connor, who write: 'Varied and long as Cosin's life was, it reveals a consistency of doctrine and purpose.[3] It seems, therefore, a worthwhile enterprise to try and determine just where Cosin stood in relation to the Puritans and Roman Catholics in the successive phases of his life, and then to see whether any shifting of his ground can in fact be discerned.

The facts of Cosin's life are well known. Born in Norwich in 1595, he matriculated at Caius College, Cambridge, in 1610, and after taking his degree, accepted the offer of a post as librarian and secretary to John Overall, then bishop of Lichfield. Overall is a rather shadowy figure, but he was an able theologian, who became Regius Professor at Cambridge, and as dean of St Paul's played a prominent part in the Hampton Court Conference of 1604. Among the early Laudians he was second only to Lancelot Andrewes, pioneering the 'back to 1549' movement which was to become the chief plank in the Laudians' liturgical platform. Cosin often calls him 'my lord and master'[4] when quoting him as an authority, and forty years later was still referring to him as 'that rare and excellent man'[5], '*vir undequaque doctissimus* (a very learned man from every angle)'.[6]

On Overall's death in 1619, Cosin returned to Cambridge for four years. During this time he studied the Book of Common Prayer with the greatest diligence, going through the text with Martin Bucer's *Censura* of 1551 and the anonymous Puritan *Survey* of 1606, recording each criticism in turn at the appropriate point. As befits a disciple of Overall, he also compared the current edition of the Prayer Book with that of 1549, copying out the text of the latter wherever it differed, usually with some approving comment. Going back further still, he made similar annotations from the Sarum service books. He was thus extremely well informed about the actual text of the Prayer Book, and this remained his outstanding interest. In the Articles for his archidiaconal visitation of 1626 he goes through the book, picking out every possible opportunity for non-observance of the rubrics; and in his proposals for the revision of 1662 he is still chiefly concerned with legality and uniformity. But this was only the practical consequence of his interest in the text. At the very same periods he was trying to reintroduce the text of 1549, and he was certainly consistent in *this* purpose throughout his life.

In 1623 Cosin became a chaplain to Richard Neile, bishop of Durham, and thus first made contact with the North of England, which was to play as large a part in his life as his native East Anglia. Preferment came rapidly: prebend of Durham cathedral in 1624, archdeacon of the East Riding in 1625 and rector of Brancepeth in 1626. These appointments gave him scope to develop two facets of his personality: a passion for uniformity in the performance of divine service and a love of beautifully carved woodwork. Those of his Brancepeth sermons that have survived show a disciple of Andrewes accommodating his learned, witty style to the simpler needs of a country congregation. In a wedding address he complains that the contents of the Prayer Book should be 'better heeded by us and known to us than they are'.[7] He then goes on to expound the Gospels for the Epiphany and the two Sundays following.

This sermon, however, was not preached at Brancepeth, but at a fashionable wedding at Datchet, near Windsor, for Cosin's activities were by no means restricted to the North. He had become a member of a little inner group of Laudians who used to meet at Durham House in London, at the invitation of bishop Neile. Laud himself used to attend, as did the fiery controversialist Richard Montague, later bishop of Chichester. In 1625, when Montague had to face a charge of 'opening a gap for popery' by his writings, it was Cosin who discovered a saving passage which enabled the duke of Buckingham to pronounce Montague innocent. During the debate Cosin scored several points against Montague's prosecutor, Thomas Morton, bishop of Lichfield. When another member of the group, Francis White, was consecrated bishop of Carlisle, the offertory was 'solemnly made by more than twenty persons, bishops, doctors and other divines of note', and Cosin preached the sermon.

It could not be long before this able young clergyman caught the eye of King Charles. In 1627 Charles invited Cosin to compile a book of devotions for the English ladies at court, so that they should not be worse off than Henrietta Maria's French ladies-in-waiting, with their Books of Hours. Cosin accordingly based his work on a publication called *Orarium*, a Latin version of the official *Primer*, which had appeared in 1560. It was this *Collection of Devotions* which won Cosin the reputation of an ardent Romanizer. Two prominent Puritans, Henry Burton and William Prynne, wrote books attacking 'Mr Cozens his couzening Devotions', in which they seized on the slightest traces of any connection with pre-Reformation spirituality.

How much truth was there in their accusations? *Was* Cosin a crytopapist, a kind of religious fellow traveller? The evidence for his early life is scanty and inconclusive. The parish of St Andrew, Norwich, in which he was brought up, had a strong Puritan tradition; but Caius College had been notorious in the 1580s as a centre of recusancy, and no doubt something of this atmosphere still remained when Cosin went up there. Clearly the Durham House group were committed Laudians, and strongly opposed to Puritanism. On a clear-cut issue such as prayer for the dead, the young Cosin comes down firmly on the Catholic side:

The Puritans think that here is prayer for the dead allowed and practised by the Church of England, and so think I; but we are not both of one mind in censuring the Church for so doing. They say it is popish and superstitious; I for my part esteem it pious and Christian.[8]

He speaks of 'that unChristian fancy of the Puritans, that would have no minister to bury their dead',[9] and criticizes them for regarding the function of the Prayer Book service as being 'to spin out the time till the preacher comes'. Puritan methods of prayer are scornfully dismissed as 'extemporal effusions of irksome and undigested prayers'.[10] His hardest words are reserved for Calvin and the Calvinists, who 'in their licentious blasphemy' regard the Real Presence as 'popish magic'.[11] The Lutherans, on the other hand, are commended for retaining exorcism.[12]

Much of Cosin's hostility towards the Puritans is aesthetic in origin; his tast in church music and church furnishings was radically different from theirs.

> For the disuse of these ornaments we may thank them that came from Geneva, and . . . suffered every negligent priest to do what him listed, so he would but profess a difference and opposition in all things (though never so lawful) against the Church of Rome.[13]
>
> Our new masters and mistresses at Geneva (have) thrust out the solemn music of David's own psalms, and other glorious hyms of holy men, from the Church, and (have given) us songs of their own altering and composing to be sung instead of them, by a company of rude people, cobblers and their wives, and their kitchen-maids, and all that have as much skill in singing as an ass had to handle an harp.[14]

The hostility was perhaps the more bitter because Cosin himself had a marked puritan element in his personality, *mutatis mutandis*: canon Martin Thornton appropriately describes him as 'a psychological puritan who hated the theological Puritans, the Catholic traditionalist who hated Rome'.[15] Certainly the name 'precisian', by which the Puritans were first known, fits Cosin like a glove.

Further, he was sufficiently sympathetic towards some aspects of Roman Catholicism to lend colour, in times of controversy, to the charge that he was a Romanizer. His very thorough knowledge of the Breviary and the Missal was by itself sufficient condemnation in the eyes of the Puritans, and indeed of Central Churchmen.

In that heated atmosphere a hostile interpretation could be placed on an incidental reference to the desirability of more frequent communion, and still more, the commending of private confession, 'a thing that the world looks not after now, as if confession and absolution were some strange, superstitious things'.[16] Cosin had exercised this ministry for bishop Neile's sister, Dorothy Holmes, and he also provided forms for its use in the *Devotions*.[17] Cosin certainly read Roman writers with avidity, notably the Spanish Jesuit Maldonatus, whose *Disputatio circa septem sacramenta* was published posthumously in 1614, and no doubt was as eagerly read in progressive circles as any work of de Chardin or Rahner today. Cosin copied out lengthy extracts on eucharistic doctrine with apparent approval of the views there expressed. Another Roman writer on whom he drew for this purpose was Georg Cassander, whose collected works appeared in 1616. Cosin pleads for a balanced attitude towards Roman Catholicism, asking:

> Is it possible that any man of judgement or conscience should think it enough to say that this or that is in the Mass, and never trouble himself to show that it is part of the corruptions contained in it?[18]

In his sermon at bishop White's consecration Cosin lists ten points about the Church of England at which the Papists are justifiably scandalized.[19] The *Devotions* gave him a chance to restore some of those passages of the 1549 Prayer Book which were omitted in 1552, and whose omission helped to give the later book its distinctively Protestant character. He also included a hymn and two prayers by St Thomas Aquinas and a prayer of St Ignatius Loyola, translated into English and unacknowledged, but indicative of the sources to which Cosin naturally turned for his spiritual enrichment.[20]

The clearest indication of his position *vis-à-vis* the Church of Rome is naturally to be found in his eucharistic doctrine, and this is set out most fully in his 'First Series of Notes' on the Prayer Book. There is a well-authenticated tradition that the longer notes, sometimes reaching the length of short essays, were in fact written by bishop Overall and merely copied by Cosin. But even if this is true, it hardly affects the issue. Cosin's devotion to his first patron extended to a wholehearted acceptance of his authority in matters of doctrine and it is entirely reasonable to take these notes as representing Cosin's own views. When he quotes a belief or practice of which he disapproves, he makes his disapproval quite plain.

His general stance appears in a note on consecration, where

he writes: 'The Mass Book hath no more than we have here', implying that it would be a defect in the Prayer Book if it lacked something that the Missal included; to a Puritan, any common ground with the Canon of the Mass was a fatal fault. Cosin holds firmly that the Church of England through the Prayer Book teaches

> the presence of Christ's body and blood in the sacrament. And though our new masters would make the world believe she had another mind, yet we are not to follow their private fancies when we have so plain and so public a doctrine as this.[21]
>
> It is confessed by all divines that upon the words of consecration the body and blood of Christ is really and substantially present, and so exhibited and given to all that receive it; and all this, not after a physical and sensual, but after a heavenly and invisible and incomprehensible manner.

He then criticizes the Lutherans and Calvinists for holding that the body of Christ is 'present only in the use of the sacrament and in the act of eating, and not otherwise. They . . . seem . . . to depart from all antiquity'.[22] In that last word we meet Cosin's acid test of doctrine and practice, the ultimate criterion by which every Church stands or falls.

The point on which he insists most strongly is that the Eucharist is the offering by us of the sacrifice which Christ made by his death, and this he finds in the Prayer of Oblation. A well-known note quotes Overall's practice of always saying this prayer *before* communicating the people, as being the offering of the sacrament to God.[23] The prayer, Cosin believes, is

> a plain oblation of Christ's death once offered, and a representative sacrifice of it, for the sins, and for the benefit, of the whole world, of the whole Church.[24]

This belief depends on the medieval interpretation of *sacrificium laudis,* 'the sacrifice of praise', as referring to the consecrated elements. The word 'representative' is crucial in Cosin's thought, implying that a *fresh* offering is made of Christ's death. The sacrifice, he quotes Maldonatus as saying, is commemorative, efficient *and propitiatory*: it avails for the living *and the dead*, and the ancient Church 'always taught as much'. No doubt it did, but the doctrine is dangerously near that condemned in Article 31 as 'blasphemous fables and dangerous deceits'. Cranmer himself classes it with transubstantiation as one of 'the two chief roots of popery'.[25] Cosin would have replied that antiquity is a better authority than Calvin-inspired articles; he goes so far as to say: 'Read a whole army of Fathers. We . . . prefer to err with so many and great authors than to speak the truth with the Puritans'(!). He rounds off his discussion by saying, in effect, 'A plague on both your houses':

> Let the schools have what opinions and doctrines they will, and let our new masters frame themselves what divinity they list; as long as neither the one nor the other can get their fancies brought into the service of the Church, honest men may serve God with one heart and one soul, and never trouble themselves with the opinions of them both.[26]

But if Cosin was clearly no Puritan, neither was he a Roman Catholic. Tart references to Papists are found alongside the lengthy quotations from Roman divines. He warns his rustic flock at Brancepeth against 'the impiety of some Christians (I mean the Papists) that are ready to persuade some of you to their own errors'.[27] Among these errors were the doctrine of transubstantiation, communion in one kind and the saying of private Masses, all of which, he claims, were contrary to the actual words of the Mass.[28]

In this first period of his career, the years of promise, Cosin took up a position in most ways centrally placed between the Puritans and the Papists, but with a definite inclination to the Roman side. He criticizes both parties and studies their writings with equal thoroughness; but his criticism of Rome is chiefly directed against recent abuses and must be seen against the background of his deep interest in, and sympathy for, a great deal of Roman teaching and practice, which he tries to reconcile with that of the Prayer Book. There is no such background to his criticism of the Puritans. On one occasion he allows himself the aside 'as Bucer well says', but that is almost the only reference of this kind. Forced to make an unequivocal choice between Rome and Geneva, the Cosin of the 1620s, it is fairly certain, would have chosen Rome.

Up to 1628 everything had gone his way, and in one sense the 1630s were years of achievement, during which he became in turn Master of Peterhouse, Cambridge and dean of Peterborough. But the enmity aroused by the publication of the *Devotions* was increased by the revelation of his high-handed introduction of Laudian ceremonial and furnishings in Durham Cathedral. There is no need to go into the Smart case all over again, but the sort of accusations which Smart made stuck to Cosin for the next thirty years. Thereafter there hung round him an aura of new stone altars, pre-Reformation copes, eastward position, elaborate church music and, above all, crossings, kissings and duckings. His conduct at Cambridge did nothing to dispel that aura. He furnished the chapel at Peterhouse which Matthew Wren had just built with the angel ceiling from which William Dowsing later removed over a hundred angels. Here there really was a new altar, with candlesticks and a crucifix on it. The last straw was the introduction of a censer which had belonged to Lancelot Andrewes.

Cosin was already in trouble with Parliament when it was dissolved in 1628, and when it met again in 1640 he was one of the first people against whom action was taken. The situation deteriorated until Cosin judged it wise to retire to France. The continued harassment, official and unofficial, can only have hardened Cosin's dislike of Puritans into open hatred. There is little fresh evidence in his writings about his churchmanship during these years, but it may certainly be assumed that the Cosin who fled abroad in 1643 will have expected to find the French Roman Catholics more congenial than the Protestants.

In fact, it was far otherwise. Apart from receiving offers of preferment if he would become a Catholic, Cosin's relations with the Roman Church during his seventeen years of exile were marked by continuous controversy and ill-treatment. Proselytization continued all through the Commonwealth period: in 1648 Cosin wrote to his old adversary, bishop Morton:

> Many times I meet here with those that are masters of popish novelties, and the professed enemies of our truly catholic and protestant religion; and many controversies I have had with them, but especially with those limiters that come creeping into our pale, and hunt for proselytes, whereof, they have not (God be thanked) been able for these four years' space to get one, unless it were a poor footman (whom they trapped with a female French bait, too) and have lost some others of more considerable quality whom they had lured into their nets before.[29]

But by far the worst blow fell in 1652, when Cosin's own son defected to Rome, for which his father never forgave him. In a letter of 1646 Cosin describes the French Catholics as 'exceeding uncharitable and somewhat worse', and goes on to say that

130

they of Geneva are to blame in many things, and defective in some: they shall never have by approbation of their doings . . . Yet I do not see that they have set up any new articles of faith under pain of damnation to all the world that will not receive them for such articles; and you know whose case that is.[30]

In these letters we see the characteristic outlines of Cosin's later attitude taking shape: the Church of England is Catholic *and* Protestant; Calvinism is not wholly bad; a distinction is drawn between Catholicism as represented by the early Fathers and, above all, the text of the Mass, for which he feels a great sympathy, and the Catholicism of the Schoolmen and the Council of Trent, the Catholicism of contemporary dogma and practice, for which he feels a great dislike.

During the years of exile, this contemporary Catholicism drew from Cosin three large-scale works of polemical scholarship, which led Thomas Fuller to describe him as 'the Atlas of the Protestant religion'. The earliest was a series of letters, ending in July 1645, on the validity of Anglican orders. Next came the *Historia Transubstantiationis Papalis*, written in 1656 and published posthumously in both Latin and English; and lastly, *A Scholastical History of the Canon of Holy Scripture*, written and published in 1657. Cosin's reputation nowadays rests chiefly on his liturgical work, but these writings reveal him as a very learned patristic scholar and a doughty controversialist. As their titles suggest, the approach is historical rather than doctrinal, the appeal to antiquity rather than to unaided reason. Cosin had managed to bring his library with him, and at first he was able to keep up his reading, as is shown by quotations from books published in 1641, 1642 and 1644. Later, he was reduced to extreme poverty, and such quotations no longer appear; but even in his worst straits, he steadfastly refused to sell any of his books.

The subject of Anglican orders cropped up shortly after Cosin's arrival in France. The prior of the English Benedictines in France, Fr Paul Robinson, had been trying to win over an exiled Anglican lady to Roman Catholicism. She appealed to Cosin to 'defend the validity of his own sacred orders', and gave an undertaking that, if his defence failed to satisfy her, she would be reconciled to the Roman Church the next morning. After some hesitation, Cosin agreed to a debate the next day, and was able to convince the lady. The argument was continued on paper, and Cosin's contribution developed into a sizeable treatise. The prior's chief points were that the Church of England had no *porrectio instrumentorum* (delivery of paten and chalice to the ordinand), and did not give its priests authority to offer sacrifice for the living and the dead; in technical terms, the Anglican ordinal had neither the essential matter nor form. Cosin deploys a formidable array of Catholic writers to show that the *porrectio* was not essential, showing himself to be well abreast of Continental scholarship, whereas Father Robinson was maintaining a position which his own authorities had abandoned. On the second point he argues that Romans and Anglicans mean different things by 'sacrifice', and that in any case the use of John 20 is sufficient form. Throughout the discussion Cosin is completely opposed to the Roman position and finds the prior illogical, lacking in sincerity and candour, and prone to seek refuge in rhetoric.

From the second of the prior's points, it was a short step to the papist doctrine of transubstantiation. Once again, Cosin was called in to frustrate attempts at conversion, this time by some Jesuits. He took up the challenge and wrote a massive criticism of the Roman teaching, which he put together between mid-June and mid-August 1655. Even while he was writing it, Puritans in England continued to accuse him of favouring popery! The Jesuits would have it that the Church of England held

> no real, but only a kind of imaginary, presence of the body and blood of Christ; but that the Church of Rome retained still the very same faith concerning this sacred mystery which the Catholic Church constantly maintained in all ages; to wit, that the whole substance of the bread and wine is changed into the substance of the body and blood of Christ, and this change was right well called 'transubstantiation' by the Council of Trent.[31]

By appealing to antiquity, while continuing to use the medieval terminology of 'substance and accident' the Jesuits were choosing to fight Cosin with his favourite weapons. Cosin maintains a 'real, true and *not* imaginary presence of Christ in the sacrament', which must not 'be understood grossly and carnally, but spiritually and sacramentally.'[32] This position is defended with the help of numerous quotations from the first thousand years of the Christian era; then the development of the doctrine of transubstantiation is traced to its final definition by the Council of Trent. Cosin has no difficulty in showing to his own satisfaction

that antiquity knew no such doctrine; it is a medieval development, and 'medieval' to him meant 'new', 'modern' and therefore undesirable.

What is new in the deployment of his argument is the vigorous
use of quotations from Protestant writers. It is no surprise to
find Andrewes, Bilson and Overall called in evidence; one
would not have expected Jewel and Poynet. A whole series of
Reformed confessions of faith is brought in; Luther and Bucer
are quoted with approval; and this remarkable verdict is pro-
nounced on the old arch-enemy, Calvin: 'His words are . . . so
conformable to the style and mind of the Fathers, that no
Catholic Reformer would wish to use any other'.[33] In these last
words Cosin repeats his belief that the Church of England is
Catholic *and* Reformed; its members are 'Protestants and Reformed according to the norm of the ancient and Catholic
Church'.[34] He was probably drawn in this direction by Georg
Calixtus, an ex-Lutheran Calvinist, whose works he had recently
acquired. Calixtus devoted all his energies to the reconciliation
of Lutherans, Calvinists and Roman Catholics; and much of his
writing is almost Anglican in tone.

Cosin's new attitude is clearly evinced in his 'Second Series of
Notes' on the Prayer Book and other writings from the period of
exile. Luther, he writes, was a very learned man, with great
strength of mind, and Calvin also has his deserved reputation,
though neither was infallible.[35] Calvin's 'hard and supercilious
censure' of the Prayer Book is now excused on the grounds that
Knox and his Scottish fellow exiles must have described it to
him 'after the most odious and ridiculous manner that they
could imagine'.[36] On the Roman front, elevation above the
priest's head is condemned on the usual ground, that it was
unknown to antiquity;[37] and lengthy articles demolish the
grounds for observing the Invention of the Cross and the
Assumption of the Blessed Virgin Mary.[38]

But Cosin's new stance comes out most clearly when this
Second Series of Notes is compared with the First in relation to
eucharistic doctrine. Here, most of all, he draws on Calixtus,
but when there is a crucial point at issue, he either modifies
Calixtus's statements by adding qualifying phrases, or states
his view in his own words.

The main issues are still the nature of the eucharistic sacrifice
and of the Real Presence. In one note Cosin quotes the Council
of Trent, *De Sacrificio Missae*:

It pleased the Synod at Trent . . . to lay their curse . . . upon all them that held the celebration of this sacrament to be a nude commemoration only of Christ's sacrifice upon the cross; or that said it was not a true propitiatory sacrifice, but a sacrifice only of praise and thanksgiving; or that taught any more, that this sacrifice profited none but those that communicated of it, and was not truly offered up for the sins, pains and satisfaction of the living and the dead . . .[39]

He then quotes Calixtus:

We do not hold this celebration to be so naked a commemoration . . . but that the same body and blood is present there . . . nor do we say, it is so nude a sacrifice of prayer and thanksgiving, but that by our prayers so added, we offer and present the death of Christ, to God, that for his death's sake we may find mercy, in which respect we deny (not) this commemorative sacrifice to be propitiatory. The receiving of which sacrament . . . we say *is* profitable only to them that receive it . . . but the prayer that we add thereunto . . . is beneficial . . . to them that are absent also, to the dead and living both . . .[40]

Cosin is in fact using Calixtus' words to express the same doctrine which he held in the 1620s, going further to meet the Tridentine position than the words of the Prayer Book really warrant. He does not hesitate to add his favourite word 'represented' to Calixtus' text, though he never discusses its meaning, and appears at times to use it as though it were synonymous with 'commemorated'.[41] There is certainly a slight haziness in his terminology which is only partly concealed by the confidence with which he uses it.

So far, then, Cosin has remained consistent to his earlier beliefs, though it is significant that he now quotes a Protestant author in support of them, rather than a Catholic. But in discussing the *manner* of the Real Presence, he takes a distinct step in the direction of receptionism, a doctrine for which in early days he had condemned the Protestant Churches as Nestorians. He now writes that the

body and blood is neither sensibly present, nor otherwise at all present, but only to them that are duly prepared to receive them, and in the very act of receiving them and the consecrated elements together . . .[42]

From this it follows that 'Christ in the consecrated bread ought not, cannot be, kept and preserved to be carried about, because he is present only to the communicants'.[43] In conformity with this startling change of mind, Cosin changes his attitude towards the remains of the consecrated bread and wine. From 1552 to 1662 the Prayer Book rubric ran: 'If any of the bread and wine remain, the curate shall have it to his own use.' In the First Series Cosin comments: 'It were but a profanation to let the curate have it home to his own use'; but in the Second Series he asks:

> Yet if for lack of care they consecrate more than they distribute, why may not the curates have it to their own use . . . for though the bread and wine remain, yet the consecration, the sacrament of the body and blood of Christ, do not remain longer than the holy action itself remains for which the bread and wine were hallowed; and which being ended, return to their former use again?[44]

However, when the Prayer Book was revised in 1661, Cosin secured the insertion into the rubric of the word 'unconsecrated', together with a direction to consume the *consecrated* remains. At the same time he would have liked to transfer the Prayer of Oblation to a position before Communion, on the grounds set out above; but here he was unsuccessful.

This discussion of Cosin's eucharistic theology arose from a consideration of his treatise on transubstantiation; we must now turn to the third and longest of his polemical works, *A History of the Canon of Holy Scripture, or the certain and indubitate books thereof, as they are received in the Church of England,* which appeared in 1657. It runs to 286 pages in the *Library of Anglo-Catholic Theology* edition, plus 36 of indexes, compared with 137 plus 7 on transubstantiation and 77 on Anglican orders. It was written at the suggestion of Peter Gunning, and its writing nearly cost Cosin his eyesight. The main object of the work, as suggested at the end of the title, is to refute the Roman claim that the Pope has the right to decide which Scriptures are canonical. An opening address *To the Reader* lists ten other errors of the Church of Rome, including transubstantiation, communion in one kind, purgatory, invocation of saints, veneration of relics and images, and indulgences.[45] Despite its academic-sounding title the work is just as controversial as the other treatises.

Cosin works through the evidence, a chapter to each century down to the seventeenth. The title page says 'compiled by Dr Cosin', and indeed it is really an enormous catena of texts, interspersed with salty comments. 'Gretser the Jesuit', counting the number of books in the Apocrypha, 'excludeth the Book of Esther, and giveth no reason for it at all; but runs . . . round with a vertigo, and counteth Esdras over again, not remembering what he said before'.[46] Cajetan was 'one of the most learned cardinals that the Church of Rome had, but he lived not to see the new canons made at the Council of Trent'.[47] Cosin's whole opinion of the latter body is very low: it consisted only of some forty Italian bishops, and perhaps twenty others, none greatly remarkable for learning.[48] Cosin's summary of his conclusions is that 'the religion of the Church of England in her article concerning the Holy Scriptures, whereunto the public Confessions of the Reformed and Protestant Churches abroad, besides the Christians of the East and South parts of the world, be agreeable, is truly Catholic'.[49] Gunning was disappointed in Cosin's handling of this article, which may be taken as a sign that Cosin himself had changed his position since Gunning had last met him, before his exile.

Cosin's claim of agreement with the Eastern Churches rests not only on the writings of the Fathers but also on 'frequent conference' in Paris with the archbishop of Trebizond. This, however, seems to have been an isolated instance. Much more frequent were his contacts with the French Protestants. Already in 1648 he could write: 'They of the Geneva fashion hear us well, and as often, as they of the Italian', even though he always preached in a surplice.[50] Cosin describes his friendly relationship with the Reformed Church at Charenton as follows:

> Many of them have been at our church, and we have been at theirs. I have buried diverse of our people at Charenton, and they permit us to make use of their peculiar and decent cemetery here in Paris for that purpose . . . I have baptized many of their children at the request of their own ministers, with whom I have good acquaintance, and find them to be very deserving and learned men . . . Many of their people . . . have frequented our public prayers with great reverence, and I have delivered the Holy Communion to them according to our own order . . . I have married diverse persons among them; and I have presented some of their scholars to be ordained as deacons and priests here by our own bishops . . . and the church of Charenton approved of it. Besides, I have been . . . to pray and sing psalms with them, and to hear both the weekly and the Sunday sermons.[51]

It is difficult to imagine the Cosin of the 1620s behaving in this way, but even now there were limits to his ecumenism: he does not say that *he* ever received the sacrament from *them*; nor that their ministers had baptized, married, buried or ordained any Anglicans. They were more ready to accept his ministrations than Anglicans were to accept theirs. Clarendon gave up going to Charenton after the execution of Charles I, and the English Ambassador refused to go there at all. Replying to an Anglican who 'seemed shy to communicate with the Protestants there upon this very scruple of their inordination',[52] Cosin did not condemn their ordinations, but suggested that his correspondent should ask the privilege of kneeling to receive and having the words of administration said to him. Again it is noticeable that Cosin does not use what would have been the obvious argument, that he himself was in the habit of communicating with them, presumably because it would not have been true.

Cosin's attitude to the ordination of Continental Protestants is derived from Overall, who

> was wont to say, though we are not to lessen the *jus divinum* of episcopacy, where it is established and may be had, yet we must take heed that we do not, for want of episcopacy where it cannot be had, cry down and destroy all the Reformed Churches abroad, both in Germany and France and other places, and say they have neither ministers not sacraments, but all is void and null that they do.[53]

This was also Andrewes's view, and it was put into practice in the first thirty years of the century. Reformed ministers who settled in England were treated as, so to speak, honorary Anglicans. Though reluctant to throw in his lot completely with the French Protestants, Cosin refers to them in a far friendlier tone than when he writes about Roman Catholics or English Puritans. A leading Protestant wrote: 'They are beasts and fanatics who suspect him of popery, from which you could hardly find anyone more alien.'[54] A short paper written while Cosin was in France and entitled *The state of us who adhere to the Church of England*, lists five points in which the Reformed Churches treated the Anglicans better than the Roman Catholics did. The Romans say 'that we are all damned . . . call us heretics . . . excommunicate us . . . not long since, they burned us alive. . . . They will allow us no other burial of our dead than the burial of a dog.' The Reformed, on the other hand, say 'that we profess and believe whatsoever is necessary to salvation . . . These acknowledge us to be true Catholics . . . They do most willingly receive us into their churches . . . They have obtained freedom for us from this kind of persecution . . . They allow us to bury our dead among theirs.'[55] Such a difference in treatment is more than enough in itself to account for the marked change in Cosin's attitude to Protestantism while he was in exile.

In the spring of 1660 Cosin returned to England. For all his anti-Roman feeling he was still eager to restore the Book of Common Prayer to its 1549 form, but Convocation, led by Gilbert Sheldon, was of another mind. At the Savoy Conference of 1661, according to Richard Baxter, Cosin 'had a great deal of talk, with so little logic . . . that no one was much moved by anything he said'. But Baxter commends him for his excellent memory for Canons, Councils and the Fathers, and because 'he would endure more freedom of our discourse with him, and was more affable and familiar than the rest'.[56] (Just imagine Cosin being affable to Peter Smart or William Prynne!) Baxter's judgement of Cosin's strengths and weaknesses as a theologian is very fair. As bishop of Durham, Cosin showed equal sternness to recusant and nonconformist alike, but was always ready to try and bring them over by reasoning with them. He was able once more to exercise his enthusiasm for beautifying God's house, and this time without opposition. Auckland chapel was rebuilt and Durham Cathedral furnished with font, screen and choir-stalls.

From all that has been said, it is clear that Cosin was all his life first and foremost a Church of England man, and in particular a Prayer Book man. In his early years he sees himself as treading the middle way between the Scylla of Puritanism and the Charybdis of Rome. The Church of England differs from both in her respect for 'the tenet of antiquity'. At this stage, however, he is definitely on the Romeward side of centre, departing from Prayer Book teaching about prayer for the dead and the propitiatory nature of the eucharistic sacrifice, and these views he held all his life. In the external surroundings of the service his taste was for a style which he would have called 'decent' and 'comely', but which to many Englishmen of the day seemed simply 'Romish'.

During the years of exile, the hostility of the French Papists and the friendliness of the Huguenots brought about a change of sympathy and some modification of his doctrinal position. He now quotes freely from Protestant writers and moves towards the Protestant belief that Christ is present in the elements only to the worthy communicant, and only for the duration of the service. Where he used to see the Church of England as neither Puritan nor Roman, he now regards it as both Protestant and Catholic. Within both camps he made distinctions: the 'new' Romans had departed from the ways of the early centuries, while French Protestants were more congenial than English Presbyterians and had much more justification for their Protestantism. But he is now prepared to treat with Puritans, and in a friendly spirit.

In his will Cosin describes himself as 'seeking after unity by preserving the bond of peace and love with all Christians everywhere', but rejecting equally Separatists, Anabaptists, Independents and Presbyterians, together with 'the corruptions and the impertinent new-fangled papistical superstitions and doctrines and new super-additions to the ancient and primitive religion and faith' of the Church. This may not seem to leave much opportunity for the pursuit of unity, but he goes on in a more practical vein: all must endeavour 'that at last an end may be put to the differences of religion, or at least that they may be lessened'.[57] But until this happy consummation should be achieved, Cosin had no doubt that the Church most in accordance with antiquity, and therefore the best Church to belong to, was the Church of England.

Note: THE TEXT OF COSIN'S *DEVOTIONS*

The edition of Cosin's *Devotions* by P. G. Stanwood and D. O'Connor (Oxford 1967) prints the text of the first edition in its earliest form, with the variant readings of later editions recorded in footnotes. A 'Commentary' supplies full texts of all passages for which Cosin gives a marginal reference, and of some of the prayers which he used as starting-points. The Library of Anglo-Catholic Theology reprint (LACT below), which is the edition known to the great majority of readers, made no attempt to trace the source of any of the prayers and was not nearly so thorough in following up the marginal references. It was also less detailed in its treatment of the later readings, merely indicating them by the *siglum 'C'*. This is nowhere explained, but comparison with Stanwood's *apparatus criticus* shows that the anonymous editor must have consulted at least the eighth edition (1672) and either the third or sixth or both, while the *'Sixth edit.'* quoted on p. 171 is Stanwood's seventh (1664). The LACT text is also that of the first edition, but in its *second* state. The only substantial difference between the two states is in the Blessing which ends the book, where the first state includes the words here italicized; *the succour of all holy Angels, and the suffrages of all the chosen of God*, be with me, now, and at the houre of death; *of thy mercy Lord I beg it*. These are omitted from the second state, though Stanwood's *apparatus* does not make this clear, as well as from all later editions. Among the variant readings, LACT (which confines itself to 'the more important') missed only three of any significance: the word 'much' on the title page, the words 'by most men' (p. 192 in Stanwood and O'Connor), and an additional sentence from Revelation 4 to be said 'prostrate before the Altar' (p. 227). On the other hand, LACT includes variant readings not found in Stanwood and O'Connor: see pp. 88, 107, 244, 272, 281, 317 and 327 in LACT.

Attention should be drawn to Dr R. C. D. Jasper's article, 'Some notes on the early life of Bishop John Cosin',[58] which shows that Cosin's parents *both* came of merchant families in the parish of St Andrew, Norwich, a Puritan stronghold. Where, then, did Cosin acquire his 'Laudian' sympathies? At Caius, perhaps; twenty years earlier, it had been known as a centre of recusancy. Stanwood has discovered that large portions of Cosin's Preface and other notes are 'lifted' from Hooker, with no more acknowledgement than the marginal note in the introduction to the Litany: 'R. H. *l*.5.' (p. 171). The *Devotions* themselves were to be quarried by no less an author than Jeremy Taylor, in *The Psalter of David* (1644).

The alterations made in the text during 1627 include some of major importance. Besides the omission of the phrases quoted above, the following alterations are specially noteworthy:

the words 'by the ministry of thy holy Angels' are omitted from the prayer 'At the Consecration'; two prayers 'to bee repeated untill the soule be departed' were originally to be said *after* its departure; and a petition that it might 'receive this dead body' in the resurrection of the just was omitted.[59]

When Cosin revised the *Devotions* for publication in 1664, he took the first edition as his general basis, but retained these changes. Another group of alterations shows Cosin modifying his more dogmatic assertions:

First edition	Second edition
after this manner published . . .	*much* after . . .
marriages are not solemnized . . .	. . . not *usually* . . .
without other Avocations . . .	. . . other *unnecessary* . . .
Christ hath instituted it . . .	Christ *arose* on it . . .
all agreeing [in fasting] . . .	*most* agreeing . . .
a writing unquestioned.	unquestioned *by most men.*
[i.e. Ignatius, *Philippians*][60]	

The editors provide a list of points in which the *Devotions* influenced the 'Durham Book', two or three of which escaped the notice of its editor. To these may be added one more: the 'Meditations whilest others are communicated' are taken from the 1549 Book, but with alterations in Luke 12.37 and Ephesians 5.1, which the 'Durham Book' reproduces in preference to the original.[61]

8

The Savoy Conference

When the Church of England prays in the Litany to be delivered from heresy and schism, we hear an echo of the century of controversy that ended with the Savoy Conference, the revision of the Book of Common Prayer, and the Act of Uniformity. Curiously little attention has been paid by historians to the Savoy Conference. It figures usually as one episode in the history of Puritanism, or of the political intrigues surrounding the Restoration, or of the evolution of the Prayer Book. In none of these is it an event of unique significance. It is, however, a convenient point at which to study one of the formative processes of the Church of England, the long debate between the Established Church and its would-be reformers. This debate remained curiously static throughout its hundred years. You can take a cross-section at various points in its course; and whether you look at Matthew Parker enforcing the surplice; at Hooker's controversy with Travers, when 'the forenoon sermon' at the Temple 'spake Canterbury, and the afternoon Geneva'; at Laud and Prynne wrangling over altars and reverences; or at the meetings in the Master's Lodgings at the Savoy, it is always the same points that are debated, the same arguments used, even the same literature reprinted. The documents of the Savoy Conference give us the most persuasive and thorough exposition of the Puritan case. Why, then, was it a failure?

On 25 March 1661, a Royal Warrant set up the Commission which we now know as the Savoy Conference. It named twelve Commissioners on either side, Bishops and Presbyterians, together with nine deputies to take the place of Commissioners who might be absent through 'age, sickness, infirmity or other occasion'. No distinction seems to have been made between the two categories in the conduct of the discussions; indeed, two or three bishops took part who were not Commissioners at all. In the preliminary negotiations of the previous year the Presbyterians had suggested that the divines chosen should be 'learned, godly and moderate'; and these qualities were largely reflected by the actual choice. Learning was represented by the inclusion, on the Bishops' side, of Gilbert Sheldon, formely Warden of All Souls; John Cosin and Humphrey Henchman, both 'excellently well versed in the Canons, Councils and Fathers', which Cosin in particular was able to quote from memory; Robert Sanderson, formerly Regius Professor of Divinity at Oxford; Bryan Walton, editor of the Polyglot Bible, in which the sacred text was printed in nine different languages in parallel columns; John Pearson, who had just published his *Exposition of the Creed*; and Anthony Sparrow, author of a learned *Rationale upon the Book of Common Prayer*. Of the nine deputies, eight were Doctors, the other a Bachelor, of Divinity. The Presbyterian list was headed by Edward Reynolds, formerly Dean of Christ Church; Anthony Tuckney, Regius Professor of Divinity at Cambridge; John Conant, Regius Professor of Divinity at Oxford; John Wallis, Savilian Professor of Geometry at Oxford; and John Lightfoot, the author of *Horae Hebraicae*, a work still quoted in commentaries. They were assisted by four other Doctors, and one Bachelor, of Divinity. The first requirement, that of learning, was thus amply fulfilled among the Commissioners; their godliness the reader may judge; the third requirement, moderation, was a virtue possessed by many of them, though not, unfortunately, by all.

Frewen, the nominal leader of the Bishops, who rejoiced in the Christian name of Accepted, was regarded even by Baxter as 'a peaceable man'; Henry King was known as a favourer of the Presbyterians in his diocese of Chichester; Benjamin Laney later treated the nonconformists of Peterborough with much leniency, 'looking through his fingers at them', and saying 'Not I, but the law', when compelled to take action. John Cosin, while in exile, had authorized an Anglican to communicate with the French Reformed Church, and himself ministered to many of their number, while his will records his great desire for unity; George Morley was 'thought a friend to the Puritans before the wars' and continued to interest himself in projects for comprehension in later years; Bryan Walton's scholarly activities had found favour under the Commonwealth; Humphrey Henchman at Salisbury 'gave no trouble or disturbance to the nonconformists'; Robert Sanderson at his death asked that the ejected ministers might be used again. Most moderate of all was John Gauden: he had been a Parliamentarian, eager for regulating the episcopacy rather than rooting it out; yet he had continued to use the Book of Common Prayer longer than anyone in his neighbourhood. In 1656 he had put forward a scheme of agreement on the basis of archbishop Ussher's *Reduction*. Baxter, the leader of the Presbyterians, says of him that 'he was our most constant helper . . . the only moderator of all the bishops' (a typical Baxter exaggeration); 'if all had been of his mind, we had been reconciled. But when . . . we had got some moderating concessions from him, and from bishop Cosin by his means, the rest came in the end and brake them all.' Gauden still persevered after the breakdown of the Conference, and with Morley's help secured the reinstatement in the Communion Service of the so-called Black Rubric, which defines the significance of kneeling at the Communion, a last-minute attempt to satisfy Puritan scruples. The deputies were more extreme in their views, with the exception of John Hackett, who had been in the Westminster Assembly, and, more especially, John Pearson, whose reasoning bred in Baxter the persuasion that 'if he had been independent, he would have been for peace; and that if all were in his power, it would have gone well. He was the strength and honour of that cause which we doubted whether he heartily maintained.'

Of the Presbyterians, Baxter himself, though antipathetic to the Bishops in personality, was not extreme in his views on the points at issue. He held kneeling at the Communion lawful; the surplice doubtful, the cross in baptism unlawful; the use of a liturgy lawful, as likewise the imposition of a worthy liturgy. The Church of England's liturgy, however, he held to be disorderly and defective, though as it contained 'no false doctrine, idolatry or false worship (and this was the mind of all his brethren but one) . . . it would be sinfully curious and uncharitable to separate from it', provided that full liberty was given for the use of conceived prayer and godly exhortation. Edward Reynolds had already gone so far as to accept a bishopric; in earlier days he had been successively one of Charles I's chaplains and a member of the Westminster Assembly. In June 1660 he had put out a paper for reconciling differences between the parties, and throughout the Conference he acted as mediator, using all his influence for moderation. John Conant had never taken the Covenant, and, though he refused conformity in 1662, he conformed, after prolonged study of the doctrines of the Church of England, in 1670. John

Wallis seems to have long had a foot in either camp, and conformed in 1662, as did also Thomas Horton and John Lightfoot; Benjamin Woodbridge conformed in 1665, though he afterwards repented of it; Matthew Newcomen had published a work entitled *Irenicum*; and Thomas Manton used the Book of Common Prayer for eighteen months before his ejection. Several of the Presbyterians had been among the fifty-seven ministers who signed a petition against the execution of Charles I; and three had been contributors to the famous manifesto of 'Smectymnuus' advocating moderate episcopacy and a reformed liturgy, the position that was probably held by the majority. Thus there were moderate men in abundance on both sides, as well as a few firebrands, and in a less heated atmosphere a settlement could probably have been reached by agreement.

For evidence about the course of the Conference, we are chiefly dependent on the account given by Baxter in his posthumous work *Reliquiae Baxterianae*, which is often vague and, where it can be checked, inaccurate. There are also letters from Henry Ferne, Prolocutor of the Lower House of Convocation, and John Hackett, one of the deputy Commissioners. Ferne seems to have attended some of the meetings and would in any case be in close touch with the Bishops. His account was written four days after the Conference ended and is therefore more likely to be reliable in matters of chronology than Baxter's version, which was composed years afterwards. The chief documents were printed at once with the title *The Grand Debate between the Bishops and the Presbyterian Divines*, while an almost identical publication is entitled *An Accompt of all the Proceedings of the Commissioners of both Perswasions*. Both are chiefly devoted to the Exceptions of the Ministers and the Reply of the Bishops.

The King's Warrant was dated 25 March and was to run for four months, thus expiring on 25 July. After naming the Commissioners, it authorized them

> to advise upon and review the said Book of Common Prayer, comparing the same with the most ancient liturgies which have been used in the Church, in the primitive and purest times . . . And if occasion be, to make such reasonable and necessary alterations, corrections and amendments therein, as . . . shall be agreed upon to be needful or expedient for the giving satisfaction unto tender consciences, and the restoring and continuance of peace and unity . . . but avoiding, as much as may be, all unnecessary alterations of

the forms and liturgy wherewith the people are already acquainted, and have so long received in the Church of England.

The comparison with ancient liturgies was never made, as the Presbyterians professed themselves unable to find any 'entire forms of liturgy within the first three hundred years . . . nor any impositions of liturgy upon any national church for some hundreds of years after'. The so-called Liturgies of St Basil, St Chrysostom and St Ambrose, they rejected as spurious or corrupt. Nor were the Bishops able to contest the point that uniformity was not a characteristic of primitive Christianity. As Baxter observed: 'Antiquity is nothing to them when it makes against them.' In fact, when the Prayer Book was revised in the autumn of the same year, no attention whatever was paid to the ancient liturgies and little to the Sarum rite. Things might have been different if Jeremy Taylor had been present: his *Forms of Prayer for use under the Commonwealth* are professedly taken out of the Greek liturgies: but he was regarded as unreliable and had been safely tucked away in an Irish bishopric. This suggestion of the Warrant was therefore stillborn, and all the energies of the Commissioners were concentrated upon the Presbyterian objections.

The warrant was received by bishop Reynolds on 1 April, but the first meeting was not held until 15 April, Easter Monday, by which time Holy Week was over, the Court had left for Windsor and the country ministers had had time to reach London. However, an election had by then revealed an overwhelming majority for the episcopal party, and the Bishops' attitude hardened correspondingly. At the opening of the proceedings, Frewen, archbishop of York, made way for Sheldon, bishop of London, who, he said, knew most the King's mind. Sheldon then said that it was the Presbyterians that had caused the holding of the Conference, not the Bishops; and therefore the Bishops had nothing to say or do until the other side brought in all that they complained of in the Liturgy in writing, together with additional forms and alterations. This was a shrewd move, tending to make the Presbyterians appear unreasonable innovators; yet they could not let their case go by default. The majority of the ministers were consequently eager for conference, urging that discussion was required by the Warrant, and would be quicker and more likely to produce an agreed settlement. This, one may surmise, was precisely why Sheldon did not want discussion; and Baxter, surprisingly, agreed with him, though for different reasons. He did not believe that the Conference was likely to succeed, and wished to appeal to posterity by means of written records.

The complaints, or Exceptions (as they called them), against the Prayer Book were drawn up by a small committee, while the composition of an alternative liturgy was entrusted to Baxter, who completed it in a fortnight. The committee was then only just beginning its work, but the Exceptions were soon prepared and handed to the Bishops at a meeting on 4 May. The Bishops considered them with great care, according to Ferne, though Baxter thinks that they were only seen by those bishops who composed the Reply. The latter was handed over about 12 June, whereupon the Presbyterians undertook a Rejoinder. Meanwhile, Baxter's Liturgy had been discussed by the other Presbyterian Commissioners, and was finally brought to the Bishops in the first week of July, as we learn from Ferne, supported by John Hackett; from Baxter's narrative one would imagine that it had been produced much sooner. Hackett, though a moderate, regarded this Liturgy as dealing the death blow to any hope of agreement, being 'so unconsonant, so quite different in the frame from our Liturgy'. It was accompanied by a lengthy Petition for Peace and Concord, drawn up by Baxter.

A week later (here Baxter and Ferne agree), the Presbyterians produced their Rejoinder to the Bishops' Reply, a composition of enormous length, written by Baxter, with a Preface by Calamy. The time had now nearly expired – ten days only were left – and Reynolds made a fresh attempt to get more concessions. This was refused, and since further discussion of particular points was obviously futile, the Bishops at last agreed to take part in a formal disputation on the question of the sinfulness of the ceremonies excepted against.

This began on 23 July. The Bishops were represented by Pearson, Gunning and Sparrow; the Presbyterians by Baxter, Bates and Jacomb. Baxter selected kneeling at the Communion as the subject of discussion, since, although he himself took it to be lawful, he held the penalty for refusing to kneel to be quite disproportionate to the seriousness of the offence. The debate was conducted in the traditional manner, and seems to us a curiously unreal, academic performance. During its course, bishop Cosin produced a paper 'as from some considerable person', offering a way out of the impasse, namely that anything in the Book of Common Prayer that was judged contrary to the

147

word of God should be pointed out and rectified; anything that was merely inexpedient should be submitted to Convocation. Baxter regarded this as a cunning snare, coming from 'someone above us, who would inquire after it', presumably Clarendon, or the King himself. He accordingly produced eight points in which the Prayer Book was contrary to the word of God, but decline to treat with Convocation, as being unrepresentative. Morley's version is that when the other brethren seemed to like a way 'tending to an amicable and fair compliance', it was 'wholly frustrated by Mr Baxter's furious eagerness to engage in a disputation'.

On the third day, the Conference was due to conclude, and it was agreed to report 'that all were agreed on the ends for the Church's welfare, unity and peace, and His Majesty's happiness and contentment, but, after all their debates, were disagreed of the means'. Baxter gives a very full, though by no means clear, account of the concluding days, from which the Bishops emerge in no favourable light. Certainly some of the remarks quoted seem foolish or offensive; but it is that kind of remark that Baxter has singled out for quotation. If the Bishops' speeches had been reported at the same length as Baxter's own, we could form a fairer judgement of the quality of the discussions. The only part of the Conference which is described by Morley (above) appears very differently in Baxter's narrative. Even the documents are one-sided. The Bishops' Reply to the Exceptions has to be extracted from the Presbyterian Rejoinder; as we have no independent source, we cannot tell whether it has been preserved in full.

And so the Conference ended; without doing any good, in Burnet's view. 'It did rather hurt', he says, 'and heightened the sharpness that was then in people's minds.' The immediate sequel was the Act of Uniformity with the revised Prayer Book attached, to which ministers had to conform, or leave their livings. Nine hundred and thirty-six are known to have been ejected, possibly more. It was the parting of the ways for the Presbyterians. They had been, first, a faction within the Church of England: then they had gained control of it: now they would not return to being a faction. They had tasted the delight of doing things as they wanted to do them and they chose rather to suffer hardship than to submit to ordinances which they deemed sinful, from which they had freed themselves seventeen years previously.

Two questions arise: could the Conference have succeeded, and was it ever intended to succeed? The King's first purpose was to delay the calling of the Conference until passions had abated, and if this purpose had been carried into effect, some kind of agreement might have been reached. In a few years' time Parliament was to become much less strongly royalist and episcopal in sentiment; several of the older bishops, who had suffered most under the Commonwealth, died in the early sixties, and a moderate party began to come to the fore. Even as things stood, proposals for a comprehension continued to be made, and a further revision of the Book of Common Prayer was attempted in 1689 with the express object of reconciling non-conformists. These considerations tend to show that a settlement was not beyond the bounds of possibility if the issue could have been left open until a calmer atmosphere prevailed. In the event, however, the Conference was called sooner than the King originally envisaged, in order to counter what appeared to be the recrudescence of anti-episcopal feeling; and again, if this impression had proved to be well founded, the Bishops might well have been found in a more compliant mood.

But it very speedily became evident that in 1661 Presbyterian influence in the country was at its nadir. The Presbyterian Commissioners were, in Trevelyan's phrase, 'leaders without an army'. The Bishops held the whip-hand, and saw no need to offer material concessions; and their intransigence exasperated the moderate Presbyterians, as it strengthened the extremer elements among their number. It certainly appears that, in the circumstances of the year 1661, a breakdown was inevitable. Some have thought that this was the result intended at any rate by Sheldon, if not also by Clarendon. Certainly there is no evidence that the Bishops ever seriously contemplated meeting the Presbyterians halfway, by adopting some such scheme as Ussher's *Reduction*. But this is not to say that the whole Conference was a sham. The Bishops were anxious, not to include all Presbyterians in a wider framework, but to win over the moderate Presbyterians to the existing order. Their first step had been offers of preferment; and when this largely failed, they resorted to the grant of minor concessions such as satisfied the consciences of the less obdurate. Seventeen of these concessions were granted explicitly during the Conference – one of major importance, the substitution of the Authorized Version for the Bishops' Bible in all liturgical reading of holy Scripture. These were entered immediately in the 'Durham Book', the first draft of the ensuing revision, though one or two were withdrawn in the later stages. Thirteen other requests were met, though not specified in the Bishops' Reply. This policy was continued in the course of revision: many of the alterations suggested by bishops Cosin and Wren and embodied in the 'Durham Book' were rejected, particularly those that reintroduced elements of the 1549 Book which had been discarded in 1552 and were therefore unlikely to be acceptable to Presbyterians. We have already noticed another instance in Gauden's revival of the rubric on kneeling at the Communion.

The success of this method is shown in the large number of ministers who conformed at once; and by the fact that about one in five of those who were ejected conformed later. This policy could never have brought about a complete comprehension; but a partial comprehension was effected, and the number of moderate men chosen to be Commissioners suggests that this had been sincerely desired. The King had always appeared as champion of a wide toleration, such as would guarantee freedom of worship by Papists, but this the Presbyterians could not stomach and thereby lost the best chance of securing their own freedom. Here, for once, they found themselves in agreement with the Bishops.

The weakness of the Presbyterians made it unnecessary to grant the large concessions required to win over the whole faction, but there were other factors hindering even the partial comprehension that was aimed at. Personal, social and economic reasons often underlie schism. All the Bishops, and Morley in particular, seem to have found Baxter's personality uncongenial; while the Presbyterians regarded the Bishops as haughty and aloof. Class distinction played a large part: the Bishops for the most part came of good family and moved freely among the nobility, while the Presbyterians sprang from the lower middle class and felt ill at ease in high society. Bishop Cosin's friendliness was sufficiently unusual to deserve comment; and on the Presbyterian side, only Baxter dared to address the Bishops as an equal, while Reynolds, though a bishop himself, was too respectful to carry much weight. The Bishops, too, belonged to an older generation; most of them had held high office before the Civil War, from which the Presbyterians had displaced them and from which they were now in process of displacing the Presbyterians. Anthony Tuckney, the Master of

St John's, Cambridge, a Presbyterian Commissioner, was made to resign this position and the Regius Professorship in favour of Peter Gunning, one of the Bishops' deputies, and that while the Conference was in full swing. The Bishops were also men of wide culture, who saw no harm in making a jest about matters which the Presbyterians treated in deadly earnest. For instance, the Exceptions asked leave to perform the whole of the Burial Service in church, to avoid the inconvenience of standing in the open air. The Bishops, who perhaps did not often officiate at funerals, replied that this difficulty, being 'for the ease, not of tender consciences, but of tender heads, may be helped by a cap better than a rubric'. Baxter was scandalized by this levity.

Finally, after we have asked whether the Conference could have succeeded and whether it was ever intended to succeed, there remains the question, what was achieved? What was gained and what lost in the settlement that ensued upon the breakdown of the Conference? If we accept the Bishops' view that the Presbyterians were still too strong to be tolerated within the Establishment on their own terms, the stand made at the Conference ensured a certain uniformity and loyalty to a particular order and discipline. It was not so much the retention of the ceremonies that the Bishops fought to secure as the right to decree their use. The Church of England that emerged from the Savoy Conference was one whose members accepted the authority of Church and State, where it was not *contrary* to the Bible. The retention of the Presbyterians would have meant that a large portion of the Church regarded the Bible as all-sufficient, and denied anyone's authority to enforce what was not *enjoined* by holy Writ. The Bishops stood firmly to Hooker's doctrine of 'things indifferent', neither enjoined nor forbidden, either explicitly or tacitly, by the Bible. These things might be enforced by the lawful authority. It would have been no fatal loss to the Church of England if some of its members had omitted the sign of the cross in Baptism; but to allow ministers regularly to ignore the directions of the Book of Common Prayer would have led ultimately to a complete alteration of the Church's character. In the words of the Prayer Book,

> the keeping or omitting of a ceremony, in itself considered, is but a small thing; yet the wilful and contemptuous transgression and breaking of a common order and discipline is no small offence before God.

Further, the Church of England was able to preserve those elements of the Catholic heritage which the Puritans wished to remove, depriving the Church alike of continuity and comprehensiveness. On the other hand, the Church was deprived of a link with the Continental Reformation and the Church of Scotland, a link which it is now trying to reforge. It lost the services of many sincere and enthusiastic ministers, whose sermons sounded the prophetic note more clearly than did those of their contemporaries within the Establishment. Finally, the pastoral zeal and practical methods of the Presbyterians were in advance of their opponents'. Their suggestions for improving the working of episcopacy have been widely adopted in the last hundred years; and their rigorist attitude to Baptism and Holy Communion also has a modern ring, though it is open to question whether this is a matter in which their counsel would have benefited the Church of England.

It is a matter for great regret that no way of reconciling the differences could be found. Politics and personalities played a larger part than scholarship or Christian charity; but the hundred-years-old controversy had to be ended somehow. The Presbyterians were too strong to be ignored, too weak to require compromise; but they might always gain strength again, so now they must either capitulate or go out into the wilderness; there was no middle way.

9

The Prayer Book in Convocation, November 1661

The first proposals for Prayer Book revision after the Restoration were made by bishops Matthew Wren and John Cosin. They were entered in the 'Durham Book' (hereafter DB), and reached their final form in William Sancroft's 'Fair Copy' (FC).[1] In November 1661 the proposals were laid before Convocation, and, as amended in debate, were entered by Sancroft in the 'Convocation Book' (CB), a folio Prayer Book of 1636, the revised text of which differs in only a few particulars from the familiar 1662 Prayer Book. A manuscript copy of the complete revised text was prepared concurrently in order to be subscribed by all members of Convocation. This was subsequently attached to the Act of Uniformity of 1662 and is known as the 'Annexed Book' (AB).[2] The course of the discussions which intervened between FC and CB remains obscure: the Convocation records are disappointingly sketchy and there is very little external evidence. From what there is of the latter and from analysis of the changes made, however, it is possible to discover the authorship of some of the alterations and additions, to identify the most influential figures in the discussions and to recover a few proposals which failed to secure acceptance.

The brief proceedings of the Upper House of Convocation have been printed more than once[3] and can be conveniently studied in a timetable constructed from them by James Parker.[4] From this it appears that the consideration of the proposals in full session of both Houses must have been rapid and superficial. The proceedings began with the appointment of a committee of eight bishops (Cosin, Wren, Skinner, Warner, Henchman, Morley, Sanderson, Nicholson) to proceed with the work of revision, meeting each evening, while the full Upper House met each morning to consider their recommendations. There is no record at all of the committee's meetings, but the Upper House required only five two-hour sittings to cover the whole of the Prayer Book as far as the Psalter, and another sitting for the Ordinal. The changes considered in the first five sittings involved an average of over 1500 words per sitting, according to Parker's computation, and those of the Ordinal, 2500 words. Yet the revision of the Ordinal in FC had been extremely tentative, compared with the rest of the book, and a great many changes were first made in Convocation. It is clear that only a very few of the changes can have been debated at any length in the Upper House; for the most part, it must have been simply a matter of approving the recommendations of the committee. One whole sitting was subsequently devoted to the General Thanksgiving, which shows what slow progress was made when there was a real debate. Nor was the Lower House any more thorough, as is borne out by two scraps of gossip recorded by E. Pearse:

> Dr *Allen* of *Huntingdonshire*, and Clerk in the Convocation, earnestly laboured with the then Bishop of *London* [Sheldon], afterwards Archbishop, that they might so refine the Liturgy, that no sober Man might make Exception. He was wished to forbear, for what should be, was concluded on or resolved.
>
> There were no debates to speak of; the greatest that I could hear of was between the *Cambridg* Professor Dr *Gunning* and the *Oxford* Professor Dr *Creed*, about (a hard point indeed) *the Age of Children to be Confirm'd.*[5]

Edmund Calamy the younger adds another anecdote:

> So very Nice and Exact were the high Party, that they would not yield so much as to forbear the Lessons of the *Apocrypha*: Insomuch, that after a long tugg at the Convocation-House about that Matter, a good Doctor came out at last with great Joy, that they had caarried it for *Bell and the Dragon.*[6]

When so much time was expended upon such small points, it is obvious that the Lower House, too, can have made only a cursory examination of most of the proposals. Thus the great bulk of the proposals added to, or varied from, those in FC must have originated in the committee.

Of the eight bishops concerned, only Wren, Cosin and Sanderson had previously shown a lively interest in questions of revision and it is precisely these three with whom suggestions can be definitely associated (three was the committee's quorum).

Wren secured the insertion of a number of points made in his *Advices* which had not found their way into DB or FC; and some of them are so minute as to render it virtually certain that he had the *Advices* before him at the time. Cosin, on the other hand, has scarcely any new entries to his credit: the two most important (the descriptions of the saints in the Calendar and the new translation of *Veni Creator*) are taken from his *Devotions* at Wren's suggestion. But a large number of alterations in DB which were passed over in FC are now reinstated; and again, many of them are wholly unlikely to have been made unless someone had DB open in front of him during the committee's meetings (a typical instance is 'O God, who art *the* author of peace . . .'); and the person most likely to have done this was Cosin, to whom the book belonged.

There is a striking resemblance between the sources drawn upon at this stage and those used in DB: fresh material is drawn from the Scottish Liturgy and the 1549 Book, though the points are too trivial for notice here; as also from the Canons (e.g. the use of the Bidding Prayer in Canon 55 for the conclusion of the Prayer for the Church). Even the Sarum Missal seems to have been kept in mind, for some of the alterations in the collects are made purely to secure a more accurate rendering of the Latin (e.g. Trinity 15, insertion of 'from all things hurtfull' to represent '*a noxiis*'). As in DB, too, new suggestions are phrased in words from other parts of the Prayer Book, as when a new collect in the consecrating of a bishop is simply a conservative adaptation of the collect of St Peter's Day. Several requests of the Presbyterians at the Savoy Conference, at that time refused by the bishops, are now granted. For example, it is no longer stated that 'the flood Jordan' was sanctified by Christ's baptism; and newly married couples are only recommended, not obliged, to make their communion the same day. In some cases these points had the support of Wren or Sanderson, as is shown by their appearance in Wren's *Advices* or Sanderson's *Liturgy*, both earlier than the conference.

Sanderson's *Liturgy in the Times of Rebellion and Usurpation*[7] was an adaptation of the Prayer Book for use under the Commonwealth. By far his most weighty contribution at this stage was his rearrangement of the Burial Service: the order of the Book of 1662 is exactly copied from the *Liturgy*, even down to the choice of psalms. Some of his suggestions failed to pass the later stages and are only preserved for us in cancelled portions of the text of

AB.[8] These variant readings have been crossed out in favour of the final text, that of CB.[9] Some are completely new, and must represent suggestions of the committee. Four of these are directly attributable to Sanderson:

PRAYER OF HUMBLE ACCESS
AB   That our sinfull bodies *and souls* may be made clean by his body, and washed through his most pretious blood.
Sanderson   That our sinful bodies and souls, being sanctified by his body, and washed through his most precious blood.

PRAYER OF CONSECRATION
AB   May be *made* partakers of his most blessed Body and Blood.
Sanderson   May be made partakers . . .

FIFTH COLLECT 'AFTER THE OFFERTORY'
AB   Which for our unworthiness we dare not *to receive*.
Sanderson   Although we are neither for our sins worthy to receive them.

WORDS OF COMMITTAL
AB   Our dear brother here departed *out of the miseries of this life*.
Sanderson   This our brother here departed out of the miseries of this sinful world.[10]

A suggestion similar to the first of these was made by the Presbyterians at the Savoy Conference and was then rejected by the bishops; but Sanderson's wording is much closer than theirs to the text of AB.

Another important piece of revision which may be attributed to the committee concerns the proposed rearrangement of the Canon after the model of the Scottish Liturgy. This is included in FC as 'Paper B', side by side with a light revision noted in the margin of the printed text, '& both left to censure'. The result of the 'censure', as Sancroft noted in DB, was that 'My LL. the BB. at Elie house Orderd all in the old Method'. But the details which he goes on to quote are exactly those of the 'light revision':

> First the prayer of Address, We do not presume, with the Rubrick When the priest standing &c the prayer of Consecration unalterd (only one for own & Amen at last) with the marginal Rubricks.

156

Then (the Memorial or prayer of Oblation omitted, and the Lord's prayer) follow the Rubricks, & Forms of Participation, & Distribution to the end of the Rubrick, When all have communicated &c altogether as in this book; only that Rubrick, In the Communion time shall be sung &c with the Sentences following, wholly omitted. And then the Lord's prayer; the Collect, O Lord, & Heavenly Father &c to the End.

As the rubrics 'When all have communicated' and 'In the Communion time shall be sung' are both suggestions of FC, it is clear that 'as in this book' must mean 'as in FC', i.e. as in the 'light revision'. But, before the writing of AB, a vigorous revision was made of the rubric prescribing the manner of administration, the actual words of administration and the rubric about further consecration. Further small corrections to the text of AB were made in CB (two are quoted in the previous paragraph). There were thus three stages subsequent to the production of FC. The most probable account of them is that the phrase 'My Lords the Bishops at Ely House' refers to a private meeting between Wren, Cosin and Sheldon which took place at the beginning of November; that the vigorous revision was the work of the committee of eight bishops; and that the final changes were made in full session of Convocation. It is true that the committee of eight was also to meet at Ely House, but it did not do so for its first meeting and it is not known whether it ever did so; and it is difficult to imagine the vigorous revision being carried through in the very brief proceedings of the Upper House.

This concludes the evidence relating to the committee's work, which was then submitted to the full Upper House, reviewed by them, sent down to the Lower House for their consideration and finally reconsidered, with the observations of the Lower House, by the Upper House. To these later stages belong some further suppressed readings in AB. In these, the original text is a faithful reproduction of FC and has been supplanted by a new reading found in CB; these CB readings must represent changes made later than in committee. For the most part, it is impossible to assign any change to any particular stage; one exception is the expansion of the form of consecration of a bishop which is attributed by Humphrey Prideaux to the influence of Peter Gunning and John Pearson in the Lower House.[11] The Convocation registers also mention some late changes made in the Commination by the Lower House; these can probably be identified in AB, where there are some entries made by a corrector.

One document, however, survives from a very late stage. This is an undated paper in Cosin's hand, now in the Bodleian Library.[12] Its contents are as follows:

Some particulars to be amended in the Booke of Common Prayer, before it be signed.

1 A Rubrick to be inserted into the Order, *How the Psalter shalbe read* viz: *It is most agreeable to a religious order & decencie in the publick service of the Church, that the Psalmes & Hymnes appointed in this Book be sung or said, one verse after another, by sides or turnes, where it may conveniently be done, the Minister, clarks & people all standing.*

2 The *Benedicite omnia opera Domini Domino* to be restored.

3 *St Chrysostomes prayer* to be used only at the End of Morning & Evening Prayer, after the *Prayers for the King &c* there printed; And the Prayer *O God whose nature & propertie &c* to be printed & used only in the End of the Litanie, after the Prayer *Wee humbly beseech thee*.

4 In that prayer, the word *righteously* to stand, rather then be changd into the word *rightly*.

5 The Hymne *Christ Rising &c* appointed on Easter day morning, to be printed by severall verses.

6 After the Collects for the King following the 10 Commandments, this Rubrick to be added,
     Then shalbe said the Collect for the day with the Epistle and Gospel there appointed.

7 Before the Gospel to be said or sung, *Glory be to thee O Lord*. And after it is ended, *Thanks be given to the Lord*.

8 During the time of distributing the Communion, Anthems & Psalmes may be used in places where they sing.

9 At the end of Baptisme, the Minister to require, that the Child &c be brought to Confirmation.

10 The Prayers for the 5th of November 30th of Jan. 29th of May, Order at the Kings Healing, & at the Mandat to be printed with the Book, & all confirmed by Act of Parliament together, besides the Order for Prayers in the King's Fleete.

11 The Epistle for St Luke's day to end with these words, *Only Luke is with me*.

The reference in the title of this paper to signing suggests a date towards the end of the session, and this is supported by the allusion to 'the Order for Prayers in the King's Fleete', which was first discussed in the Upper House on 5 December. The paper clearly consists of suggestions to be put before the Upper House after the receipt of the alterations recommended by the Lower House. Of the eleven 'particulars', four (nos. 1, 7, 8, 9) show Cosin trying to secure the restoration of suggestions made in FC and dropped in committee, while one (no. 11) revives a suggestion of DB which was not even transferred to FC: all these were rejected once more. Two (nos. 2 and 4) restore the text of the Prayer Book at points where it had been altered by the committee; the remaining four were completely new (nos. 3, 5, 6, 10). Of these six, no. 3 and 5 were also rejected; but the other four were accepted and have left their mark on the text of AB, which must have been completed before Cosin wrote his paper.

No. 2 Apparently the committee had suggested the omission of the *Benedicite*, in deference to the wishes of the Presbyterians. In AB the canticle is written out in full, so presumably the Upper House had restored it at once. However, a reference to it had also been removed from the rubric directing repetition of *Gloria Patri*; here AB originally had 'Benedictus, Magnificat and Nunc dimittis' in large letters, then erased 'Benedictus' and wrote in 'Benedicite, Benedictus' in fine writing. It is to this rubric that Cosin refers, thus incidentally revealing the otherwise unknown proposal to omit the canticle.

No. 4 Wren says that the word *righteously* has been objected to, though not by him; and it is omitted in FC, while the Scottish Liturgy and Sanderson both alter it to *justly*. AB originally had *rightly*, then erased it and wrote in *righteously*.

No. 6 After the completion of the copying of AB, the phrase '& the Collect of the day' has been removed from the rubric before the collects for the King, and Cosin's phrase has been prefixed to the rubric before the Epistle.

No. 10 A note carrying out the bulk of Cosin's suggestion is added at the end of AB in Sancroft's hand.

So much for the alterations; there remain the additions to be considered. These consist of the Preface; the prayers for Parliament and for all conditions of men; the General Thanksgiving; Baptism of those of riper years; four prayers appended to the Visitation of the Sick; the Forms to be used at sea; and the 'State Services'. All these were dealt with after the Prayer Book in its current form had been gone through. The State Services had already been approved by Convocation during its previous

159

session and required no further attention; so had the form of Baptism of those of riper years, though here there is evidence, in the final charge, of a suggestion from Sanderson:

> BCP   It is your part, and duty also, being made the Children of God, and of the Light by faith in Jesus Christ, to walk answerably to your Christian profession he hath now made.
> Sanderson   Our very Baptism and Christianity would oblige us to a holy walking, suitable to our holy calling . . . Children of God and of the Church . . . *Children of Light* . . .[13]

Sanderson is indeed the dominant figure in the additions. Isaak Walton's account of his contribution is worth quoting:

> How many of the new Collects were worded by *Dr Sanderson*, I cannot say; but am sure the whole Convocation valued him so much, that he never undertook to speak to any Point in question, but he was heard with great willingness and attention; and when any Point in question was determin'd, the Convocation did usually desire him to word their intentions, and as usually approve & thank him.
>   At this Convocation the *Common Prayer* was made more compleat, by adding 3 new necessary Offices; which were, *A form of Humiliation for the murther of King* Charles *the Martyr*; *a Thanksgiving for the Restoration of his Son our King*; *and for the baptizing of persons of riper age*. I cannot say *Dr Sanderson* did form or word them all, but doubtless more than any single man of the Convocation; and he did also, by desire of the Convocation, alter & add to the forms of Prayers to be used at Sea (now taken into *the Service Book*) . . . And lastly it may be noted, That for the satisfying all the dissenting Brethren, and others, the Convocations Reasons for the alterations and additions to the Liturgy, were by them desir'd to be drawn up by *Dr Sanderson*; which being done by him, and approv'd by them, was appointed to be printed before the Liturgy, and may be known by the Title, – *The Preface*: and begins thus – *It hath been the wisdom of the Church* –.[14]

The Preface does not, at any rate in its phraseology, reveal a close affinity with Sanderson's other writings, though the words 'too much stiffness' occur in his sermons.[15] But the emphasis on moderation is characteristic, as witness such passages as the eloquent exposition of the Anglican *via media* in Sermon *Ad Clerum* IV.[16] The 'general account' of the 'variations' may owe something to John Gauden, bishop of Exeter, who, referring to the then impending revision, points out the need for explaining obsolete words; '*quickning* and *improving* of some passages which seem less devotional and *Emphatick* than they may easily be made'; and providing more explicit thanksgivings.[17]

Walton's remarks about the 'Prayers to be used at Sea' are borne out by the parallels adduced by Brightman,[18] while further examples are dealt with below in connection with the General Thanksgiving. Stylistic analysis also reveals Sanderson's share in the prayers appended to the Visitation of the Sick. To the resemblances noted by Brightman[19] may be added the following, besides other smaller instances:

Prayer for a sick person
BCP   Give him unfeigned repentance.
Sanderson   Give him . . . unfeigned repentance.[20]

Commendatory Prayer
BCP   We humbly commend the soul of this thy servant . . . into thy hands, as into the hands of a faithful Creator and most merciful Redeemer.
Sanderson   We may . . . commit the keeping of our souls to him, both as a faithful Creator and as a powerful Redeemer, saying once more with David, *Into thy hands I commend my spirit.*[21]

The Prayer for the High Court of Parliament, originally composed in 1625, had been revised and brought before Convocation in May 1661; it seems to have been further revised in December, as it now contains a phrase, 'the advancement of thy glory, the good of thy Church, the safety, honour and welfare of our Sovereign', which is akin to Sanderson's 'the advancement of thy honour and glory, and the welfare of the people'.[22]

Almost the last item to be added was the General Thanksgiving. 'On Saturday, 14 December' (only a week before the Book was signed) 'between the hours of 8 and 10 a.m., the Reverend Father the Lord Bishop of Norwich [Edward Reynolds] introduced and delivered into the hands of the Lord President a form of a certain prayer conceived by him at another time concerning thanks to God for general mercies to be used publicly'. So the Proceedings of the Upper House of Convocation, which then tail off with the tantalizing words: 'After this prayer had been read aloud and some discussion held thereon, the Reverend Father, etc.'[23] The normal procedure in 1661 for additions, as opposed to alterations, was to entrust their compilation to a committee whose chairman duly introduced the new form, when completed, into the House of Bishops. There is, however, no trace of such a committee's being appointed to devise a general thanksgiving. By 14 December the section of AB headed *Thanksgivings* was already written out in full and no space was left for further additions. Reynolds would seem to have acted on his own initiative.

If he did so, a reason is not far to seek. The lack of thanksgivings in the Prayer Book had been a stock Puritan complaint from the days of Cartwright up to the Savoy Conference; and Reynolds, as the only Presbyterian bishop, was both sympathetic to this grievance and well placed to redress it. It is clear from the phrasing of the Convocation records that what he introduced was not an *ad hoc* composition. It had been 'conceived' (the regular Puritan term for the composition of prayers) 'at another time (*alias*) to be used publicly (*publice usitand*'). These last words must refer to the original purpose of composition; applying to Reynolds's object in introducing the prayer into Convocation, they would be quite superfluous, and the author of those records was not the man to waste even two words.

There are certain pointers to the original occasion of 'conception': first, the structure and wording. It is instructive to compare Reynolds's Thanksgiving with the 'Prayer, Thanksgiving or Blessing of the Bread and Wine' in the *Directory for the Public Worship of God* of 1644:[24]

Directory	*BCP*
God, the Father of all mercies . . . our great unworthiness . . . with humble and hearty acknowledgement . . . to give thanks to God for all his benefits and especially for that great benefit of our redemption . . . the sufferings and merits of the Lord Jesus Christ . . . and for all means of grace . . .	Almighty God, Father of all mercies, we thine unworthy servants do give thee most humble and hearty thanks for all thy goodness and lovingkindness . . . and for all the blessings of this life; but above all for thine inestimable love in the redemption of the world by our Lord Jesus Christ; for the means of grace and for the hope of glory.

Apart from the coincidences of language, there is a distinct similarity in the sequence of thought. In its later part, the General Thanksgiving goes on to the thought of gratitude expressed in service, which finds a place in both Prayer Book and *Directory*, though after the communion; in each place the word 'walk' is central.

A further pointer towards the Communion Service is afforded

162

by what is now the Third Exhortation in the Prayer Book service. Compare these phrases with the excerpt given above:

> And above all things ye must give most humble and hearty thanks to God . . . for the redemption of the world by the death and passion of our Saviour Christ.

and the concluding words of each:

Exhortation	*Thanksgiving*
submitting ourselves wholly to his holy will and pleasure, and studying to serve him in true holiness and righteousness, all the days of our life.	by giving up ourselves to thy service, and by walking before thee in holiness and righteousness all our days.

All this suggests that Reynolds's Thanksgiving was originally a eucharistic prayer. Such a prayer might well have been composed at any time during the Commonwealth, but there is one particular occasion which catches the eye. In June 1660 Reynolds, with the other Presbyterian leaders, drew up a set of proposals for the settling of differences, and among them were suggestions for the compilation of a new form of liturgy, or the revision and effectual reformation of the old.[25] Reynolds may have set his hand to the task in the prolonged interval before the convening of the Savoy Conference ten months later.

An analysis of the wording of the General Thanksgiving shows that the original draft must have undergone modification at the hands of Sanderson. First may be noted two parallels from the 'Prayers to be used at Sea', brought in ten days earlier and retouched by Sanderson:

SECOND COLLECT OF THANKSGIVING

And, we beseech thee, make us as truly sensible now of thy mercy . . . and give us hearts always ready to express our thankfulness, not only by words, but also in our lives, in being more obedient to thy holy commandments . . . that we . . . may serve thee in holiness and righteousness all the days of our life.

COLLECT AFTER VICTORY

And, we beseech thee, give us a true sense of this great mercy, as may engage us to a true thankfulness, such as may appear in our lives by an humble, holy and obedient walking before thee all our days.

With these, and with the General Thanksgiving, may be compared a phrase from Sanderson's

THANKSGIVING FOR FAIR WEATHER:

Unto unfeigned repentance and amendment of life, and to express the true thankfulness of our hearts for thine undeserved mercies by our cheerful and constant obedience to thy most holy commandments.[26]

These phrases, all expressing the same basic idea, can be seen gradually taking shape, from their first emergence in Sanderson's *Liturgy*, through their new form in the 'Sea Service', until they finally reach the familiar version of the General Thanksgiving.

The earlier part of the Thanksgiving may be compared with the *Hymns and Thanksgivings* section of the *Liturgy*:

O most glorious Lord God . . . for thy mercies every day wonderfully renewed upon us in our daily preservation . . . But especially for sending thine only-begotten Son . . . to undertake the great work of our reconciliation and redemption . . . For these and all other those innumerable mercies . . .[27]

and with

A PRAYER IN TIME OF DROUGHT:

We thy poor servants . . . for thy great and undeserved mercies vouchsafed unto us . . .[28]

(the comparison is with the passage in brackets in the Thanksgiving.)

The general design of the Thanksgiving, as well as some of its keywords, is anticipated in this passage from Sermon *Ad Populum* V:

If we be thus bound to give God thanks for these outward blessings, how much more ought we then to abound in all thankfulness unto him for his manifold *spiritual blessings in heavenly things in Christ*, for Grace and Election, for Mercy and Redemption, for Faith and Justification, for Obedience and Sanctification, for Hope and Glorification.[29]

It seems, then, that Reynolds must be given the credit for the first draft of the General Thanksgiving; and his sermons, too, supply parallels of language:

We have exhorted his servants to rejoice . . . in the graces wherewith he supplies us; in the light of his countenance; in the hope of
his glory . . . to improve this joy unto thankfulness for his benefits,
unto cheerfulness in his service. (1655)
The life of grace and the life of glory. (1657)
Continued his gospel, and the means of grace . . . among us. (1660)
The unmeasurableness of his love . . . the hope of his glory
(22.9.1661)[30]

But it is also clear that Sanderson played a large part in the
choice of words.

To find another prayer which could have been derived from
Reynolds's liturgy, it is only necessary to turn back one page, to
another last-minute addition, the *Prayer for all Conditions of Men*.
The Convocation records are not specific about the introduction
of this prayer into the Upper House, but it was almost certainly
one of the new collects read and revised on 13 December, the
day before the General Thanksgiving. The evidence of AB
points strongly in this direction. Two and a half pages were
originally left blank at the end of the section headed *Prayers*,
ready for the insertion of the Prayer for Parliament. This had
been in print since June 1661, but was being held back for
revision. It was copied in later by another hand, together with
the Prayer for all Conditions of Men and the General Thanksgiving. (That is why the former comes last in the *Prayers* and the
latter first in the *Thanksgivings*.) Clearly the two prayers were
added at approximately the same moment.

In this case, however, there is a rival candidate for the
authorship. Fifty years later, Thomas Bisse published a sermon
to which he appended an often-quoted note:

Upon the complaint of the Dissenters . . . this Prayer was added to
supply the place of the Litany . . . And therefore Bishop Gunning,
the supposed author of it, in the College whereof he was head,
suffered it not to be read in the afternoons, because the Litany was
never read then, the place of which it was supposed to supply.[31]

Consequently, the prayer is often ascribed to Gunning. But
first, Bisse does not claim that Gunning was definitely the
author, only that he was 'supposed' to be; nor does the point of
his anecdote in any way depend upon Gunning's authorship.
Secondly, although the prayer may have been originally intended to take the place of the Litany, in the event the preceding
rubric ('to be used at such times when the Litany is not appointed

to be said') makes nonsense of Bisse's story; Evensong would be a perfectly appropriate time to read the prayer. It may well be, indeed, that Gunning was the author of the *rubric*. In any case, some prayers composed by Gunning *c.* 1655 have recently come to light, whose style makes it unlikely that he wrote the Prayer for all Conditions of Men.[32]

In favour of Reynolds's authorship it may be remarked that the concern for the unity of all Christians which informs the first part of the prayer shows itself in sermon after sermon of his. The last-minute appearance of this prayer and the General Thanksgiving, and their common character of eirenic approach to Puritans, strongly suggest a common author. Hitherto, association with the Litany has tended to obscure the fact that the prayer is actually a close paraphrase of the Prayer for the Church in the Prayer Book Communion Service. Each begins with a reference to 'all men' or 'all mankind', and then goes on to pray for the Church in particular.

Prayer for the Church	*Prayer for all Conditions of Men*
Beseeching thee to inspire continually the universal Church with the spirit of truth, unity and concord:	We pray for the good estate of the Catholick Church, that it may be so guided and governed by thy good Spirit,
And grant that all they who confess thy holy Name may agree in the truth of thy holy Word, and live in unity and godly love . . . in holiness and righteousness all the days of their life.	that all who profess and call themselves Christians may be led into the way of truth, and hold the faith in unity of spirit, in the bond of peace and in righteousness of life.

In the original form petitions for the King, the clergy and the people will have followed, as in the Communion Service. They are now omitted, for the very good reason that these subjects would have been thoroughly dealt with at Mattins in the relevant 'State Prayers'. Their omission is indicated by the surprisingly early appearance of the word 'finally'. This introduces a petition for those 'who are anyways afflicted or distressed in mind, body or estate', balancing that in the Communion Service for those in 'trouble, sorrow, need, sickness or any other adversity'. In each prayer they are commended to God's 'goodness', and he is asked to 'comfort and succour' or 'comfort and relieve' them. The Prayer for all Conditions of Men ends at this point, and so did the Prayer for the Church, until the thanksgiving for the departed was added in this very session of Convocation.

All these considerations point to the conclusion that the Prayer for all Conditions of Men could well be Reynolds's equivalent to the Prayer for the Church. The hypothesis that in this prayer and the General Thanksgiving we have excerpts from a mediating liturgy composed by Reynolds fits excellently into the general situation. At the Savoy Conference, when the Presbyterians had complained of the lack of thanksgivings, the bishops had replied: 'If there be any forms wanting, the Church will provide.'[33] By December 1661 it was quite clear that no large-scale concessions to the Presbyterians were going to be made. But the addition to the Prayer Book of a long intercessory prayer and a thanksgiving, while it would not satisfy Baxter or Calamy, might well help to win over a number of waverers. If Reynolds had such prayers already drafted, what more natural than that he should now introduce them into Convocation?

10
Towards the 1928
Prayer Book

The Prayer Book in Convocation, 1909–10

On 21 June 1906 the Royal Commission on Ecclesiastical Discipline signed its Report; and on 11 November of that year Royal Letters of Business were issued to the Convocations of Canterbury and York, suggesting that they consider the desirability of revising the rubrics of the Book of Common Prayer. A joint committee was appointed to advise on the procedure to be adopted in replying to the Letters of Business. As a result of its advice, each of the four Houses set about the task independently, though not without cognizance of what the others were doing, and very occasional conference with one or other of them. Each House appointed a committee to consider what changes were necessary. The Upper House of Canterbury decided that the whole House should sit in committee, with the result that their discussions were not included in *The Chronicle of Convocation*, until such time as their report was printed, when they debated their own recommendations in full session. The Upper House of York did likewise. Luckily for historians, the standing orders of the Lower House did not allow them to adopt this procedure and their debates were printed at considerable length. As the Canterbury debates by themselves provide an abundance of material, they alone are considered here.

The committee of the Lower House of Canterbury, which included such distinguished names as dean Wace, Armitage Robinson, T. B. Strong and Hensley Henson, produced its first report early in 1909. At this period the House consisted of 24 deans, 71 archdeacons, 26 proctors for cathedral chapters and 54 proctors for the inferior clergy, a total of 175 members. It is not easy to determine its composition in terms of churchmanship. Thirty-eight voted against making the use of the Athanasian

168

Creed optional and 47 against a reconstruction of the Prayer of Consecration on the lines of 1549; and these figures probably give a fair idea of the strength of the Anglo-Catholic and Evangelical parties respectively. Neither could defeat the other without the help of the central third, a situation which ensured that the proposed changes were far from extreme in character.

When the House had been debating detailed proposals for about a year, the opponents of revision managed at last to bring about a debate on the desirability of undertaking any revision at all. The debate, which lasted two days (8–9 November 1910), was opened by archdeacon Stocks (Leicester), who was in charge of the Report.[1] He put forward three arguments in favour of revision: (1) the degree of liberty habitually exercised had become a source of danger to the Church; (2) other parts of the Anglican Communion had effected successful revisions; and (3) it was the only way to save the Book of Common Prayer. Canon Drummond (Oxford) said that there was no evidence of a majority in favour of revision. The Prayer Book held the Church together. The alternatives proposed showed the possibility of deepened party strife. Even advisable revisions cost too much. It would be better to provide a Supplement, which could be done under the Shortened Services Act and would not need to be submitted to Parliament. (This last point was denied by a later speaker.) Canon Hamilton (Southwell) deprecated the common attitude that revision was desirable, but not now; Convocation should give a lead. Canon Deane (Chichester) said that, since becoming a canon, he had broken the rubric about preaching at the Communion 'six thousand' times. Canon Allen Edwards (Southwark) had had at least fifty resolutions sent to him against revision, and not one in favour. (This was hardly surprising, since he was known to be strongly against it.) Archdeacon Fearon (Winchester) knew of several ruri-decanal conferences which were in favour, besides a very large number of silent laymen. Canon Hensley Henson (Westminster) said there was a great and urgent need of revision: (1) there was a paralysis of order in the Church of England; (2) there was a strain on the conscience in obeying the law; (3) the Prayer Book was inadequate for the needs of the modern Church; and (4) there was a conflict between the modern intellect and the Prayer Book. He was not anxious about sending the proposals to Parliament.

Dean Wace (Canterbury) pointed out that the question of

desirability was not raised in the Report on Ecclesiastical Discipline; it had been introduced by the Letters of Business. He wanted a Supplement, revision of the psalms and the lectionary, and the introduction of the most important readings of the Revised Version. He would accept any change consistent with the practice of the first five centuries, such as a reconstruction of the Canon or prayer for the dead; but he would not accept vestments. To legalize these would make Evangelical concessions impossible. It would substitute party advantage for a great principle. (The dean later took a similar position in regard to reservation, but remained faithful to the *consensus quinquesaecularis* to the end.) He wanted a Supplement rather than revision, because the present Prayer Book must be kept as a standard. The proposed addition to the Ornaments Rubric had united Evangelicals against revision; and the treatment of the Athanasian Creed had had the same effect on Anglo-Catholics. The result was that the proposals would go to Parliament with an agitation behind them to prevent them being carried into effect. (This gloomy prophecy was fulfilled seventeen years later.) Dean Strong (Christ Church) reminded the House of the Clergy Discipline bills which had been before Parliament year by year; one had finally been passed in 1903. This made it dangerous to argue that since revision would cause a split, nothing could be done. The consequence of doing nothing would be more Clergy Discipline bills.

Archdeacon Dundas (Dorset) said that if Convocation gave judgement, things would never be the same again, whatever Parliament said. (This also proved to be true.) By all means, leave the Prayer Book as a standard; but add a Schedule of permitted deviations from the text, not merely a supplement of special services. Mr Macleane (Salisbury) described the Report before the House as 'a very trivial document, interspersed with more dangerous concessions to laxity'. He then quoted ten salient points which made it difficult to accept the proposed revision, because they liberalized the Church of England. An example of these points was 'the making of the Commination Service optional'. Archdeacon Bond (Stow) said that all were agree that *additions* were needed; but addition was not enough: 'Some wise changes must be made in the body of the Prayer Book.'

Archdeacon Burrows (Birmingham), who had already exercised a great influence on the proposals, and, as bishop of Truro and later of Chichester, continued to do so right up to the final rejection by Parliament, poured cold water on the idea that there had been a liberal plot to get rid of the Athanasian Creed and the Ornaments Rubric. The committee did not sit in groups negotiating bargains between one section and another. They were not liturgical experts, and this was a good thing. The committee were representative of the practical needs of church life. Deans and archdeacons had nearly all passed through the experience of parochial life. People spoke of 'putting the Prayer Book in the melting-pot'. Out of fifty-one changes proposed, only seven affected the words of the services, and those only slightly. He also was not afraid of Parliament. In answer to those who said revision would stir up strife, he thought that the way to war lay through non-revision.

Canon Newbolt (St Paul's) said that the disorder in the Church had been much exaggerated. There was a large middle class of church with a normal form of worship. He wanted everything left as it was, with the addition of a Supplement. Archdeacon Stocks, winding up the debate, said that canon Newbolt had no belief in the power of the Church of England to legislate for itself.

The proposal to discontinue revision, which was technically before the House as an amendment confining revision to a Supplement, was then voted upon and lost by 71 votes to 44, and the House continued with the consideration of the committee's proposals.

One feature of the debates, which was prominent also in the discussions of the 1960s about Anglican–Methodist union, recurs again and again. A resolution is moved: dean Wace rises to his feet to deplore the proposed change from the Evangelical point of view, and he is followed by canon Newbolt also deploring it but for exactly opposite reasons. This was commented on by the archdeacon of Buckingham, Mr Shaw, who asked:

> How was he to account for that whole-hearted devotion to the Prayer Book upon the part of those who used and interpreted it so differently? Was it because each thought his view was the view which was the spirit of the Prayer Book; or, on the other hand, was it because the Prayer Book avowedly, not by accident nor in consequence of the decisions of the Privy Council, was so comprehensive as to include both views? He thought they could have very little doubt . . . that the former was the case, that each was

devoted to the Prayer Book because he thought his view was the true one (9 November 1910).

What united these widely differing viewpoints in opposition to change was their fear of the common enemy, liberalism, a blanket term which covered the findings of biblical scholarship and of science, a positive attitude towards Free Churchmen, and any departure from the letter of the Bible and the Prayer Book.

In the earlier stages of the discussions, two controversial subjects stand out, subjects inherited from the days of bishop Wilberforce and archbishop Tait, though of course their roots go much further back: the Ornaments Rubric and the Athanasian Creed. These matters aroused the deepest feelings and drew the weightiest speeches from the two protagonists. Attention had been specifically directed to the Ornaments Rubric by the Letters of Business. The Upper House of Canterbury had appointed a committee under bishop John Wordsworth, which had produced a detailed survey of the historical evidence, but had refrained from making any recommendation. The Lower House's own committee had suggested a resolution that 'the eucharistic vestments . . . cannot be rightly regarded as symbolic of any distinctively Roman doctrines, and . . . two alternative vestures for the minister' should be 'recognized as lawful under proper regulations' (4 May 1909). Dean Wace had refused to serve on the subcommittee which produced this resolution and had signed a dissentient report. He said that the vestments were declared illegal by the Ridsdale judgement and a large number of the clergy 'had committed a moral offence' in defying it. He quoted Darwell Stone as saying that the vestments were desired by his party 'distinctly as symbolic of the continuity of the doctrine of the Church of England with that of the Church of Rome'. They were 'indelibly associated with the doctrine of the propitiatory sacrifice in the Holy Communion'. 'If this medieval revival had not been proposed', he might have been able to come to an agreement about prayer for the dead.

Canon Newbolt said he 'disagreed with almost all the reasons put forward by the dean, but arrived at the same conclusion by another way'. He objected to the words 'recognized as lawful', because he believed that the vestments were lawful already. Some priests 'had been to prison to verify that belief'. Archdeacon Burrows said that it was time that the historical argument should be ended and both alternatives be recognized as lawful.

> There was a great third party, a party represented in that matter neither by the dean of Canterbury nor by canon Newbolt. That party was strong in numbers, and he thought that it was weighty in its earnestness and its breadth of sympathy. It was not organized, it was not very articulate, it did not readily come to the front in conferences and congresses. It waited, it listened and it thought, and he hoped it prayed; and that party, he thought, was determined on one thing at the present moment, that . . . there should be an end to this strife about ambiguous rubrics and disputable vestments, that neither extreme should drive the other out of the Church, and it was convinced that their only right policy now was to allow alternative uses.

It was finally agreed, on the motion of archdeacon Dundas (Dorset), that

> this House, holding that it is not desirable that any alteration should be made in the Ornaments Rubric, declares its opinion that in the present circumstances of the Church of England neither of the two existing usages . . . ought to be prohibited.

This was passed with only seven dissentients and a rider was added that

> no sanction is intended to be given to any doctrine other than what is set forth in the Prayer Book and Articles of the Church of England.

Despite this overwhelming majority, the procedure recommended failed of its purpose. Its adoption in the Books of 1927 and 1928 did not save either of them from rejection by Parliament and the main cause of rejection was the same disenchantment of both Evangelicals and Anglo-Catholics that manifested itself in 1909. Not until 1964 was the procedure finally adopted, in the Vestments Measure of that year.

Over the Athanasian Creed the main contest was between the Anglo-Catholics, who regarded its retention as 'almost a matter of life and death', and the central churchmen, who voiced the widespread dislike of the damnatory clauses (4 May 1909). Dean Furneaux (Winchester) said that 'no thinking man now used the words of those clauses in the sense in which their author meant them'. As archdeacon Stocks remarked, the Creed 'demanded more as a profession of faith from mixed congregations than it was wise for the Church to demand'. On this occasion the balance was held by the Evangelicals. The resolution before the House simply substituted 'may' for 'shall' (be sung or said) in the rubric. Dean Wickham (Lincoln) introduced this as 'the simplest, kindest and safest way' of dealing with the Creed. Dean Wace, who had at first been in favour of the resolution, came to the conclusion that it would not be passed and therefore supported an amendment by dean Furneaux to transfer the Creed to the end of the book. Canon Newbolt said that

> it would be impossible to silence the Creed ... In many churches it would be the fashion to use it without restriction, on the part of those who felt that they could not submit to the silencing of a creed which was one of the joys and delights of their life.

Various speakers gave conflicting accounts of the popularity or unpopularity of the Creed. Some wanted a new translation; others felt that this would not solve the problem. The amendment (to transfer) was carried by 56 votes to 38.

Canon Johnston (Oxford) then moved that a form without the warning clauses be provided. (This the Anglo-Catholics termed 'mutilation'.)

> The alternatives were either the silencing of the Creed altogether, or the continued distress of many good people and the alienation of many more by the compulsory public recitation of words which ... went beyond what ought to be stated.

Dean Armitage Robinson (Wells) preferred to keep the Creed intact and append a Synodical Declaration 'to show what the Church did or did not mean in regard to the warning clauses'. He wanted to 'encourage the use of those portions which dealt with the Trinity and the Incarnation'. Canon Johnston's amendment was carried by 48 votes to 29. (The 1928 Book provides rubrics carrying out Armitage Robinson's wishes, and a revised translation. Since then, however, the Creed has simply fallen into desuetude.)

Other subjects which produced vigorous debates in this Convocation were reservation, which eventually proved the greatest stumbling-block of all; and the third question put to deacons, which raised the question of biblical inspiration. But the most important issue was the reconstruction of the Prayer of Consecration, to which we now turn.

The process described as the reconstruction of the Canon was initiated by the Lower House of Canterbury Convocation on 19 February 1914 in these terms:

> That the Prayer of Humble Access be removed from its present position and be placed immediately before the Communion of Priest and People; that the *Amen* at the end of the present Prayer of Consecration be omitted, and that the Prayer of Oblation follow at once (prefaced by the word *Wherefore*), and then the Lord's Prayer.

This proposal had already been put forward by W. H. Frere in his book *Some Principles of Liturgical Reform* (1911)[2] and was carried by an overwhelming majority (79 to 8). Nevertheless, on 28 April 1915 both Houses of Bishops rejected it almost as decisively (15 to 3 in Canterbury and 6 to 1 in York). On 7 February 1918, however, the Canterbury bishops reversed their decision by 13 votes to 7, while adding the anamnesis of 1549 as a stronger link than the single word 'Wherefore'. This was acceptable to the Lower House of York, but not to the bishops, who were predominantly Evangelicals. That party objected, among other things, to the construction put by Anglo-Catholics on the phrase 'our sacrifice of praise and thanksgiving' as referring to the consecrated elements, and to the offering of 'ourselves, our souls and bodies' *before* communion.

In October 1918, when all four Houses held a joint meeting to produce the final proposals for revision, this 'reconstruction' was the only point on which agreement was not reached and it was referred to a conference of wider membership. Frere, then at Mirfield, approached Dr Drury, bishop of Ripon, a leading Evangelical, and the two together hammered out a compromise form which was put to the conference and passed with only five votes against. Even this, however, was not acceptable to the Northern bishops.

Soon afterwards, the Church Assembly was brought into being, which meant that the proposals for the entire Book had to come before the new body. A committee which reported in June 1922 rejected the Frere–Drury compromise and virtually restored the 1918 proposals, with minor amendments. The Northern bishops had by now lost their power of veto, but this time the reconstruction was rejected by the House of Clergy. After an unofficial conference held in the Jerusalem Chamber on 13 October 1923, the chairman reported:

It was agreed on all sides that, if it were possible, there should be one form of Canon only in the Alternative Book, but what emerged from the discussion seemed to be the impossibility of one form of Canon being accepted either by the conference or by the House of Clergy as a whole; and there was the danger that if a proposal for a single form of Canon were passed, it would only be carried in the face of a very considerable and important minority, which, in the opinion of the conference, would be disastrous. [Therefore] there would have to be two forms of Canon in the Alternative Book.

The conference met again the next day and still could not 'arrive at any agreement for a single form of Canon'; they 'had therefore applied themselves to the preparation of two forms':

They had drafted a form of Canon which would be acceptable to those who represented the Green Book, and which the representatives of the Grey Book felt in no way trespassed upon the doctrinal principles of the Church of England. They were also submitting another form which was accepted by those who represented the Grey Book and to which the representatives of the Green Book would not wish to raise objection.

'The Green Book' was put forward by the traditional Anglo-Catholics of the English Church Union, 'the Grey Book' by the successors of the Life and Liberty movement. In fact, the first canon (1924 A below) is almost identical with 1549, the second (1924 B) with that in the Grey Book.

Dean Wace said that he and his party could not accept the form which had the approval of the representatives of the Green Book. Earlier that year (2 May 1923) he had rejected the idea of alternative forms of Holy Communion as, from the point of view of simple people, 'a positive monstrosity'. Separation of the Canon from reception entirely altered the meaning, opening the way to the Roman doctrine of the sacrifice of the Mass. In the same debate Canon Sparrow Simpson preferred comprehensiveness to uniformity. No one rite would satisfy the three main parties. The Green Book was a party book and 'that was a virtue, not a defect'. It would be better to have three alternatives which could happily be used than enforce one which satisfied nobody. Canon Darwell Stone said that the Green Book was highly permissive and therefore not a party book.

The House of Laity, though willing to accept *one* canon as an alternative to 1662, drew the line at allowing two alternatives (17 February 1925). Many of the clergy shared this view, and since it was understood that the Jerusalem Chamber conference might have been able to agree on a single canon if more time had been available, another unofficial conference was held at Farnham in April 1926.[3] This conference, under the guidance of the Revd R. G. Parsons, managed to combine the two Jerusalem Chamber canons into one (1925 below). In the final stage of revision, the House of Bishops produced the form which appeared in the Proposed Book of 1927. No change was made in the Canon after the first rejection of the Book by Parliament, the form proposed in 1928 being identical with that of 1927.

The first part of the Prayer of Consecration shows at once the influence of Frere, who by the 1920s had become by far the most important figure in the process of revision. He held that consecration of the elements was effected by giving thanks over them: this involved the whole prayer, not merely the words of institution, and required the inclusion of an epiclesis, which gave a satisfactorily trinitarian basis to the prayer. This was bitterly resisted by both Anglo-Catholics and Evangelicals, who saw in it a weakening of the action of Christ in the words of institution. Frere also wished to restore the unity of the anaphora by 'bonding' the beginning of the prayer on to the Sanctus. The later revisions therefore begin the prayer with the words 'All glory and thanksgiving be to thee', thus picking up the word 'glory' from the end of the Sanctus and establishing thanksgiving immediately as the keynote of the prayer. The phrase first appeared in 1924 A and B. 1926 also opted for including 'thanksgiving', but the bishops removed it in 1927. The only other change in the opening sentence was the insertion after the words 'didst give thine only Son Jesus Christ' of 'to take our nature upon him and (to suffer death . . .)'. This phrase first appeared in the South African draft form and was adopted in the Grey Book and in 1924 B, but again was removed by the bishops, though it is in keeping with the incarnational emphasis of the theology of the day.

The second sentence of 1662 ('Hear us, O merciful Father . . .') is restored by 1924 A and 1926 to its original form in the 1549 Book, which included a sort of epiclesis, except that now there is no allusion to God's 'Spirit and word'. Thus it is an invocation of the Father, not of the Spirit, to bless and sanctify the elements. 1926 omits the word 'gifts' here, because it is to be used later on, in the anamnesis; and also rounds off the sentence with a phrase deriving from 1662, 'that all who shall receive the same may be partakers of his life'; 'life' is introduced to avoid repetition of

177

'Body and Blood'. However, the bishops in 1927, following 1924 A, refused to have an epiclesis here and omitted the second sentence altogether.

No single change was made in the words of institution at any stage of the revision.

All the proposed canons continue with an anamnesis, in every case including elements of 1549. 1920 and 1923 have already had the 1662 phrase, 'according to thy Son our Saviour Jesus Christ's holy institution' before the words of institution, so they omit the very similar phrase of 1549 here. 1924 A and B, 1926 and 1927/8 all omit the 1552 phrase above; 1924 A alone has the 1549 version at this point; 1924 B has it in the middle of the Prayer of Oblation; 1926 and 1927/8 have a shortened form after 'glorious ascension'. 1920 and 1923 both add a reference to the Second Coming.

Again, 1920, 1923 and 1924 B omit 'do celebrate and make here before thy divine majesty with these thy holy gifts the memorial which thy Son hath willed us to make'. The Anglo-Catholic liturgist J. H. Srawley described this phrase as 'contentious . . . innocent as it is, [it] arouses so much hostility'.[4] It is the words 'and make' which are unacceptable as adding something to the work of Christ. 1926 omits them, while 1927/8 substitutes 'set forth', both retaining the rest of the phrase, which they bring down to follow the remembrance of 'the precious death and passion . . . mighty resurrection and glorious ascension'. Their order is both traditional and logical. Only 1924 A gives the 1549 anamnesis verbatim.

After the anamnesis, 1920 inserts an epiclesis which owes more to the early liturgies than to 1549, invoking the Holy Spirit 'upon us and upon these thy holy gifts'. It is clear from speeches made in 1920 that Drury and Frere had rather different understandings of the text. Drury said: 'The prayer . . . really did not mean more than the words in the Baptism Service, "Sanctify this water . . .".' In the same debate it was recalled that Dr Frere had said: 'This will prove to be a bridge between the Eastern and Western Church.'[15] Though this epiclesis disappeared in 1923, it was not without influence on the epiclesis of 1927/8, which is placed at the same point and also includes a reference to the Spirit as giver of life. The rest of the 1927/8 epiclesis is derived from 1549, with the addition of some words from 1926, leading into a quotation from the Catechism suggested by archbishop Lang.

All the canons except 1920 now proceed with the first half of the Prayer of Oblation (down to 'benefits of his passion'). Drury felt that this procedure raised 'the storm-centre of our unhappy divisions',[6] and so, at his insistence, 1920 keeps the whole prayer in its 1662 place after communion. 1923, 1924 A and 1927/8 add the remainder of the prayer as well; 1924 A also restores a phrase from 1549 which was omitted in 1552. 1924 B inserts the phrase 'offering ourselves to thee in communion with him' from the Grey Book, while 1926 vigorously rewrites the latter half of the prayer, substituting 'We pray thee to accept this oblation of thy Church, through the ministry of our great High Priest', an obvious attempt to win the support of the representatives of the Green Book. Both 1924 B and 1926 are then able to incorporate the latter half of the prayer within the Prayer of Thanksgiving.

1920 introduces an entirely new doxology, which is replaced in 1923 by that of 1662 which remains thereafter.

It will be seen from this analysis that the problem of revision was immensely complicated by Frere's insistence on introducing an epiclesis. Frere himself came to realize this:

> There is a widespread desire for some recognition of the work of the Holy Spirit in the blessing of the elements. But there is so much difference of opinion as to the nature, meaning, effect and position of such an invocation that it seems doubtful whether any agreement can be reached at present.[7]

This was written in 1923 and the succeeding years merely bore out the correctness of Frere's conclusion. Probably he over-estimated the strength of the desire for an epiclesis. Even liturgical experts such as Armitage Robinson and Srawley, though well aware of the primitive Eastern view of consecration, clung to the primacy of the words of institution, which they saw to be threatened by the inclusion of an epiclesis.

Without such an addition, the process of drafting would have been far simpler and a great deal of controversy would have been avoided. As we have seen, there was no epiclesis in the prayer agreed on in 1918 and revived in 1923. In 1920 and 1927/8 an epiclesis is placed between the anamnesis and the Prayer of Oblation; in 1924 A and 1926 immediately before the words of institution; in 1924 B between the first half of the Prayer of Oblation and the doxology. The first of these positions is the traditional Eastern one; the second has no precedent among the great Eastern liturgies: it derives entirely from 1549. This position Srawley felt to be disastrous and Frere readily agreed with him.[8] (It is interesting to note that most recent eucharistic prayers have followed this innovation of Cranmer's.) The third position has no precedent at all. Frere put forward a suggestion for the sake of those who resisted the introduction of an epiclesis, that there should be two alternative clauses (the quasi-epiclesis of 1662 and an epiclesis of Eastern form and effect), only one of which would be said. This suggestion won no support at all.

By now it has become obvious that the dominant model for the revision was the 1549 Prayer Book. The Canon of this book is presented in the writings of liturgical scholars such as Frere and Brightman as a genuinely Catholic prayer, purged of the excesses of the Middle Ages and more logically constructed than the Roman Canon. It is not surprising, therefore, that the possibility was often canvassed of simply authorizing the 1549 Canon as it stood, or without the Prayer for the Church, as an alternative to that of 1662. Lord Halifax, who always used 1549 in his private chapel, was the protagonist of this suggestion, which won the support of many leading churchmen, including archbishop Lang. Indeed, with two or three tiny changes, the Canon 1924 A reproduces 1549 verbatim, adding nothing and omitting only one phrase which also appears in the Prayer of Humble Access, and the petition for our prayers to be brought by the angels to God's holy tabernacle, which was never included in any published revision. However, the complete restoration of the 1549 Canon, even without the Prayer for the Church, proved to be unacceptable, being rejected by the House of Laity on 17 February 1925 by 132 votes to 101.

Note: 'THE GREY BOOK'

The official title of this publication was *A New Prayer Book: Proposals for the Revision of the Book of Common Prayer and for Additional Services and Prayers, drawn up by a Group of Clergy*. It was nicknamed 'the Grey Book' to distinguish it from the English Church Union's proposals, which were nicknamed 'the Green Book'. It is often associated with the name of William Temple, who wrote a foreword to it, though he writes expressly, 'I have had no share in framing' these suggestions. In a copy formerly belonging to a member of the group, canon Cyril Hepher, this list was written on the flyleaf:

This group consisted of the following persons.

Dr Bell	afterward Bishop of Chichester
Dr Dearmer	afterward Canon of Westminster
F. C. Eeles FSA	
Cyril Hepher	Canon of Winchester
R. G. Parsons	afterward Bishop of Middleton
Guy Rogers	Canon of Birmingham
R. L. H. Shepherd*	afterward Dean of Cantuar
E. S. Woods	afterward Bishop of Croydon
Canon Dwelly	Dean of Liverpool

Sic: i.e. H. R. L. Sheppard

Sigla

1920   Frere–Drury canon as finally accepted by Convocation

1923   The Canon proposed by a Committee of the Church Assembly

1924 A The two Canons drawn up by the Jerusalem Chamber Conference as accepted by the Houses of Clergy and

1924 B Laity

1926   The Farnham Conference Canon

1927/8 The Canon printed in the Deposited Books

Words in italics represent a change from the previous canon (in the case of 1924 B, this is 1923 and not 1924 A).

The note '(*cf. p. 000*)' means that the equivalent section in the canon concerned will be found on the page indicated.

1920	*1923*	*1924* A

		All glory and thanksgiving *be to thee*, Almighty God, our
Almighty God, our heavenly	Almighty God, our heavenly	
Father, who of thy tender mercy didst give thine only Son Jesus Christ,	Father, who of thy tender mercy didst give thine only Son Jesus Christ,	heavenly Father, *for that thou* of thy tender mercy didst give thine only Son Jesus Christ,
to suffer death upon the cross for our redemption; who made there (by his one obla- tion of himself once offered) a full, perfect and sufficient sacrifice, oblation and satisfaction for the sins of the whole world; and did institute and in his holy Gospel command us to continue a perpetual memory of that his precious death, until his coming again; Hear us, O merciful Father, we most humbly beseech thee; and grant (*cf. p. 184*)	to suffer death upon the cross for our redemption; who made there (by his one obla- tion of himself once offered) a full, perfect and sufficient sacrifice, oblation and satisfaction for the sins of the whole world; and did institute and in his holy Gospel command us to continue a perpetual memory of that his precious death, until his coming again; Hear us, O merciful Father, we most humbly beseech thee; and grant	to suffer death upon the cross for our redemption; who made there (by his one obla- tion of himself once offered) a full, perfect and sufficient sacrifice, oblation and satisfaction for the sins of the whole world; and did institute, and in his holy Gospel command us to continue, a perpetual memory of that his precious death, until his coming again; Hear us, O merciful Father, we most humbly beseech thee; and *vouch- safe to bless and sanctify* these thy *gifts and* creatures of bread and wine, *that they may be* *unto us the* Body and Blood of thy *most dearly beloved* Son, Jesus Christ.
that we receiving these thy creatures of bread and wine, according to thy Son our Saviour Jesus Christ's holy institu- tion, in remembrance of his death and passion, may be partakers of his most blessed Body and Blood: Who, in the same night . . . (*as in 1662*) in remembrance of me. Wherefore, O Father,	that we receiving these thy creatures of bread and wine, according to thy Son our Saviour Jesus Christ's holy institu- tion, in remembrance of his death and passion, may be partakers of his most blessed Body and Blood: Who, in the same night . . . (*as in 1662*) in remembrance of me. Wherefore, O Lord and heavenly Father,	Who, in the same night . . . (*as in 1662*) in remembrance of me. Wherefore, O Lord and heavenly Father, *according* *to the institution of thy* *dearly beloved Son our* *Saviour Jesus Christ,*
we thy humble servants,	we thy humble servants,	we thy humble servants *do celebrate and make* *here, before thy divine* *majesty, with these thy*

1924 B	1926	1927/8

All glory and thanks-giving be to thee, All-mighty God, our heavenly Father, *for that thou* of thy tender mercy didst give thine only Son Jesus Christ, *to take our nature upon him and* to suffer death upon the cross for our redemption; who made there, by his one oblation of himself, once offered, a full, perfect and suf-ficient sacrifice

for the sins of the whole world; and did institute and in his holy Gospel command us to continue a perpetual memory of *him-self, wherein we do pro-claim* his death until his coming again.
(cf. pp. 185–6)

All glory and thanks-giving be to thee, Al-mighty God, our heavenly Father, for that thou of thy tender mercy didst give thine only Son Jesus Christ to take our nature upon him and to suffer death upon the cross for our redemption; who made there (by his one oblation of himself once offered) a full, perfect and suf-ficient sacrifice, *and propitiation* for the sins of the whole world; and did institute, and in his holy Gospel command us to continue, a perpetual memory of that his precious
death until his coming again; Hear us, O merciful Father, we most humbly beseech thee, and vouch-safe to bless and sanctify these thy creatures of bread and wine, that they may be unto us the Body and Blood of thy Son *our Saviour* Jesus Christ, *to the end that all who shall* receive *the same*

All glory be to thee, Al-mighty God, our heavenly Father, for that thou of thy tender mercy didst give thine only Son Jesus Christ,
to suffer death upon the cross for our redemption; who made there (by his one oblation of himself once offered) a full, perfect and suf-ficient sacrifice, obla-tion and satisfaction for the sins of the whole world; and did institute and in his holy Gospel command us to continue a perpetual memory of that his precious
death, until his coming again;
(cf. p. 185)

---

may be *made* partak-ers of his *life*:

Who, in the same night . . .
(as in 1662)
in remembrance of me.
Wherefore, O Lord and heavenly Father,

we thy humble servants,

Who, in the same night . . .
(as in 1662)
in remembrance of me.
Wherefore, O Lord and heavenly Father,

we thy humble servants,
(cf. below)

Who, in the same night . . .
(as in 1662)
in remembrance of me.
Wherefore, O Lord and heavenly Father,

we thy humble servants,
(cf. below)

183

1920	*1923*	*1924* A
		holy gifts, the memorial which thy Son hath willed us to make, having in remembrance *his blessed passion and* precious death, his mighty resurrection and glorious ascension;
having in remembrance before thee the precious death of thy dear Son, his mighty resurrection and glorious ascension, looking also for his coming again,	having in remembrance the precious death of thy dear Son, his mighty resurrection and glorious ascension, looking also for his coming again,	
do render unto thee most hearty thanks for the innumerable benefits which he hath procured unto us.	do render unto thee most hearty thanks for the innumerable benefits which he hath procured unto us;	render*ing* unto thee most hearty thanks for the innumerable benefits procured unto us *by the same.* (*cf. p. 182*)
And we pray thee of thine almighty goodness to send upon us and upon these thy gifts thy Holy and Blessed Spirit, who is the Sanctifier and Giver of life, (*cf. p. 186*)		
	And we entirely desire thy fatherly goodness mercifully to accept this our sacrifice of praise and thanksgiving; most humbly beseeching thee to grant, that by the merits and death of thy Son Jesus Christ, and through faith in his blood, we and all thy whole Church	And we entirely desire thy fatherly goodness mercifully to accept this our sacrifice of praise and thanksgiving; most humbly beseeching thee to grant, that by the merits and death of thy Son Jesus Christ, and through faith in his blood, we and all thy whole Church
	may obtain remission of our sins, and all other benefits of his passion.	may obtain remission of our sins, and all other benefits of his passion.

having in remembrance the precious death of thy dear Son, his mighty resurrection and glorious ascension,	having in remembrance the precious death and passion of thy dear Son, his mighty resurrection, and glorious ascension, *according to his holy institution do celebrate*	having in remembrance the precious death and passion of thy dear Son, his mighty resurrection and glorious ascension, according to his holy institution, do celebrate *and set forth* before thy divine

having in
remembrance
the precious death
of thy dear
Son, his mighty resur-
rection and glorious
ascension,

having in
remembrance
the precious death and
passion of thy dear
Son, his mighty resur-
rection, and glorious
ascension, *according to
his holy institution
do celebrate
            before thy divine
majesty with these thy
holy gifts, the memori-
al which he hath will-
ed us to make,* rendering
unto thee most hearty
thanks for the innum-
erable benefits
which he hath procured
unto us.
(*cf. p. 182*)

having in
remembrance
the precious death and
passion of thy dear
Son, his mighty resur-
rection and glorious
ascension, according to
his holy institution,
do celebrate *and set
forth* before thy divine
majesty with these thy
holy gifts, the memorial
which he hath will-
ed us to make, rendering
unto thee most hearty
thanks for the innum-
erable benefits
which he hath procured
unto us.
Hear us, O merciful Father,
we most humbly beseech thee,
and with thy Holy and Life-
giving Spirit vouchsafe to
bless and sanctify both us
and these thy gifts of
bread and wine, that they may
be unto us the Body and
Blood of thy Son, *our Saviour*, Jesus Christ, to the end
that we, receiving the same,
may be *strengthened and
refreshed both in body and
soul.*

                    do render
unto thee most hearty
thanks for the innum-
erable *blessings*
which he hath *assured*
to us.
(*cf. p. 182*)

And we entirely desire
thy fatherly goodness
mercifully to accept
this our sacrifice of
praise and thanksgiv-
ing; most humbly be-
seeching thee to grant,
that by the merits and
death of thy Son, Jesus
Christ, and through
faith in his blood, we
and all thy whole
Church, *offering our-
selves to thee in
communion with him,*
may obtain remission
of our sins, and all
other benefits of his
passion.
Hear us, O merciful
Father, we most humbly
beseech thee, and with thy

And we entirely desire
thy fatherly goodness
mercifully to accept
this our sacrifice of
praise and thanksgiv-
ing; most humbly be-
seeching thee to grant,
that by the merits and
death of thy Son Jesus
Christ, and through
faith in his blood, we
and all thy whole
Church

may obtain remission
of our sins, and all
other benefits of his
passion.
(*cf. p. 183*)

And we entirely desire
thy fatherly goodness
mercifully to accept
this our sacrifice of
praise and thanksgiv-
ing; most humbly be-
seeching thee to grant,
that by the merits and
death of thy Son Jesus
Christ, and through
faith in his blood, we
and all thy whole
Church

may obtain remission
of our sins, and all
other benefits of his
passion.
(*cf. above*)

(*cf. below*)

And here we offer and
present unto thee, O
Lord, ourselves, our
souls and bodies, to be
a reasonable, holy and
lively sacrifice unto
thee; humbly beseeching
thee; that
        all we, who
are partakers of this
Holy Communion,

        may be
fulfilled with thy
grace and heavenly
benediction. And al-
though we be unworthy,
through our manifold
sins, to offer unto
thee any sacrifice, yet
we beseech thee to ac-
cept this our bounden
duty and service;
not weighing our merits,
but pardoning our of-
fences;
through Jesus Christ
our Lord, by whom, and
with whom, in the unity
of the Holy Ghost, all
honour and glory be
unto thee, O Father
Almighty, world with-
out end.

   The Lord's Prayer
   The Communion

And here we offer and
present unto thee, O
Lord, ourselves, our
souls and bodies, to be
a reasonable, holy and
living sacrifice unto
thee; humbly beseeching
thee, that
        all we, who
are partakers of this
Holy Communion, *may*
worthily receive the
most precious Body and
Blood of thy Son, and be
fulfilled with thy
grace and heavenly
benediction. And al-
though we be unworthy,
through our manifold
sins, to offer unto
thee any sacrifice, yet
we beseech thee to ac-
cept this our bounden
duty and service;
not weighing our merits,
but pardoning our of-
fences;
through Jesus Christ
our Lord, by whom, and
with whom, in the unity
of the Holy Ghost, all
honour and glory be
unto thee, O Father
Almighty, world with-
out end. Amen.

   The Lord's Prayer
   The Communion

---

to whom with thee and
thy Son Jesus Christ
be ascribed by every
creature in earth
and heaven all bless-
ing, honour, glory and
power, now, henceforth
and for evermore.
Amen.
   The Lord's Prayer
   The Communion
O Lord and heavenly
Father, we thy humble
servants entirely
desire thy fatherly
goodness . . .
    (*as in 1662*)
world without end.
Amen.
       and/or

Holy Spirit bless and
sanctify both us and
these thy gifts of bread
and wine, that we receiving
them according to thy Son
our Saviour Jesus Christ's
holy institution may be
partakers of his most
blessed Body and Blood:

And *humbly* offe*ring*
ourselves unto thee, O
*Father Almighty, we pray
thee to accept this ob-
lation of thy Church,
through the ministry of
our great High Priest,* that
in the power of thy life-
giving Spirit all we who
are partakers of this
Holy Communion

And here we offer and
present unto thee, O
Lord, ourselves, our
souls and bodies, to be
a reasonable, holy and
living sacrifice unto
thee: humbly beseeching
thee, that
                all we, who
are partakers of this
Holy Communion,

                may be
fulfilled with thy
grace and heavenly
benediction.

                may be
fulfilled with thy
grace and heavenly
benediction. And al-
though we be unworthy,
through our manifold
sins, to offer unto
thee any sacrifice, yet
we beseech thee to ac-
cept this our bounden
duty and service;
not weighing our merits,
but pardoning our of-
fences;

By whom, and
with whom, in the unity
of the Holy *Spirit*, all
honour and glory be
unto thee, O Father
Almighty, world with-
out end. Amen.

Through Jesus Christ
our Lord, by whom, and
with whom, in the unity
of the Holy *Ghost*, all
honour and glory be
unto thee, O Father
Almighty, world with-
out end. Amen.

through Jesus Christ
our Lord, by whom, and
with whom, in the unity
of the Holy Ghost, all
honour and glory be
unto thee, O Father
Almighty, world with-
out end. Amen.

The Lord's Prayer
The Communion

The Lord's Prayer
The Communion

The Lord's Prayer
The Communion

1920

Almighty and everliv-
ing God, we most heart-
ily thank thee . . .
        (*as in 1662*)
world without end.
Amen.

1923

Almighty and everliv-
ing God, we most heart-
ily thank thee . . .
        (*as in 1662*)
world without end.
Amen.

1924 A

Almighty and everliv-
ing God, we most heart-
ily thank thee . . .
        (*as in 1662*)
world without end.
Amen.

1924 B

Almighty and everliv-
ing God, we most heart-
ily thank thee . . .
    (*as in 1662*)
world without end.
Amen.

1926

Almighty and everliv-
ing God, we most heart-
ily thank thee . . .
    (*as in 1662*)
world without end.
Amen.

1927/8

Almighty and everliv-
ing God, we most heart-
ily thank thee . . .
    (*as in 1662*)
world without end.
Amen.

Notes

Chapter 1

1. *Edward VI and the Book of Common Prayer* (1890).
2. *A New History of the Book of Common Prayer* (1901), p. 34.
3. *The English Rite* (1915), i, pp. lxxvi–lxxviii (hereafter referred to as *ER*).
4. Vol. 50, *Cranmer's Liturgical Projects* (1915).
5. Ibid., p. xvii.
6. *Cranmer and the Reformation under Edward VI* (1926, reprinted 1973), pp. 74–7.
7. *Miscellaneous Writings and Letters* (Parker Society 1846), pp. 366–7: my italics.
8. 'The Liturgical Work of Archbishop Cranmer', *Journal of Ecclesiastical History*, 7 (1956), p. 194; reprinted in *Liturgical Studies* (1976), p. 189.
9. *Cranmer's Liturgical Projects*, pp. 212 (*ad* p. 53), 215 (*ad* p. 68).
10. Ibid., pp. xix, xx, 222–30 (*passim*).
11. Ibid., p. xvii.
12. Ibid., p. 17.
13. Ibid., pp. 54, 213.
14. Ibid., pp. 168–97.
15. Ibid., p. 16.
16. For a detailed comparison, see *ER* i, pp. lxxvi–lxvii.
17. *incommode*.
18. *coetu*.
19. *vetustatis et venustatis*.
20. *deflorari*.
21. Τὰς θεοπνευστὰς γραφὰς.

Chapter 2

1. The original readings of the 1534 edition of Marshall, which Burton first discovered at a late stage of publication, were added in footnotes.
2. *Venite* is, of course, strictly speaking, not a canticle but an invariable psalm.

Chapter 3

1. 'Reformed Doctrine in the Collects of the First Book of Common Prayer', *Harvard Theological Review*, 57 (1965), pp. 49–68.
2. J. Wickham Legg, *Cranmer's Liturgical Projects*, pp. lxii ff., 210 ff., 224.
3. Ibid., pp. 125, 225.
4. *ER*, i, p. xcvii.
5. C. Lloyd, *Formularies of Faith* (1825), p. 238.
6. Ibid., pp. 231–2.
7. Ibid., p. 229.
8. Ibid., p. 234.
9. Ibid., p. 243.
10. E. H. Fellowes, *English Cathedral Music* (1941), p. 57; 2nd edn (1969), p. 54.
11. *ER*, i, p. xciv.

Chapter 4 (see Bibliography on p. 90 for full titles)

1. *Annals of the Reformation*, II, i (Oxford 1824), p. 293.
2. Varrentrapp, i, p. 36.
3. Ibid., ii, p. 120.
4. Ibid., i, p. 39.
5. b. 1503.
6. *ER*, i, pp. lv–lvi.
7. *Appellatio*, A vi b.
8. *Defensio*, 5.
9. Ibid., 2.
10. Ibid., 4.
11. Ibid., 3.
12. *Antididagma*, Preface.
13. *Appellatio*, B i b.
14. Varrentrapp, i, p. 148.
15. *Defensio*, 4.
16. *Antididagma*, Preface ('*mutatis quibusdam*').
17. Varrentrapp, i, p. 177 (*Deliberatio*, Preface, iii a: '*post diligentem deliberationem et correctionem, quantum brevi in tempore fieri potuit*').
18. *Defensio*, 14.
19. *Deliberatio*, Preface, ii b.
20. *Defensio*, 14.
21. Drouven, p. 173 (*ER*, i, p. xlviii, is wrong here; cf. p. xlvi).
22. Varrentrapp, i, p. 178, n. 1.
23. Anon, (i.e. F. E. Brightman), 'Capitulum Coloniense', *Church Quarterly Review* 31 (1891), pp. 419–36.
24. *STC*, 13213.

25. *STC*, 13210.
26. *STC*, 13214.
27. T. Cranmer, *Miscellaneous Writings* p. 415, n. 5.
28. *Workmanship of the Prayer Book* (1902), p. 169.
29. *ER*, i, p. lxxx.
30. *ER*, i, p. xlvi, n. 2.
31. *ER*, i, p. lxxii.
32. Drouven, p. 172n.
33. I adopt Brightman's symbol **H** to denote the Church Order for Cologne, without distinguishing between the German and Latin versions or between the contributions of Hermann and Bucer.
34. *Further Studies in the Prayer Book* (1908), p. 46.
35. *ER*, ii, p. 698; Lloyd, *Formularies of Faith* p. 260.
36. *Workmanship of the Prayer Book*, p. 26.
37. R. C. D. Jasper and G. J. Cuming, *Prayers of the Eucharist* (1975), p. 119.
38. *ER*, ii, p. 662; i, p. ccxxx (1921 edn only); *Deliberatio*, ff. 95a, 95b, 97a.
39. See also ff. 84b, 96b, under 'The Book of 1552', p. 87.
40. *ER*, i, p. xcii; **H**, 91b.
41. *Further Studies in the Prayer Book*, pp. 47–53.
42. *ER*, i, p. cxviii.
43. *ER*, ii, pp. 778–86.
44. Dowden, *Workmanship of the Prayer Book*, p. 260; *Further Studies in the Prayer Book*, pp. 283–5.
45. *ER*, i, p. cxxiii.
46. *ER*, ii, p. 800; **H**, 105b.
47. *ER*, ii, p. 860; **H**, 112b.
48. *ER*, ii, p. 858; **H**, 72b.
49. *ER*, i, p. clviii; **H**, 91b.
50. **H**, 70b.
51. *ER*, i, p. clx.
52. '*communicent*' is rendered 'be partakers' in the *Consultation*.
53. ed. A. Beesley, in *Journal of Ecclesiastical History*, xix (1968), pp. 83–8; but cf. *ER*, i, p. clxi (*re* p. 667).
54. *ER*, ii, p. 745; **H**, 71b.
55. *ER*, ii, p. 755; **H**, 72b.
56. *ER*, ii, p. 795; **H**, 82a.
57. *ER*, ii, p. 797; **H**, 79a.
58. *ER*, ii, p. 873; i, p. clxiv; **H**, 112b.

Chapter 5

1. *ER*, ii, pp. 684, 686; C. Lloyd, *Formularies of Faith*, pp. 231–2, 243.
2. *ER*, i, p. xlix.
3. *ER*, i, p. cvi.

4. E.g. C. W. Dugmore, *The Mass and the English Reformers* (1959), p. 160; G. J. Cuming, *A History of Anglican Liturgy* (1969), p. 79.
5. *Defence*, v. 3: ed. Jenkyns, pp. 448 ff.; quoted at length, G. Dix, *The Shape of the Liturgy* (1945), p. 654.
6. Quoted from *ER*, i, p. cvi.
7. *Answer* (Parker Society), pp. 79, 271.
8. *Defence*, v. 3: ed Jenkyns, p. 413; Dix, op. cit., p. 650.
9. Migne, *Patrologia Latina,* CCXVII.891 (wrongly given by Brightman *ER*, i, p. cxi).
10. *ER*, i, pp. cvii–cx.
11. *ER*, ii, p. 692; 'The New Prayer Book Examined', *Church Quarterly Review*, 104 (1927), pp. 240–2.
12. *ER*, i, pp. liii–lvi.
13. C. Lloyd, *Formularies of Faith*, pp. 263–4.

Chapter 6

1. Most recently by Colin Buchanan, *What did Cranmer think he was doing?* (Grove Books 1976).
2. *Works*, VII, p. 287.
3. Ed. P. G. Stanwood and Daniel O'Connor (Oxford 1967), p. 284.
4. G. J. Cuming (ed.), *The Durham Book* (1961), p. 167.
5. Ibid., p. 179.
6. Ed. cit., p. 230.

Chapter 7

1. *A Life of John Cosin*, 1913.
2. *Eucharistic Doctrine in England from Hooker to Waterland*, 1942.
3. p. xxi; cf. p. xlvii, n. 18.
4. *Works* (Library of Anglo-Catholic Theology edn) V, pp. 114, 127 etc.
5. IV, p. 475.
6. Epitaph in Norwich Cathedral.
7. I, p. 46.
8. V, p. 169.
9. V, p. 168.
10. *Devotions* (ed. Stanwood and O'Connor), p. 11.
11. I, p. 132.
12. I, p. 139.
13. V, pp. 42–3.
14. V, p. 63.
15. 'John Cosin: Foundation or Embarrassment?', *The Month* (Jan. 1975), p. 13.

16. I, pp. 28–9.
17. Ed. cit., pp. 235ff.
18. V, p. 413.
19. I, p. 97.
20. Ed. cit., pp. 230, 284; 102, 103, 229.
21. V, p. 104.
22. V, p. 131.
23. V, p. 114.
24. V, p. 119.
25. Quoted from G. Dix, *The Shape of the Liturgy*, p. 647.
26. V, p. 120.
27. I, p. 145.
28. V, pp. 109, 112, 98, 126–9.
29. IV, p. 472.
30. IV, pp. 385–6.
31. IV, p. 151.
32. IV, p. 155.
33. IV, p. 41; cf. p. 166.
34. IV, p. 18; cf. p. 156.
35. IV, p. 349.
36. V, pp. 306–7.
37. V, p. 340.
38. V, pp. 199–218.
39. V, p. 335.
40. V, p. 336.
41. V, pp. 343, 350.
42. V, p. 345; cf. p. 131.
43. IV, p. 174.
44. V, pp. 130, 356–7.
45. III, pp. xxvii–xxxi.
46. III, p. 20.
47. III, p. 134.
48. III, p. 278.
49. III, p. 285.
50. IV, p. 387.
51. IV, p. 397–8.
52. IV, p. 401.
53. IV, p. 449.
54. IV, p. 399.
55. IV, pp. 337–8.
56. M. Sylvester, *Reliquiae Baxterianae*, 1696.
57. IV, p. 527.
58. *The Bishoprick*, 30 (1954), pp. 5–9.
59. pp. 230, 281.
60. pp. 2, 37, 46, 189, 192.
61. p. 233.

Chapter 9

1. See further G. J. Cuming, *The Durham Book* (1961); 'The Making of the Durham Book', *Journal of Ecclesiastical History*, vi (1955), pp. 60–72.
2. CB and AB have both been reproduced in facsimile.
3. E.g. E. Cardwell, *Synodalia* (Oxford 1842), ii, pp. 638ff.
4. *Introduction to the History of the Successive Revisions of the Book of Common Prayer* (1877), pp. cccix, ccx.
5. *The Conformists' Plea for the Nonconformists* (1682), pp. 28, 32; 'Dr Allen' is Giles Aleyn DD.
6. *Abridgment of Mr Baxter's History* (1713), p. 159.
7. Printed in W. Jacobson, *Fragmentary Illustrations of the History of the Book of Common Prayer* (1874).
8. There are no intentional divergencies in the Ordinal, so presumably CB was available by the time the copyists of AB reached that point.
9. About one-third of these readings are printed in *ER*, i, pp. cc, cci. The cancelled readings are represented here by italics.
10. Jacobson, op. cit., pp. 26, 27, 21, 37.
11. *The Validity of the Orders of the Church of England* (1688), p. 42.
12. MS. Tanner 48 (1): *not* 43, as in Parker, op. cit., p. ccccxvi.
13. *Works* (Oxford 1854), II, p. 383.
14. *Life of Dr Robert Sanderson* (1678), f. 15.
15. E.g. *Works*, I, p. 28.
16. *Works*, II, p. 115.
17. *Considerations touching the Liturgy of the Church of England* (1661), p. 22.
18. *ER*, i, p. ccxxiii.
19. *ER*, ii, p. 840.
20. Jacobson, op. cit., p. 21.
21. *Works*, I, p. 191.
22. Jacobson, op. cit., p. 8.
23. E. Cardwell, *Synodalia*, ii, p. 685 (my translation).
24. Jasper and Cuming, *Prayers of the Eucharist*, pp. 176–7.
25. G. Gould, *Documents relating to the Act of Uniformity* (1861), p. 17.
26. Jacobson, op. cit., p. 17.
27. Ibid., p. 6.
28. Ibid., pp. 13, 14.
29. *Works*, III, p. 210.
30. *Works*, ed. A. Chalmers (1826), IV, pp. 405, 461; V, pp. 285, 360.
31. *ER*, i, p. 192.
32. Cambridge University Library, Add.MS.7977.
33. Gould, op. cit., p. 156.

Chapter 10

1. Quotations from debates are taken from *The Chronicle of Convocation* and *The Proceedings of the Church Assembly* for the dates mentioned in the text.
2. Frere, *Some Principles of Liturgical Reform*, pp. 187–91.
3. *Walter Howard Frere, His Correspondence on Liturgical Revision and Construction*, ed. R. C. D. Jasper (1954), pp. 103–4.
4. Ibid., p. 85.
5. W. K. Lowther Clarke, *The Prayer Book of 1928 Reconsidered* (1943), p. 81.
6. Frere, *Correspondence*, p. 68.
7. *A Survey of the Proposals for the Alternative Prayer Book* ('the Orange Book'), p. 36.
8. Frere, *Correspondence*, pp. 114, 118.

Index

197